SHAKESPEARE SURVEY

ADVISORY BOARD

SHAKESPEARE SURVEY

AN ANNUAL SURVEY OF
SHAKESPEARIAN STUDY AND PRODUCTION

26

EDITED BY
KENNETH MUIR

CAMBRIDGE
AT THE UNIVERSITY PRESS
1973

Published by the Syndics of the Cambridge University Press
Bentley House, 200 Euston Road, London NW1 2DB
American Branch: 32 East 57th Street, New York, N.Y.10022

© Cambridge University Press 1973

Library of Congress Catalogue Card Number: 49–16391

ISBN: 0 521 20216 7

Shakespeare Survey was first published in 1948. For the first
eighteen volumes it was edited by Allardyce Nicoll under the
sponsorship of the University of Birmingham, the University
of Manchester, the Royal Shakespeare Theatre and the
Shakespeare Birthplace Trust

Printed in Great Britain
at the University Printing House, Cambridge
(Brooke Crutchley, University Printer)

EDITOR'S NOTE

As previously announced, the central theme of *Shakespeare Survey 27* will be 'Shakespeare's Early Tragedies'. The theme of Number 28 will be 'Shakespeare and the Ideas of his Time'. Contributions on that or on other subjects, which should not normally exceed 5,000 words, should reach the Editor (Department of English Literature, University of Liverpool, P.O. Box 147, Liverpool L69 3BX) by 1 September 1974. Contributors are required to provide brief summaries of their articles and they should leave generous margins, use double-spacing, and follow the style and lay-out of articles in the current issue. A style-sheet is available on request. K. M.

CONTRIBUTORS

NIGEL ALEXANDER, *Senior Lecturer in English Literature, University of Nottingham*

JAMES BLACK, *Associate Professor of English Literature, University of Calgary*

KEITH BROWN, *Lecturer in English, University of Oslo*

JOHN DOEBLER, *Professor of English Literature, Arizona State University*

CECIL S. EMDEN, *Emeritus Fellow of Oriel College, Oxford*

R. A. FOAKES, *Professor of English Literature, University of Kent*

C. H. HOBDAY, *Bristol*

CYRUS HOY, *Professor of English Literature, University of Rochester*

MARY LASCELLES, *Honorary Fellow of Somerville College, Oxford*

CLIFFORD LEECH, *Professor of English Literature, University of Toronto*

HARRY LEVIN, *Professor of English and Comparative Literature, Harvard University*

RICHARD PROUDFOOT, *Lecturer in English Literature, King's College, University of London*

NORMAN SANDERS, *Professor of English Literature, University of Tennessee*

LEAH SCRAGG, *Lecturer in English Literature, University of Manchester*

J. L. SIMMONS, *Professor of English Literature, Tulane University*

PETER THOMSON, *Lecturer in Drama, University College, Swansea*

GLYNNE WICKHAM, *Professor of Drama, University of Bristol*

CONTENTS

PLATES

STUDIES IN SHAKESPEARIAN
AND OTHER JACOBEAN TRAGEDY,
1918-1972: A RETROSPECT

CLIFFORD LEECH

It is difficult to know how to start this retrospect, how to decide what to include, what to leave out. It is today almost impossible to write about Shakespeare without making some reference to his Jacobean contemporaries and successors, or to write about any of them and yet omit mention of their supreme fellow. Webster and Ford, to take the two most obvious examples, manifestly echo patterns and speeches that they found in him; Fletcher, with or without Beaumont, delighted in giving us ingenious variations on what he offered. In comedy Jonson made a commensurable contribution to his successors' writing, but in tragedy there was only one fount from which the Jacobeans and Carolines drew their lifeblood. Only Chapman, perhaps, is almost entirely *sui generis*: the rest, even when they are most different from Shakespeare, as for example Fletcher is, are writing with Shakespeare to some extent in mind. Moreover, any book or article on the nature of tragedy itself can hardly be written without bringing in more than one early seventeenth-century dramatist. So what can be offered here comprises only a few comments on the way that, in the writings of the last fifty years, the critic or historian has linked in his mind the major tragedies of Shakespeare and other tragic drama from around 1600 to the closing of the theatres.

Yet it seems legitimate to comment on a paradox that has come to manifest itself of recent years in the academic writing in this field, which I think is intimately related to trends in university curricula and to what are, I believe mistakenly, regarded as dominant student-preferences. There was a time when it would have been inconceivable for a student to 'specialise' (or 'major') in English without some not inconsiderable study of several of the Elizabethan and Jacobean tragic writers. For the past ten years I have been teaching in North America, and my information is now fuller in relation to that scene than to that of the United Kingdom, though I suspect that, just as Chapman in *Bussy d'Ambois* made Montsurry say that before long the English court would come to imitate the French in its manners as already in attire, so England and Scotland and Wales (perhaps Ireland too) are doubtless catching up or climbing down. Perhaps I may illustrate this from a personal experience. Eight years ago I was asked, on a visit to a United States university, to talk informally to an undergraduate class on *Hamlet*. The regular instructor, thanking me with all courtesy, said: 'Of course, I don't suppose they understood those references to Kyd.' Yet probably never before has there been so much scholarly work on Shakespeare's fellows than we have seen in the last fifty years. I shall refer to a number of the major books, but there are major periodicals too, including *Renaissance Drama* and *Studies in English Literature*, which every year gives one of its four issues to Elizabethan and Jacobean drama; and of course articles in this field appear elsewhere with overwhelming frequency.

Partly, of course, this is due to the demands for 'Ph.D. research' and for the continuing evidence of publication in a young university teacher's career. This is likely, at least for a time, to be in the field where he wrote his thesis. It has often had a bad effect. The thesis can go sour, but the young scholar feels committed: he has to plough his furrow for what it is worth, however increasingly infertile the ground begins to appear. In the area we are considering there is some recent writing which is either tired or even resentful. It might be a good thing if every successful Ph.D. candidate were persuaded to turn at once to a new area, and to come back to his Ph.D. only when the sourness has worn off (if it does). It is appalling that he is so often bullied into publishing at once. This is particularly true because when, for example, a young man or woman has written about Webster in the dissertation, he or she is no longer easily able to teach Webster's plays to undergraduates – which is the best way, surely, for the thing to remain vital to him. Only a few undergraduates will 'opt' for Jacobean tragedy apart from Shakespeare; if we want the generality to know about it, we must demand that they study it: then they may become marked for life through the knowledge thrust upon them. Let us brood in silence for a moment on the situation of the student who knows Shakespeare only in a vacuum.

Between the wars

Nevertheless, despite all its limitations, our period of some fifty years has been a major time for writings in this field. And let me begin this retrospect by a slight antedating of the announced starting-point. Perhaps Rupert Brooke's *John Webster and the Elizabethan Drama*[1] is not so much read now as it should be. It was written in 1911–12 as a dissertation which won Brooke his fellowship at King's in 1913. His view of Webster as a whole is probably not ours: we are no longer likely to

agree that 'A play of Webster's is full of the feverish and ghastly turmoil of a nest of maggots' (p. 158), though there are perhaps now people from certain universities who are getting back to that. But let us listen to him for a moment on Shakespeare's relation to his fellows:

The relation of Shakespeare with the whole of this period, of which he, then at his greatest, was, to our eyes, the centre, is curious. His half-connections, the way he was influenced and yet transmuted the influences, would require a good deal of space to detail. But in this, his 'dark period' – whatever it was, neuralgia, a spiritual crisis, Mary Fitton, or literary fashion, that caused it – he was not unique or eccentric in the *kind* of his art. His humour was savage, he railed against sex, his tragedies were bloody, his heroes meditated curiously on mortality. It was all in the fashion.
(pp. 66–7)

The tone is no longer what we are used to, but Brooke is open-minded enough: he does not simply believe in Mary Fitton's influence or in the fact of a 'spiritual crisis' or in 'literary fashion'; all he insists on is that Shakespeare belonged to the time of the other major writers of English tragedy and was not, in 'kind', essentially different.

What we needed in those times was more readily accessible information. We had, in a fashion, the texts, for the Old Mermaids were easily enough available in second-hand copies (green and brown) and in rather tatty reprints. But we needed people who would explore the field and chart its pattern. The major event which has given to subsequent criticism a firm base was the publication of E. K. Chambers's *The Elizabethan Stage*[2]: its four volumes gave us the facts, which later research has been able to correct only on comparatively small matters of detail. And Chambers, in exploring the Elizabethans and the early Jacobeans, had always Shakespeare in view. His work achieved its long-envisaged summit when *William*

[1] London, 1916.　　　[2] Oxford, 1923.

Shakespeare: A Study of Facts and Problems appeared seven years later. From this point on there was no excuse for ignorance. Some years ago John Dover Wilson, addressing a small group at the Shakespeare Institute at Stratford-upon-Avon, described Chambers's *William Shakespeare* as marking the great watershed in Shakespeare studies in our century. Very soon after *The Elizabethan Stage* was published, Allardyce Nicoll in *British Drama*[1] explored the drama of the English Renaissance in relation to the whole body of drama in England, and he was later to extend his frame in *World Drama*.[2] The importance of these books is partly as frequently-consulted works of reference, and partly too in making a wide public aware of the changing dramatic pattern over the centuries. Nicoll had little room for detailed criticism, but his books have laid a broad foundation on which others could build their more idiosyncratic structures. Moreover, it should after this have been difficult to think of a writer, a genre, or a period in total isolation. For those who were at school in the 1920s, it is strange to look back and recall the slack and facile clichés often, but not by Nicoll, used in referring to the Elizabethans and Jacobeans apart from Shakespeare. Shaw's labelling of Webster as 'the Tussaud laureate' stuck for a long time, and is still occasionally found when a production of a Webster play is being popularly reviewed; Jonson was, it was said, too 'learned' for the stage; Marlowe was a poet who was unfortunately led to the theatre through economic circumstance; 'damned dull' was a comment on Chapman's tragedies from a young teacher of my undergraduate time. No large claim can be made that we have in all respects improved, but at least our present clichés are uttered in the face of a wide range of thoughtful writing.

T. S. Eliot's brief essays on Elizabethan and Jacobean dramatists, which first appeared during the years 1918–34, have in retrospect an air of *sprezzatura*, brilliant and sometimes brilliantly misguided things that a fresh reading of the texts had led him to give utterance to. Although he was familiar with the then 'literature of the subject', he could be influenced by writers whose reputation has not stood the test of time (as in the case of J. M. Robertson), and his application of Freudian psychology to *Hamlet* is now generally seen as facile. But it was these essays that set many a young mind alight in the 1920s, and today they should be constantly re-read. We can pass over their 'shots in the dark' (often indeed 'near-misses'); we shall again and again be brought up against comments as challenging as this:

Chapman appears to have been potentially the greatest of all these men [the others being Webster, Tourneur, Middleton]: his was the mind which was the most classical, his was the drama which is the most independent in its tendency toward a dramatic form – although it may seem the most formless and the most indifferent to dramatic necessities.[3]

In broad terms, the 1920s gave us the map. It was in the 1930s that critical exploration became truly searching. Of course, the nineteenth century had here and there its enthusiasm for the Jacobeans: we can think of Swinburne, and of Symonds and Ellis in their Mermaid introductions. But M. C. Bradbook's *Themes and Conventions of Elizabethan Tragedy*[4] and Una Ellis-Fermor's *The Jacobean Drama: An Interpretation*[5] drew on the more exact knowledge by then made available. These were books written with a deep sense of the value of wha was being discussed, yet with that sense of fact that Eliot in his 1923 essay on 'The Function of Criticism at the Present Time' had insisted on as basic to good criticism. Yet the burden of the past could not be easily discarded. It seems likely that Muriel Bradbrook would not now,

---

[1] London, 1925. [2] London, 1949.
[3] 'Four Elizabethan Dramatists' (1924); reprinted in *Selected Essays* (London, 1932).
[4] Cambridge, 1935. [5] London, 1936.

as she did then, use the heading 'The Decadence' for her discussion of Beaumont and Fletcher and Ford. She was echoing the use of the word in S. P. Sherman's introduction to the first volume of W. Bang's *Materialen* edition of *John Fordes Dramatische Werke*.[1] Of course, we have it with us still, but in this notably decadent age in which we now write it seems at least impertinent to use it of major Jacobean and Caroline writers, who are not so good as Shakespeare, who wrote in his shadow, but who nevertheless gave us something of their own with astonishing skill and insight. Occasionally we might wish for a more precise wording. Miss Bradbrook is excellent in relating the sub-plots to the total structure of some of the plays, giving hints which Richard Levin has thoroughly developed, for Shakespeare and many others, in *The Multiple Plot in English Renaissance Drama*,[2] but she surely makes too easy an equation when she declares of the sub-plot of *The Changeling*: 'It acts as a kind of parallel or reflection in a different mode: their relationship is precisely that of masque and antimasque, say the two halves of Jonson's *Masque of Queens*' (p. 221). 'Precisely'? The sub-plot does not precede, prepare the way for, the main action, nor is it a grotesque contrast to a noble entry of main masquers: rather, despite its mad-house setting, it ends in the establishment of common sense, which is hardly visible in the world of Middleton's noble family. Such matters apart, it is difficult to think of a more generally rewarding 1930s book on its subject, unless it is perhaps Una Ellis-Fermor's almost coincident one. Boldly Miss Ellis-Fermor put two quotations from Webster on her title-page. 'Tussaud laureate' indeed! For her he was properly a major dramatist and poet, and not all the source-hunting, and declared moral shock, of recent years have made any serious dint on that verdict. It is true that she softened Webster's effect by interpreting 'Look you, the stars shine still' as consolatory, which we are not

likely to do; and we may query her statement that Ford was essentially a Jacobean, for if ever a specifically Caroline drama truly flowered it was surely in *Perkin Warbeck* and *The Broken Heart*. In these two books there is learning and humanity, a sense of what Shakespeare was, a sense that his Jacobean contemporaries are worth studying, and not merely as men who point to his superiority. Not until Robert Ornstein's much later book, which will be commented on below, have we had work of equal range and perceptiveness. Ornstein has had the advantage of building on Miss Bradbrook's and Miss Ellis-Fermor's groundwork, but *Themes and Conventions* and *Jacobean Drama* remain books we rely on and recommend.

With a disregard for the convenient chronological division, Miss Ellis-Fermor's later book *The Frontiers of Drama*[3] should here be mentioned. It contains, I think, her most mature critical writing. Its range was over drama in general, and, although her references to Shakespeare's contemporaries in tragic writing are here incidental, they contribute powerfully to the book's total effect.

In this time we acquired information in a way other than those already mentioned. This was through the publication of truly scholarly editions of the plays of Shakespeare's contemporaries. There were F. L. Lucas's edition of Webster[4] and Allardyce Nicoll's Tourneur,[5] following the pioneer work of T. M. Parrott's *The Plays of George Chapman*.[6] Again by-passing the chronological sub-division, we are bound to think of the more recent editions by Fredson Bowers of Dekker[7] and, under his general editorship, of Beaumont and Fletcher.[8] Professor Bowers's methods of editing are of course very different from those known in the 1920s: the 'new bibliography', which he so

[1] Louvain, 1908.   [2] Chicago, 1971.
[3] London, 1945.   [4] London, 1927.
[5] London, 1929.   [6] London, 1910–13.
[7] Cambridge, 1953–61.   [8] Cambridge, 1961– .

outstandingly embodies today, has given all editing an increased self-consciousness, an increased awareness of the magnitude of the task undertaken. This applies even where the editorial procedures have taken lines different from those that Bowers stands for. One result has been that thorough editing (as in the New Arden Shakespeare and the Revels Plays) has taken much longer to come into print – and that is in the long run a genuine gain. The non-Bowers editions just mentioned, and some comparable others, will be referred to in the following section. What we still sadly lack are up-to-date editions of Ford and Middleton. Some years ago several North American presses could have managed these without difficulty: now they are pressed for money. However, an edition of Massinger, edited by Philip Edwards for the Clarendon Press, is promised, and a Shirley, of lesser but real importance for tragedy, is apparently to appear from the same publisher.

The period of this section was notably enriched by the first *A Companion to Shakespeare Studies*, edited by Harley Granville-Barker and G. B. Harrison,[1] which included a paper by Bonamy Dobrée on 'Shakespeare and the Drama of his Time'. He paid a special tribute to Chapman, where he reiterates the sense of the uniqueness of that dramatist which has been noted already:

It is more to the point to study the dramatists who had made their appearance at the end of the [sixteenth] century, not because they had much or any effect on Shakespeare – it is, rather, the other way about – but because they developed further than Shakespeare did certain aspects of the drama in which they specialised, using material which he was content to handle as side issues in his wider sweep. The greatest of these is no doubt Chapman, the nearest approach to a 'metaphysical' poet in the drama of the time.   (p. 255)

It is curious that Peter Ure, in his chapter on 'Shakespeare and the Drama of his Time' in *A New Companion to Shakespeare Studies*, edited by Kenneth Muir and S. Schoenbaum,[2] concentrates much more on the Elizabethan contemporaries, but he does say of Shakespeare's plays that 'none is without some kind of contextual relationship to other plays of the time' (p. 220).

After 1939

In view of what has been said above about the increasing undergraduate ignorance of Shakespeare's contemporaries, it is ironic that the past generation has had more ways of increasing its knowledge than ever before. There is no need to refer to the big anthologies of Elizabethan and Jacobean plays, though some of them have been most carefully edited: unless, however, they are 'adopted' for a class, they are not likely to be much consulted. But several series have made Jacobean plays, especially tragedies, easily available in comparatively inexpensive form. They can here be mentioned in chronological order of appearance: the Revels Plays (1958–   ), the Regents (1964–   ), the New Mermaids (1964–   ), the Fountainwell series (1968–   ). These editions are in every case anxious to present the chosen play in relation to what Shakespeare was doing or had done, and the best of the introductions to these volumes have provided major illumination on the connection or the absence of it.

Scholarship, as distinct from criticism, has done us a most signal service in these years, as in the 1920s. Gerald Eades Bentley's *The Jacobean and Caroline Stage*[3] in its splendid seven volumes has continued Chambers's work in *The Elizabethan Stage*, carrying the record on to 1642. Now we have all the information we need for Shakespeare's immediate successors, and can disregard it only at our peril. Other works of reference are legion, but reference should be made here to *The Reader's Encyclopedia of Shakespeare*, edited by Oscar James Campbell,[4] which is of course mainly

[1] Cambridge, 1934.   [2] Cambridge, 1971.
[3] Oxford, 1941–60.   [4] London, 1966.

concerned with Shakespeare but includes informative entries on other writers of tragedy up to 1642. Also in this category should be noted F. S. Boas's *An Introduction to Stuart Drama*,[1] a book of minor importance critically, but splendid for reference purposes.

One of the most distinguished of post-war critical writings was also one of the earliest. It was F. P. Wilson's *Elizabethan and Jacobean*,[2] based on the Alexander Lectures he gave at Toronto in 1943. It is unnecessary to search for suitable words of praise for a book to which all of us owe much. It is enough to recall that its last two chapters were respectively titled 'Drama' and 'Shakespeare', and that the author talks of the tragic writers with wisdom as well as with enthusiasm and discrimination, feeling it unnecessary to rebuke the dramatists for their strong imaginings.

Two major and wide-ranging books came at the beginning of the 1960s: R. H. Ornstein's *The Moral Vision of Jacobean Tragedy*[3] and Eugene M. Waith's *The Herculean Hero in Marlowe, Chapman, Shakespeare and Dryden*.[4] Beginning with a chapter on 'Tragedy and the Age', Ornstein proceeds to examine the varieties of the tragic view embodied in each major dramatist between 1600 and 1642. Shakespeare is reserved for the last chapter, so that when we arrive there we have been led more strikingly to a comparison than is frequently the case. There are many shrewd insights into the individual dramatists, and there is also much careful consideration of the age's modes of thinking (as for example when a distinction is made between 'ideas which are at the vital centre of late Renaissance creative thought and those which are cherished as intellectual pieties'). The tragic writer and the preacher are seen as having basically different approaches to the human condition, and on the book's last page we have this firm and compelling statement: 'To accept the affirmations of tragedy we must have the cour-

age to cherish beauty as it is being destroyed and to rejoice in the fulfillment of human greatness no matter how indifferent to man's fulfillment or annihilation is the universe.' The book has been much studied and widely admired, and its influence can I think be traced in a number of subsequent writings. Yet it is curious that so balanced and broad a view of Jacobean tragedy appears to have had no impact at all on some critics during the years that have followed. After twelve years it surely remains the best and most comprehensive treatment of this body of drama.

Waith's scope is both smaller and larger. He does not attempt to take in the whole field of Jacobean tragedy, but looks backwards to Marlowe and forwards to Dryden. He is indeed one of those rare people thoroughly at home with Restoration along with Renaissance drama. His discussion may seem one-sided, for he is manifestly arguing a case which he feels has been neglected: he wants us to respond to Marlowe's and Shakespeare's and Chapman's and Dryden's heroes as emblematic of the Herculean ideal, and he makes a thoroughly good case. We may say 'but yet', but we have to accept his insistence on the hero's magnitude, are surely compelled to reject a mere denigration as a tenable way of dealing with any of his heroes. He has formidably continued the argument in *Ideas of Greatness: Heroic Drama in England*,[5] where again Shakespeare is related to the whole seventeenth-century context. If at times he holds back from recognising that the Jacobean hero has a littleness as well as a greatness, he has made us more deeply conscious of the greatness, however flawed. Both here and elsewhere in his writing Waith has, moreover, shown himself able to deal with English and French drama in revealing juxtaposition.

[1] Oxford, 1946.   [2] Oxford, 1945.
[3] Madison, 1960.   [4] London, 1962.
[5] London, 1971.

Earlier than this, Madeleine Doran published *Endeavors of Art: A Study of Form in Elizabethan Drama*.[1] It must be briefly saluted here, for it has been properly influential on much later writing. But Miss Doran's special concern stops with the turn of the century, though with some glances forward: she observes the efforts of the dramatists to master the form that had come to them from varied sources, medieval and classical, notes the importance of medieval and Renaissance rhetoric in the plays' composition, and emphasises the debate-element which could mirror unresolved oppositions and sometimes confusion. The relevance of this for the Jacobeans needs no underlining.

Some further notable books are: Irving Ribner's *Jacobean Tragedy: The Quest for Moral Order*,[2] which perhaps errs on the side of making the dramatists look like *bien-pensants*, but draws on Ribner's extensive knowledge of the field and is a companion volume to the author's *Patterns in Shakespearian Tragedy*;[3] John F. Danby's *Poets on Fortune's Hill*,[4] which links Sidney with Beaumont and Fletcher and with Shakespeare's last plays, with a special recognition of irony in the so-called 'romances'; and Bernard Spivack's *Shakespeare and the Allegory of Evil*,[5] which is principally concerned with the relation of Iago to the Vice-figure but includes an occasional reference forward: it could provide a basis for a study of Iago's successors. But one of the most influential books of these years has been Alfred Harbage's *Shakespeare and the Rival Traditions*,[6] which has provided the main basis for a distinction between the repertories of the public and private theatres in the late sixteenth and early seventeenth centuries. We can argue that he discriminates too curiously; he is obviously unhappy about *Troilus and Cressida*; he does not sufficiently allow for the exchange of plays between the two sorts of theatres (*The Spanish Tragedy* and *The Malcontent*, for example); he avers that he is making no qualitative judge-

ment, but he obviously has a preference for the 'democratic' public theatre. Even so, he has made us aware, more fully than anyone before, of the fact of there being two separate theatres in Shakespeare's time, a dichotomy that became even more noticeable when the King's Men took over the Blackfriars and were followed soon after by other adult companies in occupying theatres that were technically 'private'.

Now a less happy note must be struck. People are still with us who wish to denigrate once again the corpus of Jacobean drama, revering Shakespeare of course but using him as a whip for the scourging of his earlier and later contemporaries. Here we need to refer to T. B. Tomlinson's *A Study of Elizabethan and Jacobean Tragedy*.[7] This writer shows some true insights: when he refers to 'Marlowe's imagery of definition and limitation rather than of growth and possibility', he seems indeed right, though we may be puzzled why he should think this a distinction of quality; he wins applause when he insists on the unique character of every considerable play, which makes a too easy (the two words need underlining) generalisation about Elizabethan and Jacobean tragedy a nugatory exercise; he is good too in bringing out the special fascination which the stuff of existence can exert on Tourneur and Middleton, fusing with the repugnance each feels respectively for the lust-ridden and money-ridden world. Yet, in contrast with his belief in each play as a world in its own right, he propounds the view that Shakespeare and Tourneur and Middleton (the last of these so modish a name now) achieved a norm by which others may be judged. He dislikes any dramatist who in any way shows an aloofness from the particular (one is reminded of an Australian critic who objects to

[1] Madison, 1954. [2] London, 1962.
[3] London, 1960. [4] London, 1952.
[5] New York, 1958. [6] Bloomington, 1952.
[7] Cambridge, 1964.

Patrick White's *The Tree of Man* because, along with similar things, a dog is commonly referred to as 'the dog' instead of 'Rover' or whatever): such an aloofness leads to his being 'sterile' (Marlowe) or 'irresponsible' (Fletcher) or 'dangerous' or 'decadent' (Chapman and Ford): his adjectives seem to become, even in his hands, oddly respectable. Here we seem to have the 'Cambridge' school at its most desperate: we should read 'George Eliot, Lawrence and others' (so beautifully vague) in order to recognise the 'breadth, depth and substance' that English literature later achieved. Well, we can value George Eliot and Conrad, Lawrence too, without wanting to put *The White Devil* (which Tomlinson despises, for no compelling reason) away. Curiously, he is oblivious of the work done on the texts of the plays he discusses.

David L. Frost's *The School of Shakespeare*,[1] is also a surprising book. It argues, as if there were anything new about this, that Shakespeare had a major influence on the dramatists who succeeded him. Middleton is again the great name here: some of us can admire him without despising the rest of the Jacobeans. It remains perplexing that Frost finds Middleton the one Jacobean writer who correctly followed in Shakespeare's steps. Of course, we can see Shakespeare behind *The Changeling* and *Women Beware Women*, but there is surely a greater difference in general attitude between these plays and Shakespeare's tragedies than there is between, say, Webster's and Ford's plays on the one hand and Shakespeare's on the other. Probably all that is meant is that Middleton is 'acceptable', as Shakespeare is and Webster and Ford are not. Frost's bad people are 'anti-Shakespearian', expressing bewilderment and confusion in place of Shakespeare's 'moral certainty'. This point is worth arguing for a sentence or two. Shakespeare's 'moral certainty' (see the comment on Ornstein's book above) surely limited itself to the recognition that certain ways of behaviour are evil and others

good (e.g., Cordelia's, Kent's, Cornwall's First Servant's, however rash these people may be): it did not extend to any sureness about the universe, or about the possibility of more than the most fleeting reward. Webster and Ford have that same degree of 'certainty', as exhibited in the figure of Webster's Duchess – we may see, for example, Gunnar Boklund's *The Duchess of Malfi: Sources, Themes, Characters*[2] for its insistence on the true marriage of the Duchess and Antonio, despite Antonio's and the Duchess's blunders and at least the man's incapacity for his insecurely-achieved high place – and in the baroque nobility of Ford's Princess Calantha. Webster is capable of making us recognise a kind of goodness in the ending of a life, formerly a 'black charnel', with insight and firmness; Ford is surely not wrong in wanting us to see Giovanni, for all his guilt (I do not mean merely incest), as splendid in facing his death's-men. In Frost's book there is, I think, a mere prudishness, a refusal in fact to look in the face either the Jacobean world or the world of today. Oddly, he is one of those who think *The Revenger's Tragedy* is Middleton's, which should destroy his case. Surely there could be no play so fiercely virulent, so fully urging an animus against the establishment – unless perhaps *Timon of Athens*?

A book on similar lines is Wilbur Sanders's *The Dramatist and the Received Idea: Studies in the Plays of Marlowe and Shakespeare*,[3] which begins by castigating Marlowe for *The Massacre at Paris*; but this is outside my period and should therefore not be commented on further: it is mentioned only as another example of what contemporary criticism can do when it sets out to denigrate Shakespeare's contemporaries in tragedy.

I hope it has been made clear that these three books all contain good things, are indeed the

[1] Cambridge, 1968.   [2] Cambridge, Mass., 1962.
[3] Cambridge, 1968.

products of vigorous and sometimes sensitive minds. What worries me is that the writers appear to dislike so much of the drama they write about. Fortunately the theatre is here a good corrective: Webster and Marlowe are there, surely to stay; so of course are Middleton and the author of *The Revenger's Tragedy*.

Meanwhile, less angry work goes on. We can note, for example, the *Festschriften* for Hardin Craig and Baldwin Maxwell: *Essays on Shakespeare and Elizabethan Drama*, edited by Richard Hosley,[1] and *Studies in English Drama*, edited by Charles B. Woods and Curt A. Zimansky:[2] both of these link Shakespeare with his contemporaries and successors. In the Craig volume, the following seem to be particularly appropriate here: Allardyce Nicoll's '*The Revenger's Tragedy* and the Virtue of Anonymity', which poses an interesting point, perhaps ultimately derivative from I. A. Richards's experiments in 'practical criticism': if we really cannot say who wrote the play, it has to stand by itself and be responded to without any *a priori* consciousness of an author: the article may make us wonder if it would be good if we could look, say, at *Timon of Athens* and *Troilus and Cressida* like that; the articles on Heywood and Massinger, respectively by Arthur Brown and Philip Edwards, are also to be welcomed. The Maxwell volume has a wider range: R. A. Foakes on Marston (though we may still wonder whether 'fantastical' is wholly the right word for the *Antonio* plays) and Allardyce Nicoll on Chapman give us articles which are presented side by side with writing on Shakespeare, Marlowe, and the drama from the Restoration to the late nineteenth century. Another collection of high value is *Jacobean Theatre*,[3] the first volume in the Stratford-upon-Avon Studies, edited by John Russell Brown and Bernard Harris: of particular note in a generally outstanding volume are Maynard Mack's now famous paper 'The Jacobean Shakespeare', J. R. Mulryne's on Webster's two major tragedies, and Peter Ure's on Chapman.

J. W. Lever's *The Tragedy of State*[4] deals with major things in Jacobean tragedy and does not neglect Shakespeare: unlike some recent writers, he puts to the forefront the violence of Jacobean times and makes us remember that this violence also belongs to us. It was absurd when a *Times Literary Supplement* reviewer rebuked him for suggesting that Italy's violence was not to be thought of in the more favoured land that the Jacobeans themselves knew. It seemed highly appropriate that he began this book by referring to Alfred de Musset's *Lorenzaccio*, revived with strong effect at the Festival Theatre, Stratford, Ontario, in 1972.

This retrospect began by indicating the writer's realisation that he hardly knew what to leave out. At an early stage in its planning he became conscious that monographs on the particular writers of Jacobean tragedies should not be mentioned unless to make a point in relation to a book of more general scope. Even so, he is very conscious that the field has been lightly skimmed. It may be best to end with a mention of a book which brings the historical position once more before us: Gerald Eades Bentley's *The Profession of Dramatist in Shakespeare's Time, 1590–1642*.[5] Here, as indeed we have come to expect from Bentley, is the large view, the original research, the putting of us in the picture, the giving of an ever more substantial basis for the work of the critic.

[1] London, 1963.   [2] Iowa City, 1962.
[3] London, 1960.   [4] London, 1971.
[5] Princeton, 1971.

© CLIFFORD LEECH 1973

'FORM AND CAUSE CONJOIN'D': 'HAMLET' AND SHAKESPEARE'S WORKSHOP

KEITH BROWN

That certain analogies exist between the opening and closing scenes of *Hamlet* is a commonplace of criticism. Everyone sees that the figure of Old Hamlet – in his Polack-defeating armour – at the start of the tragedy is balanced by the armed figure of Fortinbras at the play's end, fresh from his own Polack wars, restoring the *status quo*. And similar parallels have been pointed out, for instance, between the *platform* of I, i, on which the ghost of the murdered king makes his silently-eloquent appearance, and the *stage* on which the silently-eloquent body of his son (again with Horatio present as messenger and interpreter) is to make its last appearance after v, ii.

But what does not seem to have been generally recognised, whether in the study or in the theatre, is quite how far such apparent symmetries can be traced on further into the play; certainly far enough, at all events, to make it unlikely that in doing so one is doing nothing but finding pictures in the fire.

It is convenient to plot this underlying parallelism scene by scene; indeed, the very extent to which that is possible seems in itself to say something about 'Shakespeare's workshop'.

Since the opening and closing scenes have already been referred to, let us begin by juxtaposing the second and the penultimate scenes:

I, ii – V, i

(*An uneasy wedding ceremony
An uneasy funeral ceremony.*)

...both cases where the royal will has overruled conventional ecclesiastical decorum. Moreover, thanks to Gertrude's 'I thought thy bride-bed to have deck'd, sweet maid, / and not have strew'd thy grave' (v, i, 239–40), the wedding–funeral association of ideas is also present on both occasions. (Seen in this light, of course, Hamlet's leap into Ophelia's grave makes rather better sense than is allowed by those who would dismiss it as merely a crude piece of vulgarisation, likely to derive rather from Burbage than Shakespeare. Essentially, it continues, however brutally, the parallel wedding–funeral entanglements.)

It is interesting, too, to see how the *sequence* of I, ii – formal court occasion / departure of King, Queen and Lords / glum ruminations by Hamlet / bitter humour, tinged with social satire, from Hamlet / conversation – is in fact repeated, in *inverse* order, in v, i. Compare II, i and IV, v in this respect, or the way the beginning of I, iii seems to pair up with the end of IV, vii.

(*third scene*) *I, iii –
IV, vii* (*third from last*)

The first of these scenes presents Ophelia to us: the latter, the story of her death. I, iii *begins* with Laertes warning Ophelia of the dangers of involvement with Hamlet; while IV, vii *ends* with Laertes learning of the end to which the Prince has indirectly brought her.

In both scenes the triangle of affection within the Polonius family is the dominating factor. In I, iii, their concern for each other is expressed through well-meant but somewhat sadly heavy-handed advice. IV, vii, is given over to the blundering determination of the survivor to do his useless best for the other two by at least avenging them.

(*fourth scene*) I, *iv and* 'v'[1]
IV, *vi* (*fourth from last*)

It might at first sight seem absurd to 'pair' a scene of 281 lines with one of 32 lines. Yet the parallel between their places in the map of the action is perfectly clear. Claudius despatches both Hamlets: Old Hamlet to Purgatory, Young Hamlet to an intended death in England – naturally not expecting either to be able later to tell the story of their journeys. But first Old Hamlet does so (four scenes from the beginning of the play): then his son does the same (four scenes from the end.)

(*fifth scene*) II, *i* ———

Begins with Polonius seeking information about his son.

Ends with Ophelia's vivid description of a Hamlet clearly as near mad as makes no difference: 'mad for thy love?' ... no, but distracted by a grief and horror certainly complicated by his feelings for Ophelia.

——— IV, *v* (*fifth from last*)

Ends with Laertes' furious search for information about the death of his father.

Begins with the presentation of an Ophelia driven mad: by a grief and horror certainly complicated by love/amorous feeling for Hamlet. (Cf. the mildly bawdy note of the St Valentine's Day song.)

It is likely, too, that Ophelia in IV, v is wearing some sort of female equivalent to the kind of dress that Hamlet is wearing (in her story) in II, i. For this was an accepted sign of madness, and Laertes grasps that she is mad before a word has been spoken.

(It is perhaps also worth noting that while the *presented* happenings of I, iv-v were matched by *reported* adventures in IV, vi, the converse happens in this immediately adjacent pair of scenes. There are other examples of this in the play.)

(*sixth scene*) II, *ii* ———

Is the last time we hear of Fortinbras and his Polack campaign until IV, iv.

Rosencrantz and Guildenstern *arrive*, at the King's behest, from Wittenberg, to keep an eye on Hamlet. (Are surprised to find the latter thinks Denmark a prison.)

———IV, *iv* (*sixth from last*)

Fortinbras and his Polack campaign are heard of again.

Rosencrantz and Guildenstern *depart*, at the King's behest, for England (with Hamlet as virtually their prisoner.)

***

We have now carried this pairing of material, scene by scene, right through the two first acts. (It is interesting to find, therefore, that in the judgements – *inter alios* – of the editors both of the Arden and of the old Harvard editions of

[1] The First Folio is surely correct, whether accidentally or not, in omitting any scene-division between I, iv and I, v. For in their movement, and anxious open-air encounters, they are obviously analogous to those sequences of separate exchanges with which Elizabethan playwrights tended to represent battles; and it appears originally to have been quite normal to

the play, we have also carried it right through the tragedy's last two acts as well. The old Harvard edition actually changes the standard act-divisons, delaying the start of act IV so that the normal 'IV, iv' becomes IV, i. The Arden editor states that only the inconvenience of upsetting a traditional scheme of textual reference stops him following suit. 'Harvard' act-divisions will be assumed throughout this present discussion, except when identifying specific scenes or making detailed textual references.) Even the apparent major 'loose end' represented by the various passages in II, ii about actors and acting (often felt by critics to be slightly digressive) seem to fall into place if one is willing to pursue the pattern apparently being traced here on into the central act.

The central act. It is not, of course, strictly necessary to pursue the 'pattern' on into act III at all. Instead, it might be argued, perhaps, that all we have really been analysing so far is just Shakespeare's rough tidying of the four outer acts of *Hamlet* into a kind of more-or-less regular frame for act III as a whole. But obviously the kind of ABC/CBA symmetry that we have been tracing does tempt one to think in terms of a progression onwards – and inwards – to some specific centre.

This is interesting for several reasons. Take, first, our general notions of the structure of Shakespearian tragedy. To a quite remarkable extent, these still derive from Bradley, the near-definitiveness of whose superb opening lectures can be measured by the degree to which we continue to reproduce his basic ideas today, even when attempting to challenge them. Characteristic in this respect, for instance, is Professor Marco Mincoff's 'The Structural Pattern of Shakespeare's Tragedies'[1] – a re-thinking of the issue that chances to afford an especially convenient starting-point for the line of thought to be followed here.

Bradley himself, constantly using metaphors of *rising* and *falling*, saw the essential form of Shakespearian tragedy as a sort of stepped pyramid. Within a broad three-part division of the action, he finds 'the usual scheme' to be 'an ascending and descending movement of one side in the conflict'. This 'rise' reaches a 'zenith' in a 'crisis' (e.g., the Mouse-trap in *Hamlet*) soon followed by a 'counter-stroke' beginning a 'descent'. The stepped profile of this broad rise and descent comes partly, he suggests, from a regular minor oscillation of fortune between the opposing parties in the conflict, and partly from 'a constant alternation of rises and falls...in the emotional pitch of the work'. The 'centre' of the action – it is curious how completely Bradley takes for granted the naturalness of looking for this in a Shakespeare play, and the possibility of finding it – can lie either in the 'crisis' or in the 'counter-stroke': or in both jointly, since sometimes the latter follows on without any pause.[2]

At first sight, Professor Mincoff's own analysis looks very different, for he rejects the notion of tripartite structural division, and differs from Bradley, too, in finding that one specific play – *Hamlet* – manifests the 'true' Shakespearian structural pattern. Yet he again is dominated by the metaphor of rise-and-fall, writing interestingly of Shakespeare's tendency to give scenes a 'pyramidal' structure, forming

regard such sequences as constituting a single scene. (See W. W. Greg, *The Shakespeare First Folio* (Oxford, 1955), pp. 142–3.) In any case, momentum and sheer continuity plainly make I, iv and 'v' into a single unit even irrespective of such formal criteria.

(The other conventionally accepted scene-numberings in the text, despite their late date, correspond much better to the facts of the play, and to Elizabethan practice.)

[1] *Shakespeare Survey 3* (Cambridge, 1950), pp. 58–65.
[2] A. C. Bradley, *Shakespearean Tragedy* (London, 1904), Lecture II, 'Construction in Shakespeare's Tragedies'.

separate units, carefully contrasted. Admittedly, some 'Shakespearian' structural patterning can often equally well be found in Shakespeare's contemporaries; but distinctively Shakespearian Professor Mincoff too agrees, is the achievement of a kind of rhythmic pulsation of emotional tension; and also – this begins to go beyond Bradley – a marked 'centring and emotional stressing of the turn of the action'. Unlike his predecessors ('who on the whole left the pattern of the play to take care of itself, or at least paid small attention to a centring climax or definite turn of the action...and still less to making such a turn coincide with the maximum of emotional tension') Shakespeare establishes 'a definite apex', with the play's tensions 'so graduated as to lead up to and down again from that peak'. Here is an interesting flowering of Bradley's casual allusions to the 'centre' of the Shakespearian tragic structure; and one made all the more persuasive by the context in which Professor Mincoff presents it:

It would seem...correct to ascribe this effect [*viz*: the centring of the turn of the action] to that completeness of structure...exemplified in so much sixteenth century art, in the closed, symmetrical composition of the Renaissance painters, and – a much nearer parallel – in so many of the more complex lyrics of the sixteenth century, such as Wyatt's *To his Lute*, Surrey's *Complaint of the absence of her Lover*, Spenser's *Prothalamion*, *Epithalamion* and *Ditty in Praise of Eliza*, which work up to the height of lyrical emotion in the exact middle and then fall slowly to the end, often in such a way that the first and last, second and penultimate verses or groups of verses are parallel.

(p. 65)

Yet how valid, really, is this use of the metaphor of rise-and-fall, when applied to *Hamlet*?

Certainly Hamlet's fortunes do in some senses 'rise' until about the middle of the play, declining thereafter. And naturally various parts of various scenes are pitched at varying emotional levels. But that is very different from claiming to find a sequence of recurrent

tensions 'so *graduated* as to lead *up to*' an '*apex*' and then *down* again. Is not this, perhaps, rather something that one can persuade oneself that one has felt, after the event, on the basis of an abstract theory, than something actually experienced in the theatre? – parts of I, v, for instance, to take only one of many possible examples, can surely reach a pitch of intensity, on stage, that nothing later outdoes.

In any case, as the reference above to painting underlines, centric effects in sixteenth-century art were achieved by many means. Emotional 'apex-ing' (surely the least practicable of all for dramatists, interested in holding their audience's attention throughout every act, to imitate) was only one such device, itself commonly built, as Professor Mincoff notes, over a formal pattern of ABC/CBA symmetries – i.e., very much the type of patterning that we seem to have been tracing through four acts of *Hamlet*. On the other hand, such formal patternings do not necessarily carry any very strong emotional correlate. It seems not impossible, therefore, that Professor Mincoff may have made the right link between *Hamlet* and Elizabethan non-dramatic poetry, but chanced to stress the wrong aspect of that link.

That possibility is not diminished by some of the studies of formal, mannerist patternings in Elizabethan art and literature that have appeared since Professor Mincoff's own article was printed. Take, for instance, Alastair Fowler's recently-published *Triumphal Forms*.[1] Although Professor Fowler has raised a number of hackles, not least by some perhaps too-rapid theorising about the Sonnets, his book remains for all that an admirable exploration of the interplay of three aspects of Elizabethan aesthetics: (i) the liking for closed symmetrical constructions noted by Professor Mincoff; (ii) the pervasively spatial character of Renaissance thought – the sort of thing which could lead Drayton to feel that he had justified the

[1] Cambridge, 1970.

use of a particular stanza form by showing that it possessed the same proportions as 'the pillar which in architecture is called the Tuscan', or that could lead Jonson to define 'action' in drama as answering to 'place' in a building, with its own 'largeness, compass and proportion'; (iii) the preoccupation, so general and persistent as to amount almost to a nervous tic in the culture of the age, with the idea of the sovereign mid-point. These three elements Professor Fowler interestingly shows to be integrated in the iconography of the Roman triumph (stylised into a procession tending to be symmetrically arranged about a central triumphator) – an image which exerted a pervasive influence on art and ceremonial in the period. For, to quote Professor Fowler himself:

the spatial tendency of renaissance thought facilitated direct control of ideas by formal organisation; and conventions of centralised symmetry naturally carried over from political protocol into poetry, as they did into architecture. Poets developed the habit of distributing matter through the metrical structure with careful regard to the centre's sovereignty. Almost as a regular practice, they would devote the central place to some principal figure or event, or make it coincide with a structural division. (p. 62)

'Almost as a regular practice': it is not too strong a claim. It is astonishing how often one does find poets of the period marking the centre of their poems – most often by some image of, or allusion to, the ideas of sovereignty or triumph, even when these can have only the most perfunctory relationship to the general tenor of the poem in question. This remains true even when one has made full allowance for the ease with which wishful thinking can 'manufacture' centres. The habit seems quite marked enough to leave little doubt that the more sophisticated Elizabethan reader would himself tend to be on the look-out for such indications of the mid-point: which further strengthens the likelihood (for which anyway there is plenty of other evidence) that he would

also notice, and savour, even quite complex formal patternings – especially when these were in fact symmetrically disposed around the central point. Nor is there any reason to suppose, either, that such a reader could not also have enjoyed the various kinds of finesse between *double* centres which Professor Fowler further analyses in sixteenth-century poetry (meeting doubts that he is being over-subtle by pointing to parallel examples of the same practice in Renaissance architecture).

Even the most sceptical will see the temptation to relate all this, however tentatively, to *Hamlet*. For – quite apart from any question of 'pairings' or symmetries – the whole weight of our critical tradition clearly tends towards seeing that play, too, as a double-centred structure. Nearly every traditional-style critic seems to feel that the tragedy *has* a centre or central turning-point: though disagreeing in locating it sometimes in the Mouse-trap and sometimes in the Bedchamber scene (though seldom anywhere else).

Yet 'why not both'? Both *are*, quite literally, formal mid-points, both identifiable by means current in the mannerist patternings of the period: the play's half-way mark[1] is reached

[1] Since *Hamlet* contains many prose passages and broken lines, it would be absurd to imagine Shakespeare ever attempting to locate the *precise* metrical centre (i.e., the line exactly at the half-way point) of either the play as a whole or of individual scenes. But it is not unreasonable to consider the possibility of his having located the play's half-way mark in some looser fashion: perhaps by making some rough computation of running-time, or (more likely) by counting MS. pages – much as many readers of this essay may well have done themselves when preparing a talk or lecture.

It is in this looser sense that the business of the *Murder of Gonzago* will be found to lie across 'the play's half-way mark' – as a page-count of any facsimile Q2 will show – even though one cannot precisely locate that notional point itself. (The episode is long enough for its physically central position not to be significantly brought in doubt by any of the various uncertainties that plague textual studies of *Hamlet*.)

[*note continued overleaf*

during the central episode of III, ii; while the Bedchamber scene is numerically central (tenth of nineteen scenes).[1] An accident? Perhaps. But at least a singularly happy one: especially in view of the persistent Elizabethan association of centrality with sovereignty. For a while the tragedy abounds in actual or potential royalty (even Laertes has the popular vote for the job) it is clear, nevertheless, that it contains only one truly sovereign figure: Old Hamlet. Speech after speech enhances our sense of his majesty. Not only does he rule the drama through a call for revenge which makes him the *primum mobile* setting in action all the wheels of the plot; but he is also the last 'true' King of Denmark in the quite simple sense that his successor unjustly owes his throne to poison. As we watch him trying to protect his wife, admonishing his son, and determined still to settle scores with his brother, there is no doubt who is still the effective head of the royal family of Elsinore.

How striking, then, that this royal figure (present nowhere else in act III) should chance to be associated – and in such clearly-differentiated ways – with *both* the play's customarily-identified 'centres'. For what routs King Claudius in III, ii? An image (as he sees it) of his murdered brother, the rightful sovereign. Yet this image was 'counterfeit': he yields the stage to a mere player-king – at what many critics see as the 'strategic centre' (the phrase is Anne Righter's) of a tragedy whose fundamental metaphor is itself a pun upon two different senses of the verb *to act*. But is there not something illusory, even so, about the 'Mouse-trap's' seemingly focal role? It does not, after all, enable *Hamlet* to sweep to his revenge; and Claudius was already planning to ship his nephew off to England anyway. Even Miss Righter, convinced of the scene's 'strategic' centrality, and showing fascinatingly just *how* fully the whole idea of that scene may be regarded as the 'natural, almost inevitable

consequence' of the conversations about theatre-matters in II, ii, still feels obliged to allow that those same conversations (partly omitted, of course, in Q2) were nevertheless 'perhaps a trifle intrusive' in a play 'concerned with fate and character in mediaeval Denmark'.[2]

And so they are. Not just in immediate

There are other Shakespeare plays, too, whose underlying structure might be thought to become clearer when one has made this sort of loose identification of their half-way mark. *Love's Labours Lost* – which also seems to exhibit symmetrical 'pairings' – is one case in point.

[1] Many people seem to find the idea of Shakespeare counting scenes, or otherwise consciously planning in scene-units, as absurd as the notion of him totalling up individual lines. There is an apparent tendency to be hypnotised by the undeniable fact that no edition of any Shakespeare play published during the poet's lifetime ever carried a full apparatus of numbered scene-divisions. Yet really that proves very little: after all, numbering is not counting. Even early texts of Renaissance works with an acknowledged number-symbolism content are not always equipped with any numbering or other typographical aid to the detection of that symbolism. More significant, surely, is the fact that surviving Elizabethan/Jacobean theatrical 'plots' do mark scene-divisions – and all the evidence suggests that authorial plots commonly did the same. Hamlet's own praise of a play for being 'well-digested in the scenes' seems extremely suggestive in this context, too.

As W. W. Greg points out, scene-division on the Elizabethan stage was structural, and followed directly from the action. So long, therefore, as the directions were clear, there was the less need to mark or number scene-divisions in the actual manuscript. (See Greg, *The Shakespeare First Folio*, pp. 142–5).

It may be added that *Hamlet* is not the only play in which there is evidence of Shakespeare's willingness to think and plan in scene-units. However one reacts to Prof. Battenhouse's numerological theories, for instance, it is hard not to share his feeling that it is unlikely to be entirely a coincidence that twenty-one scenes lead up to, and twenty-one follow, the turning-point of the Battle of Actium in *Antony and Cleopatra*. (See Roy Battenhouse, *Shakespearean Tragedy: its Art and its Christian Premises* (Bloomington, 1969), pp. 180–1.)

[2] Anne Righter, *Shakespeare and the Idea of the Play* (London, 1962), p. 159.

subject-matter, but also – *inter alia* – in disrupting our sequence of 'pairings', which after this point cease to be bracketings of scenes, although in other respects they seem to continue to narrow down, tidily enough, on to the (numerically central) Bedchamber scene.

The Bedchamber scene has of course been endlessly discussed: even those who find the tragedy's turning-point in the play-within-the-play still note the crucial importance of the hold which the murder of Polonius gives Claudius over Hamlet. Both Freudian interpretations and readings of the play in terms of the 'minister' / scourge-of-God distinction equally point to it as the drama's heart (while it might be argued that Freudian analyses only really put more dramatically something that in more general terms has always been grasped anyway). View the play as the presentation of a *world*, rather than an *action*, and the result is the same. A recent study of the 'shape' of the Elizabethan play has shown very well how regularly dramatists employed ('on a stage well matched to the purpose') a structure which places

the individual and private person and private or personal action at the center, surrounds that action with the action belonging to a city or state, and that public action with an international action, and finally that whole earthly action (not always, but often) with an unearthly action or area for action...Whereas in later drama we are usually made aware of only one or two of these spheres, in the Elizabethan we are usually made sharply aware of all...the scheme suggests, as it appropriately should, the concentric spheres of the Ptolemaic system.[1]

Hamlet itself strongly enforces precisely this schematisation upon us. Not only is the enclosure of a private, family tragedy within a separate nationally-relevant crisis there especially well-marked, but the country which is the scene of this troubled story is also set within a particularly well-defined ring of other kingdoms, to each of which some manifestation of the power centred at Elsinore reaches out. This

effect must have been further reinforced for Shakespeare's original audience by the precision with which it dovetailed with their own image of Denmark, as the (still somewhat menacing) power at the centre of 'the Northern Regions' – to them a more-or-less distinct division of the globe. Elsinore itself, too, was well-known as the cross-roads of this whole northern world: that famous place to which, in Mercator's phrase, the ships of all nations were compelled to come 'as to one common centre'. And at the centre of this centre was the fortress/palace of Kronborg, with the private royal apartments at its heart: in reality as in the play.

To that 'heart', in the play and at the play's own heart, comes Hamlet. (Not, it should be noted, to a 'bedchamber', despite the traditional label of III, iv, but to his mother's '*closet*'. Just how elegantly apt this choice of setting was for the tragedy's focal scene, even a glance at the *OED* will show.) And at the metrical centre of the scene itself, inevitably, appears the sovereign figure of Old Hamlet – not dimly intimated by a play-king, this time, but in his proper person, still advising and commanding: the true King at the play's true centre, setting both his son and the action of the drama back on the rails again.

Or is that too glib? Claudius at least *acts* the King most convincingly: so would not something more immediate than abstract retrospective plot analysis be needed, therefore, clearly to mark the Ghost's appearance in III, iv as the more *truly* 'sovereign' role?

Of course it would: were it not that this 'something more' seems in fact already firmly provided by the preceding scene. For, apart from duplicate information,[2] what does III,

[1] T. B. Stroup, *Microcosmus: the shape of he Elizabethan play* (Lexington), 1965, p. 41.

[2] We already knew that Claudius was having trouble with his conscience (III, i, 50) and that Hamlet shall to England (III, i, 169ff.) while we shall see for ourselves that Polonius is going to hide behind the arras – and hardly needed to be told why. Of course

iii contain? Only the non-stabbing of Claudius at prayer; and two static, sermonising speeches on kingship by Rosencrantz and Guildenstern – speeches that might almost have wandered into the play text from one of the Histories. That of Rosencrantz, in particular, is peculiarly un-dramatic, holding up the action like an aria in an opera (Claudius does not even find it necessary to reply) just to embroider, in melodiously varied ways, upon an idea already presented by Guildenstern anyway. Together, the two speeches constitute only a sevenfold repetition, prefaced by insistence on its 'holy and religious' significance, of that received Tudor truth that the monarch is the hub of the wheel of society, upon which all else depends. Nowhere else – not only in *Hamlet*, but indeed in the whole Shakespeare canon – is there anything quite like the same limited, insistent repetition of this one particular point. Con-sidering the general density of ideas which *Hamlet* otherwise manifests, it seems quite beyond belief that so enormous a punctuation mark occurs at this point just by chance. It has, surely, all the appearance of a cue or marker.

And what it points to is not obscure. Its very ominousness tilts the emphasis back to Old Hamlet. 'The cease of majesty dies not alone …but both draw / what's near it with it'; yet this, we know, the death of the late King has yet to do. More than that, the two speeches firmly re-state a crucial test, which the rest of the scene is devoted to showing that Claudius fails, but which Old Hamlet passes uniquely well: thus clearing the ground for the latter's reappearance in the next scene. For no aspect of the Renaissance concept of kingship had been more hammered home for Shakespeare's contemporaries than the notion of the monarch as God's vice-gerent. Yet Claudius, as we are carefully shown, cannot even communicate with God, cut off from prayer by the retention of a crown which for this very reason is not altogether a true crown – as he himself knows.

For 'above', as he tells us, 'there is no shuffling; there the action lies / In his true nature' (III, iii, 61–2). By contrast Old Hamlet, returning to his kingdom only because supernatural powers allow it, to pursue the (obviously divinely-approved) tasks of ending the pollution of the sacred 'royal bed of Denmark' and punishing a sinner above the reach of human law, fulfils this aspect of the royal role to a degree that, in fact, no *living* man could ever do. No-one suspects in III, iv that here, too, might be a player-king: truth lies with the illusion.

'The true king / at the true centre.' Again we come back to the double assertion. As has recently been made clear, it would be quite consonant with Elizabethan literary practice to mark a sovereign mid-point by a royal presence *without* necessarily constructing any wider pattern of supporting symmetries around it at all. Nonetheless, having inspected the (pre-sumptive) keystone, it is natural to build up the rest of our arch. Take, then, the odd affair of Polonius' body: an element in the play on which the plethora of commentators have been unusually silent. Why is so much of the second half of act III taken up with looking for it? To the present writer, at least, this episode has always seemed to have about it a touch of perverse irrelevance.

True, that is precisely what makes it so dramatically effective: its very unexpectedness, and the bustle of the search, clearly help prevent too great an anticlimax after the excitement of the Closet scene. And certainly it is all plausible enough: Hamlet, presumably, drags the body into some neighbouring room and simply abandons – rather than hides – it there. Then in the ensuing alarm (and darkness? these elements of III, iii are not therefore just *redund-ant*: they do serve a dramatic purpose, as part of a build-up of excitement ensuring that we know before it begins that III, iv is going to be important. But that only reinforces the general case for III, iv's intended centrality.

...it is midnight) the obvious place is over-looked and the conclusion is jumped to that mad Hamlet has hidden the body deliberately, Hamlet himself ironically playing along with the assumption. An effective piece of naturalistic observation, it might be said, spiced with residual doubts that perhaps Hamlet did, half hysterically, hide the body on purpose: just the sort of unsuitable bye-comedy that real life does often generate.

Yet is there not still a seeming break here, for good or ill, with a certain decorum? For while individual Shakespearian tragedies certainly vary profoundly, they do at least all give one the sense that some process, some sort of ritual, is darkly going forward, to which every event along the main line of action contributes. Of course wryly humorous observation is also there; but it is normally either smelted into something quite different ('pray you, undo this button') or else is as it were 'encapsulated' (the Gravediggers). It is from this point of view that the business of 'Hamlet, where's Polonius?' seems faintly odd. For though it is interwoven into the main line of the action at a crucial moment of the play, nothing comes of it. 'Hamlet, where's Polonius?' Eventually, he tells them; and that is that. It does not seem to carry the 'ritual' forward and hence has at first sight no very obvious place in the rites. Why did Shakespeare bother with it? Just to meet the sort of technical needs sketched in above? These could have been met in a score of ways.

Whether such a *problemstellung* is thought acceptable or not, the fact remains that this part of the action does fall more plainly into some sort of 'ritual' place when oriented in relation to a central crisis. Although those who would reject all 'centric-' or ritual-minded approaches to the play can perfectly well deny the fact to be of any significance, it is undeniable that up to III, iv Polonius *is* hidden from (or talking about plans to hide from) Hamlet for most

of act III – except during the 'false' centre provided by the Mouse-trap scene – whereas after III, iv he is instead hidden from Claudius. Thus when Hamlet's rough demand of Ophelia, 'Where's your father?' converts into 'Hamlet, where's Polonius?' it is at least not absurd to feel that one movement of a sinister ballet is being completed.

Claudius's failure to achieve prayer in III, iii, too, surely finds its own place in this same sombre dance. Claudius, living, cannot make successful appeal to Heaven: but Polonius' murdered body must and will do so. No cliché is more familiar in the rhetoric of Elizabethan melodrama than that of the murdered man whose-every-wound's-a-mouth-to-cry-to-Heaven. How tidy, then, that the Closet scene, which is *preceded* by (abortive) *prayer*, should be *followed* by the order to convey the old man's corpse *to the chapel*. Hamlet's instinctive, slightly hysterical evasion of surrendering the body falls more into place when seen in this perspective, too.

In short, it does seem arguable that a centric view of act III (as here defined) better activates what might perhaps seem otherwise to be an unusually 'inactive' section of the tragedy. Meanwhile acceptance of even a few pairings of course automatically opens up further, more tentative possibilities. There is much in the play that, while it could hardly be used to demonstrate, in its own right, any centred symmetry underlying the drama, nonetheless does fit comfortably with such a concept if that concept once gains acceptance by other means.[1] Not that every line and passage locks into a dead symmetry: an apter image would

[1] An example of this in the part of the play we have just been analysing, is the attack on Rosencrantz and Guildenstern as 'sponges'. If this passage is put side by side with the praise of Horatio in III, ii, then one has something that might approximately be said to be the obverse and reverse of one coin...but only approximately, so that it is only in the context of other pairings that it catches the eye.

be that of a statue constructed upon a symmetrical armature – not every part of which is likely to be covered with an equal depth of 'flesh', if the statue is to have life and momentum. In *Hamlet,* this symmetry / asymmetry dichotomy precisely parallels (and is indeed, I would suggest, intimately related to) that other dichotomy which everyone sees in the play, between its ritual quality and its contrasting vein of naturalism.

Obviously one large question remains. Could the analogy thus traceable between the organisation of *Hamlet* and that of some non-dramatic Renaissance works 'simply' be the reflection of subconscious pressure upon Shakespeare's mind from the general artistic climate of the day? If not, does it concern only the play's 'back-stage carpentry'; or is it something meant to be discerned by the judicious spectator (. . . or reader)?

Hamlet's structural tidinesses do seem often too marked to have escaped at any rate the conscious attention of the playwright himself, working as he was for a theatre alive to scene-divisions. Moreover, play-texts were much read; while *Hamlet*'s unpractical length does suggest that for Shakespeare this play perhaps grew into something to be valued more nearly as an autonomous literary object than as an actor's production-script. It might thus not be necessarily absurd to envisage him composing partly with an eye to the 'wiser sort' of reader rather than spectator. (For that matter, a pro-duction carefully worked out for some special audience or occasion *could* have pointed-up the play's 'tidinesses', via groupings, costumes, hangings, music, etc.)

But that is mere speculation. Still, it is at least worth noting (i) that Shakespeare does show evidence at times of wishing to challenge more socially-advantaged intellectuals in their own arena; (ii) that one of the 'worlds' of Hamlet is very much that of young-gentlemen-around-a-university;[1] (iii) that for no other play is explicit boast made of production at both universities;[2] (iv) that Gabriel Harvey noted the esteem of university-educated connoisseurs for the play – which he brackets for praise, as it happens, with the work of several poets who seem to have used numerological or patterned centric structures.[3]

[1] One passing remark of Hamlet's, apparently not altogether understood by commentators, which contributes to this general flavour of what might be called 'fashionable intellectualism' in the play, is his mocking reference (v, ii, 115–16) to Renaissance memory systems. Any Elizabethan audience qualified to relish that sort of allusion were surely qualified, too, to appreciate centric patternings, the taste for which was very much part of the same intellectual climate as the interest in 'memory theatres', etc.

[2] In Ch. 11 of *Shakespeare's Occasional Plays* (New York, 1965), J. M. Nosworthy presents an extremely thorough review of all the reasons for thinking that the Q2 version of *Hamlet* must have been prepared at least partly with a potential academic audience in mind.

[3] See his comments as quoted in E. K. Chambers, *William Shakespeare* (Oxford, 1930), II, 197.

© KEITH BROWN 1973

THE ART OF CRUELTY:
HAMLET AND VINDICE

R. A. FOAKES

Hamlet admits to cruelty only when he is about to encounter his mother in the Closet scene, and then he seeks to qualify the term

> O heart, lose not thy nature, let not ever
> The soul of Nero enter this firm bosom,
> Let me be cruel not unnatural.   (III, ii, 396–8)

The cruelty he seeks to permit himself is to be kept under a restraint, not let loose with the tyrannical savagery of which Nero served as a type. So again, at the end of the interview, Hamlet cries, 'I must be cruel only to be kind', claiming that his cruelty serves its opposite, kindness. What Hamlet seems anxious to do here is to prevent himself from inflicting cruelty for its own sake; and the fact that he alone articulates this idea in the play suggests both the measure of success he has in controlling himself, and also his awareness, so to speak, of possibilities for cruelty within himself.

If Hamlet is not at this point recalling the Ghost's speeches to him in act I, his concern about his mother, and the re-appearance of the Ghost in the Closet scene, make the link for spectator and reader. Then the Ghost had ended his account of the murder by exhorting Hamlet to revenge, but warning him too:

> Howsomever thou pursues this act,
> Taint not thy mind, nor let thy soul contrive
> Against thy mother aught...   (I, v, 84–6)

It might be said that Hamlet's mind is already tainted, as the first soliloquy, 'O that this too too sullied flesh would melt', has already shown him brooding on suicide and disgusted by the speed of his mother's remarriage with a man he despises; but the Ghost himself may be seen as tainting Hamlet's mind in another way. For the Ghost, like Hamlet in his soliloquy, dwells imaginatively on what has happened in such a way as to emphasise by elaboration what is most gross and nasty. In this the Ghost and Hamlet are alike: what the Ghost speaks may be seen as articulating what is already there in Hamlet. So, like Hamlet, the Ghost dwells on remarriage in language that is itself revolting,

> So lust, though to a radiant angel linked,
> Will sate itself in a celestial bed
> And prey on garbage   (I, v, 54–6)

There is a kind of self-indulgence in this, a relish of nastiness which does not relate to the Claudius and Gertrude we have seen in action. The Ghost continues with his account of the murder:

> Upon my secure hour thy uncle stole
> With juice of cursed hebenon in a vial,
> And in the porches of my ears did pour
> The leperous distillment, whose effect
> Holds such an enmity with blood of man
> That swift as quicksilver it courses through
> The natural gates and alleys of the body,
> And with a sudden vigor it doth posset,
> And curd, like eager droppings into milk,
> The thin and wholesome blood. So did it mine,
> And a most instant tetter barked about,
> Most lazarlike, with vile and loathsome crust,
> All my smooth body.   (I, v, 61–73)

The Ghost seems fascinated by the details of what happened, and dwells especially on the effects of the poison, producing that 'tetter' or eruption which covers his skin with a 'loathsome crust'; it is this above all that the speech renders with the force of particularity, and which informs that great cry.[1]

> O, horrible! O, horrible! most horrible!
>
> (I, v, 80)

In other words, the Ghost does not just tell us *what* happened, but recreates imaginatively *how* it happened, the horrible atrocity of a murder which could, presumably, have been relatively quick and simple, a stab with a dagger, or smothering with a pillow. A passage from Dostoevsky's *The Brothers Karamazov* may be helpful at this point, for this is a novel much concerned with the nature of cruelty; at one point in it Ivan tries to explain to Alyosha why he cannot love his neighbours, and this passes into an extraordinary account of human cruelty, in which he tells Alyosha a story:

'By the way, not so long ago a Bulgarian in Moscow told me', Ivan went on, as though not bothering to listen to his brother, 'of the terrible atrocities committed all over Bulgaria by the Turks and Circassians who were afraid of a general uprising of the Slav population. They burn, kill, violate women and children, nail their prisoners' ears to fences and leave them like that till next morning when they hang them, and so on – it's impossible to imagine it all. And, indeed people sometimes speak of man's 'bestial' cruelty, but this is very unfair and insulting to the beasts: a beast can never be so cruel as a man, so ingeniously, so artistically cruel. A tiger merely gnaws and tears to pieces, that's all he knows. It would never occur to him to nail men's ears to a fence and leave them like that overnight, even if he were able to do it. These Turks, incidentally, seemed to derive a voluptuous pleasure from torturing children, cutting a child out of its mother's womb with a dagger and tossing babies up in the air and catching them on a bayonet before the eyes of their mothers. It was doing it before the eyes of their mothers that made it so enjoyable. But one incident I found particularly interesting. Imagine a baby in the arms of a trembling mother, surrounded by Turks who had just entered her house. They are having great fun: they fondle the baby, they laugh to

make it laugh and they are successful: the baby laughs. At that moment the Turk points a pistol four inches from the baby's face. The boy laughs happily, stretches out his little hands to grab the pistol, when suddenly the artist pulls the trigger in the baby's face and blows his brains out... Artistic, isn't it? Incidentally, I'm told the Turks are very fond of sweets.'[2]

Ivan observes that man is distinguished from beasts by his artistry: we speak casually of 'bestial' cruelty, but no animal is as cruel as men can be, who do it for enjoyment and to display their skill as artists, while others, looking on as spectators, take pleasure in watching, and in this case, enjoy the anguish the murder of the baby causes to its mother.

Something of this artistry in cruelty seems to be shown in the murder of old King Hamlet, as the Ghost describes it; the poison chosen by his brother was one that visibly corrupts and makes horrible the body of the dying man. Even the Ghost, who speaks of it as if he had been an onlooker at his own murder, is fascinated by the details of the process of dying, horrible as they are. He says he was sleeping at the time, and so not conscious, but he narrates what happened as if Claudius, in the manner of Dostoevsky's artists in cruelty, had staged it so that old Hamlet would at once suffer and be a spectator at his own death.

The Ghost calls on Hamlet to revenge,

> Revenge his foul and most unnatural murder,
>
> (I, v, 25)

and to pursue it by any means so long as he leaves his mother to Heaven. Although the Ghost does not explicitly command him to kill Claudius, this is what, in effect, 'revenge' means, since it is the only way Hamlet can

[1] This line functions too in relation to the idea immediately preceding it, of dying, 'With all my imperfections on my head', and that following in the reference to 'luxury and damned incest', but it seems to me to carry most weight as a rhetorical climax to the account of the murder as a whole.

[2] The quotation is from the translation by David Magarshack (Harmondsworth, 1958), I, 278–9.

obtain satisfaction and repay the injuries received by his father. So Hamlet is required to contrive another killing, a deed ironically condemned in the very next words of the Ghost,

> Murder most foul, as in the best it is.
>
> (I, v, 27)

In her study of revenge,[1] Elinor Prosser 'found no evidence to indicate that Elizabethans believed the law required blood revenge. The Law was absolute: murder, as such, was never justified.' The play shows Hamlet to be an artist, an actor–dramatist, ingenious contriver, and player of many parts; the Ghost, even as he condemns murder, demands that he put that artistry into the service of a cruelty Hamlet sees, at any rate in the Closet scene, as potentially there in himself.

This may seem a strange perspective when it is set against that view of Hamlet, which many hold, as a character imbued with a moral idealism or governed by a sense of moral scruple. It has been said, for example, very recently by Ivor Morris, in a careful account of Hamlet, that

Goodness and simple humanity are Hamlet's ideal. More truly than the heroic, it is the moral that confers nobility on man...Human excellence for Hamlet does not imply a self-aggrandizement, but rather the forsaking of an instinctive self-will, and the disciplining of the aspiring consciousness according to values which, though humble and familiar, are yet of a power to transcend. The chief passion of Hamlet's soul, therefore, is the precise antithesis of the heroic.[2]

Well, yes – but isn't this much too simple and clear-cut? For Hamlet sees his father in an heroic image, and finds a model for himself in Horatio, more an antique Roman than a Dane. It is true that Hamlet disparages himself in saying that Claudius 'is no more like my father than I to Hercules'; yet much of his idealism is bound up with the warrior-figures of the Ghost at the beginning and Fortinbras at the end, so that it is important to notice how these figures are presented in the play.

Some think of the military imagery in the play as being there to 'emphasise that Claudius and Hamlet are engaged in a duel to the death',[3] or that it exists to call attention 'to the issues of public life, to the state of the nation'.[4] It may serve these purposes, but when the Ghost appears in armour from head to foot, and accompanied by indications of past triumphs, as when he smote the sledded Polacks on the ice, other connotations are at work too; for war here does not, of course, have its unpleasant modern associations, but rather a ring of chivalric heroism in the thought of personal encounters, personal courage and skill. Old Hamlet appears in a 'fair and warlike form', as 'valiant Hamlet', who, challenged to combat,

> Did slay this Fortinbras, who by a sealed compact,
> Well ratified by law and heraldry,
> Did forfeit (with his life) all those his lands
> Which he stood seized of, to the conqueror.
>
> (I, i, 86–9)

The word 'heraldry', referring vaguely to heraldic practice, suggests an almost medieval ceremony, an ancient practice, no longer meaningful in the new Denmark of Claudius, the modern politician, negotiating through ambassadors. Later on Hamlet sees another image of chivalric heroism in that 'delicate and tender prince', young Fortinbras, passing through on his way, like old Hamlet, to fight the Poles, merely for honour, and driven by a 'divine ambition'. It is enough to make him give Fortinbras his dying vote for the succession to the Danish throne.

[1] *Hamlet and Revenge* (Stanford, 1967), p. 18.
[2] *Shakespeare's God. The Role of Religion in the Tragedies* (London, 1972), p. 371.
[3] Nigel Alexander, *Poison, Play and Duel* (London, 1971), p. 25. This stimulating book in some measure provoked the present essay.
[4] Maurice Charney, *Style in Hamlet* (Princeton, 1969), p. 30.

Hamlet in this combines a nostalgia for a past that seems better than the present with the idea of a great soldier as simple, good and truthful. An audience sees also that Fortinbras is wasting his country's youth on a trivial and useless campaign; and if the Ghost really represents Old Hamlet, then he was also vindictive and morally perverse, condemning all murder, yet urging Hamlet to commit one. Hamlet's image is a partial one; Fortinbras and his father take on in his mind's eye grander proportions and finer qualities than are evidenced in the play, and Claudius appears worse to him than he does in the action:

> So excellent a King, that was to this
> Hyperion to a satyr,   (I, ii, 140–1)

the sun-god compared with one who is half-beast. The heroic ideal Hamlet thinks he sees in his father merges into those classical figures that spring to his lips for a comparison, Hyperion, Mars, Mercury, Caesar, Hercules, Aeneas, and others, and all help to suggest imagined models for Hamlet himself, and to exemplify to him that possibility of the godlike in man embodied in 'What a piece of work is a man!' Hamlet tends to disclaim comparison between himself and his heroes, yet there is much of the heroic in him too,[1] complicated by other qualities, as he is more fully of the Renaissance, a man of all talents and so much less the mere warrior-hero. Trained at a university, he retains the habit of sifting evidence, even the habit of taking lecture-notes ('My tables, meet it is I set it down'). He writes more than other Shakespearian protagonists; King Lear could have been illiterate, but Hamlet is clearly an intellectual, au fait with classical literature, able to turn off a few lines for Ophelia, however much he is 'ill at these numbers', and to pen a speech for the players, a dozen or so lines of verse. Hamlet the writer reflects Hamlet the thinker and scholar, but he is also an accomplished swordsman, who

throughout conveys a sense of absolute fearlessness, so that at the end it seems entirely appropriate when he is accorded martial honours, as four captains bear his body, 'like a soldier' to the stage.

Hamlet is a very complex character, and it won't do to say that 'goodness and simple humanity are Hamlet's ideal'. Insofar as he locates his ideal in his father and Fortinbras, it seems to be partly a longing for a simpler world, in which problems could be honourably settled in combat; and it is based on an un-critical association of these figures with a chivalric heroism. Hamlet's idealism is confused, and this confusion prevents him from seeing at once the contradiction in the Ghost's exhortations to him to do the very thing for which the Ghost condemns Claudius. Hamlet shows at times a moral delicacy and scrupulousness that mark him off from the world of Claudius, and this is brought out by the comparison with Laertes sweeping unhesitatingly to his revenge; but he is confused in his moral stances too, and fails to discipline his consciousness, or to remain, as Ivor Morris claims, 'morally consistent'.[2] He does not directly question the Ghost's command, although he avoids pursuing it, and has recourse to play-acting, to an antic disposition, and to the play within the play. Some see this as a substitute for real action, for killing Claudius, and put emphasis on Hamlet's delay, but it is as much a device to penetrate the mask of Claudius in order to discover his true nature and to expose his guilt. Beyond this it is also, more importantly, a means to accommodate himself to what he feels he has to do; the Ghost has emphasised in detail the horror of the murder of his father, and in order to accomplish his revenge, he

---

[1] See G. K. Hunter's analysis of 'The Heroic in Hamlet', in *Hamlet*, edited J. R. Brown and Bernard Harris (Stratford-upon-Avon Studies 5, London, 1963), especially pp. 103–4.

[2] *Shakespeare's God*, p. 383.

needs to act like Claudius, and face a similar horror.

In the course of the play he makes a series of moral adjustments, notably after he stabs Polonius through the arras, and so marks himself with a blood-guilt. He assigns the responsibility for this to 'heaven', as if he has been appointed a divine agent:

> For this same lord
> I do repent; but heaven hath pleas'd it so
> To punish me with this, and this with me,
> That I must be their scourge and minister.
>
> (III, iv, 172–5)

The terms 'scourge' and 'minister', it seems, 'are so contradictory that they are irreconcilable', for 'God elects as his scourge only a sinner who already deserves damnation', while a 'minister' would be a true agent and servant of God.[1] Hamlet could not be both at the same time, and the moral confusion present here is brought out further in his recognition in the same speech that, 'This bad begins, and worse remains behind.' This confusion is marked too in the way he seems to convince himself after his return from the sea-voyage in act v that it would be 'perfect conscience' to kill Claudius:

> Does it not, think thee, stand me now upon –
> He that hath kill'd my king and whor'd my
> mother,
> Popp'd in between th' election and my hopes,
> Thrown out his angle for my proper life,
> And with such cozenage – is't not perfect
> conscience
> To quit him with this arm? And is't not to be
> damned
> To let this canker of our nature come
> In further evil? (v, ii, 63–70)

Though Claudius has done these things, including the attempt to have Hamlet done to death by sending him to England bearing a commission for his own execution, Hamlet is not thereby given moral freedom to kill Claudius, to practise murder most foul, 'as in the best it is'.

In fact his claims that heaven has appointed him as its agent, and that he would be damned for not killing Claudius, do not issue in any determined action. Hamlet might be interpreted here as cheering himself up; whatever he says, he still does nothing, and rather at the end resigns himself to providence. However much he may justify murder to himself, there is no sign that he can bring himself in action to face the horror of doing it. After the encounter with the Ghost in act I, Hamlet cries out that the commandment to revenge shall alone live in his mind, but what he does is to adopt that 'antic disposition', which allows him to play any part, notably those of fool and madman. The Ghost's commandment brings out the artist in Hamlet, his concern with play-action, which is stimulated too by the entry of the players, and Shakespeare focuses our attention on these through much of acts II and III. When Hamlet first meets the players, he asks for a speech, recalling the opening of it himself: ''twas Aeneas' tale to Dido, and thereabout of it especially where he speaks of Priam's slaughter'. It is appropriate for him to have remembered this speech from a play that was 'caviare to the general', a play for the educated, based on Virgil's *Aeneid*, and so associated with that heroic world with which Hamlet likes to link himself, and which emerges especially in references to and images drawn from classical history, literature and myth. As has been skilfully shown by Nigel Alexander,[2] the player's speech also provides subtle analogies for Hamlet, as it acts out the successful vengeance of Pyrrhus upon Priam, and the destruction of a kingdom brought about by lust.

But the speech has another kind of significance which I want to emphasise; it describes

---

[1] The quotations are from Elinor Prosser's analysis of this passage in *Hamlet and Revenge*, pp. 199–201.

[2] *Poison, Play and Duel,* p. 97.

Pyrrhus raging through the streets of Troy to revenge the death of his father, until eventually he finds and hacks to pieces the aged and defenceless Priam:

'Head to foot
Now is he total gules, horridly trick'd
With blood of fathers, mothers, daughters, sons,
Bak'd and impasted with the parching streets,
That lend a tyrannous and a damned light
To their lord's murder. Roasted in wrath and fire,
And thus o'er-sized with coagulate gore,
With eyes like carbuncles, the hellish Pyrrhus
Old grandsire Priam seeks.'   (II, ii, 460–8)

The language of this is inflated, but not too much so for its content and occasion, and the overall impression it makes is powerful. Of its kind, it is a good speech, vigorously presenting an image of Pyrrhus as literally covered in blood that is dried and baked on to him, so that he is 'impasted' or encrusted with it, through the heat generated by his anger ('roasted in wrath'), and slaughters fathers, mothers and sons at random. In other words, Pyrrhus images an ultimate in cruelty, beyond all control, and exemplifies the kind of pleasure in atrocity which Dostoevsky observes, as he goes on to make 'malicious sport' in mincing Priam before the eyes of Hecuba. If it is a reminder to Hamlet of what he feels he must do, it recalls also the Ghost's account of his murder, when the poison Claudius administered caused his skin to become covered with a 'vile and loathsome crust'. Like the Ghost's speech, this one dwells on the particularities of the event, recreating imaginatively the horror of it, and like that, it wins for a moment Hamlet's wholehearted involvement. In each case, however, the horror of the deed is made bearable to Hamlet through its presentation in art, in a kind of play within the play, where it is aesthetically distanced.[1] The point I would make about these scenes, is that they show how Hamlet can involve himself imaginatively in play-acting or dramatising the act of cruelty, but

cannot do it. Briefly now he whips himself into a heat of passion:

Is it not monstrous that this player here,
But in a fiction, in a dream of passion,
Could force his soul so to his own conceit,
That from her working all his visage wanned,
Tears in his eyes, distraction in his aspect,
A broken voice, and his whole function suiting
With forms to his conceit; and all for nothing?
                              (II, ii, 554–60)

In fact, it is the fiction or art that makes it possible for Hamlet to face this image of cruel murder, and it provokes him not into acting like Pyrrhus, but into arranging a performance of another play, the murder of Gonzago.

It is not 'monstrous' to 'force the soul' to display the imagined passion; it would be monstrous rather to put that passion to work in earnest. Again Hamlet's moral confusion emerges, as he forces his own soul into a rage and unpacks his heart with words in this soliloquy. For Hamlet's moral idealism emerges not in what he tries to will himself to do, which is to abandon scruple and drive to his revenge (consciously, so to speak, this is what he thinks he is doing, as is evidenced in his confusions or rejections of morality); it is revealed rather in the energy with which he can respond to or recreate the horror imaginatively. In this the aesthetic passes into the moral; he confronts the image of what, on one level, he would like to make himself, at such a pitch of imaginative intensity, that it disables him from practising cruelty himself. His full imaginative involvement brings home to him and us the horror of what Claudius did, and of the carnage wrought by the 'hellish Pyrrhus'; so, even when he has a perfect opportunity, finding Claudius at prayer, Hamlet cannot do it, and

[1] In *Shakespeare the Craftsman* (London, 1969), p. 129, M. C. Bradbrook has argued that the First Player here was made up to look like Burbage playing Hamlet, so that during the Pyrrhus speech Hamlet was watching, as it were, a reflection of himself.

neglects the chance to kill him. The reasons he gives have some plausibility, but behind them we sense his radical inability to become 'monstrous' or 'hellish' in deed, and carry out a willed murder.

When he does kill, it is in a fit of excitement, and an unpremeditated act, stabbing blindly through the arras, not a planned murder. The death of Polonius fastens a guilt on him, and makes it easier for him to send Rosencrantz and Guildenstern to their deaths by forging a new commission to the King of England. Even this, though ingenious, is not a direct deed of cruelty, and on his return to Denmark, it is in a condition of resignation: 'If it be now, 'tis not to come; if it be not to come, it will be now; if it be not now, yet it will come – the readiness is all.' He appears to be talking about his *own* death – but he is talking also about the death of *Claudius* – for he abandons plotting, the thought of acting as revenger, of being a Pyrrhus; and the death of Claudius happens in a muddle at the end, and only after Hamlet has his own death-wound. Horatio speaks with reason here

Of accidental judgments, casual slaughters,
Of deaths put on by cunning and forced cause,
And, in this upshot, purposes mistook,
Fallen on the inventors' heads.
                                    (v, ii, 380–3)

It is all clumsy, casual and, on the part of Hamlet, unplanned and unprepared – he never does become a revenger, unless he might be thought one in that moment when, having given Claudius his death-wound with a venomed sword, he then forces him to drink the poisoned wine. Its effect, however, is to despatch Claudius at once, not to protract his death, or make it more horrible, and Laertes guides our response:

He is justly served;
It is a poison tempered by himself. (v, ii, 325–6)

Hamlet shows a kind of cruelty twice in the play, once when he turns on Ophelia, recognising that she is a decoy, and later when he speaks savagely to his mother. He lashes verbally the two women he loves, and his behaviour here is not, as is sometimes argued, merely a reflection of his revulsion against sex, or of his hatred of the corruption he sees around him; it relates also, and more deeply, to his imaginative engagement with, and recoil from, the horror within himself. The cruelty expressed in words is also a substitute for action, an outlet for what he knows is in him, and might perhaps be seen too as vicariously satisfying the conscious urge to drive himself to a deed of cruelty, to revenge. His attack on Ophelia springs from an inquisition into himself, beginning in the soliloquy 'To be or not to be', in which, amongst other things, a dejected Hamlet attempts to reckon with the need for action, the task of taking arms against Claudius, in the recognition that 'the pale cast of thought' is inimical to action; the self-inspection deepens into the hyperbole of his words to Ophelia:

I am very proud, revengeful, ambitious, with more offences at my beck than I have thoughts to put them in, imagination to give them shape, or time to act them in.   (III, i, 125)

He has a sense of a potential in himself for unimagined, or unimaginable offences, but those we are aware of in him exist mostly in his mind or imagination. So when he confronts his mother in the Closet scene, it is to recreate in imagination, and with a nastiness belonging to his conception, to him more than to the deed itself, the activity of sexual relations between Claudius and his mother:

Nay, but to live
In the rank sweat of an enseamed bed,
Stewed in corruption, honeying, and making love
Over the nasty sty...   (III, iv, 91–4)

The obscenity is inside Hamlet, and bursts out in a savagery of words; if these help to bring Ophelia to suicide, and afflict Gertrude so that she cries

> These words like daggers enter in mine ears,
>
> (III, iv, 95)

nevertheless, these attacks are essentially different from the deed this line recalls, Claudius pouring poison into the ears of Old Hamlet. Ophelia cannot comprehend what Hamlet says, and both she and, initially at any rate, Gertrude, are inclined to think his outbursts are expressions of madness. I think rather that Hamlet gives rein to his tongue as an alternative to the action he cannot face; and his ability to give bitterness vent in words to them, and yet refrain from a willed or planned killing, is exactly what we might expect.

The presentation of Hamlet in this way is worth comparing to that of Vindice in *The Revenger's Tragedy*, who is also something of an artist, and likes to see himself as dramaturge, even as writer of his own play. Even in the opening speech over the skull, he already uses it as a stage-property in his own dramatisation of the court, and when he is not playing the disguised roles of Piato and a malcontent, adopted to deceive Lussurioso, he is to be found stage-managing playlets of his own, most notably in the famous scene in which the skull is again introduced, now dressed in 'tires', fitted with a head-dress as if alive. As he brings it on, Vindice uses it consciously again as a property, saying to Hippolito;

> Now to my tragic business, look you, brother,
> I have not fashioned this only for show,
> And useless property; no it shall bear a part
> E'en in its own revenge... (III, v, 103–6)

The skull itself is a reminder of Hamlet in the graveyard, but though Hamlet plays many parts, and fancies himself as an actor with the visiting company in Elsinore, there is a radical difference, namely that Hamlet is wholly involved in the decision whether to revenge, in those questions to do or not to do ('Now might I do it pat...'), and to be or not to be, that reverberate in the play; but Vindice has made his decision already before his opening speech; his attention is engaged by the question, 'How can I effect my revenge in the cleverest way?' not, 'How can I do it at all?' Because his attention is on the means rather than the end, he becomes pleased with his own cleverness, designing the little play within the play in which he murders the Duke.

While Hamlet is concerned with the nature of revenge and the horror of the act of cruelty, we see in Vindice a growing detachment from the nature of what he is doing, a detachment which is made to take effect fully as part of the play's serious action. At the beginning, his moral indignation at the corruptions of the court invites our sympathy and assent. In the opening scene, his independence from the court is imaged in the visual separation of Vindice from the procession he watches and describes, but by act III, when he contrives the murder of the Duke, he has taken his place among the courtiers, and joins those he so despised at first, crying

> 'Tis state in music for a Duke to bleed
> The dukedom wants a head, tho' yet unknown.
> As fast as they peep up, let's cut 'em down.
>
> (III, v, 224–6)

Vindice's anger at the beginning is justified insofar as he is in a position similar to that of Hamlet, unable to obtain justice for a murder in a court which seems corrupt; but when Vindice uses the skull to poison the Duke in act III, Hippolito applauds him not for a moral achievement, but more appropriately for his cleverness:

> I do applaud thy constant vengeance,
> The quaintness of thy malice. (III, v, 108–9)

It is an ingenuity ('quaintness'), an artistry, put into the service of 'malice', of cruelty, as

Vindice enjoys poisoning the Duke in a kiss even while he watches his own wife and bastard son making love.

It is their self-satisfaction in their skill which leads Vindice and Hippolito to boast at the end of their 'wit' in murdering the Duke, and so brings on their arrest and execution. By act v, their enjoyment in plotting has reached the point where they congratulate each other on watching an innocent nobleman carried off to execution suspected of a murder they have carried out:

Hippolito.
Brother, how happy is our vengeance!
Vindice.   Why, it hits
Past th' apprehension of indifferent wits.

(v, ii, 133–4)

In relation to this delight in cruelty, it is important to notice how much of the play is funny; its general cleverness emerges in a kind of grisly humour, as in the joking of the Duchess's youngest son as he expects release from the scaffold, a release which never comes, or in the hiring of Vindice by Lussurioso to kill his *alter ego*, Piato; or in the double masque of revengers at the end. In spite of the burning moral indignation of some of Vindice's speeches, the world of the play offers an image of human existence which excludes the possibility of the heroic and moral idealism present in *Hamlet*; it is a world in which money, power, and sex dominate, and for Vindice, intelligence and artistry replace morality. The humour is necessary to make such a vision of human cruelty through ingenuity bearable. At the same time, the play shows in Vindice an 'artist', the stage-manager and writer of his own playlets, becoming so absorbed in his skill that he treats life merely as an exercise for his art, and so loses all moral sense. When he confronts his mother in act IV, it is not to threaten her with words like daggers (compare Hamlet's, 'I will speak daggers to her, but use none'), but to hold a real dagger to her breast,

so that when she echoes Gertrude's 'Thou wilt *not* murder me', it is with a difference: Gratiana asks, 'What, *will* you murder me?' and there seems every reason to suppose Vindice and Hippolito may do so.

To return then to *Hamlet*: there is one moment in the play when Hamlet, like Vindice, yields to a sense of pleasure in the skill of plotting:

'tis the sport to have the engineer
Hoist with his own petar, and 't shall go hard
But I will delve one yard below their mines,
And blow them at the moon: O, 'tis most sweet
When in one line two crafts directly meet.

(III, iv, 206–10)

This occurs after the death of Polonius, and when he learns he must go to England; but in fact, Hamlet practises craft in this way only once. All his artistry in the first part of the play is aimed at understanding himself and making apparent the guilt of Claudius; he stabs Polonius in a fit of passion, and not knowing what or who is behind the arrras; and at the end he declines to plot against Claudius, putting his trust in providence. Only once, in the boat to England, is he prompted to try his craft, when he alters the message Rosencrantz and Guildenstern are carrying to avoid his own death. There is no instance at all of Hamlet initiating a plot to kill anyone.

Although he is as much of an artist as Vindice, Hamlet does not confuse art and life; indeed, he has his theory of the art of playing, and his famous formulation is worth noting: 'whose end both at the first, and now, was and is, to hold as 'twere the mirror up to nature, to show virtue her own feature, scorn her own image, and the very age and body of the time his form and pressure' (III, ii, 20). The 'end' or aim of art is to reflect what is there, and presumably by reflecting, to reveal to him what the spectator may not otherwise see; but its success in doing this depends on the apprehension of the spectator, as Vindice knew, on his sensitivity and understanding, and Hamlet's theory says nothing of his. It does not work too well for Claudius; the play within the play shows twice, first in dumb-show and then in action, something closely resembling the murder of old Hamlet, and Claudius is not much troubled by this mirror held up to nature; what does seem to stir him is Hamlet's identification of the murderer as 'one Lucianus, nephew to the King', and a few lines later, Claudius walks out, calling for lights, and 'marvellous distempered'. What he saw acted before him was not the murder of Old Hamlet so much as an image of a secret fear, the killing of himself by his nephew, Young Hamlet.

The theory works better for Hamlet himself: the play within the play seems to him to mirror Claudius's deed, and to cause him to reveal his guilt; in addition, it provides yet one more artistic expression of the nature of that murder, which is also reflected in the Ghost's speech, and in the First Player's speech on the 'hellish Pyrrhus'. Hamlet's playing dwells on the image of a murder which reflects the cruelty of the deed and the horror of revenge; and so reveals to us what is not apparent to Hamlet himself, his moral revulsion from the task he feels the Ghost has imposed on him. This fascinated loathing of the horror in its imagined recreation finds one more outlet in the Graveyard scene, when he broods on the skull of Yorick, and after drawing out the commonplaces appropriate to that *memento mori*, passes on to Alexander, another classical hero:

Hamlet. Now get you to my lady's chamber, and tell her, let her paint an inch thick, to this favour she must come, Make her laugh at that. . .Prithee Horatio, tell me one thing.
Horatio. What's that, my lord?
Hamlet. Dost thou think Alexander looked o'this fashion i'th' earth?
Horatio. E'en so.
Hamlet. And smelt so? pah!
Horatio. E'en so, my lord.

Hamlet. To what base uses we may return, Horatio! Why may not imagination trace the noble dust of Alexander till'a find it stopping a bung-hole?
Horatio. 'Twere to consider too curiously, to consider so. (v, i, 187–200)

Why may not imagination trace the dust of Alexander in this way? Horatio's answer carries weight – because it is to speculate too nicely, to go too far, to become, he might have added, self-indulgent; but there are more things in heaven and earth than Horatio sees, and his response is a limited one; Hamlet's effort to trace in imagination the full consequences of physical decay in death parallels his ability to face imaginatively the full horror of revenge; the element of indulgence in both is less significant than the power they have to work as vehicles of Hamlet's deepest moral awareness; he is right to reply here to Horatio's ''Twere to consider too curiously' with the phrase 'No, faith, not a jot!'

The greatness of *Hamlet* may be measured against the more limited, if splendid, achievement of *The Revenger's Tragedy*, in which Vindice so falls in love with his art as to commit himself entirely to it. Unable then to see its moral implications for himself, he uses it, most notably in his device with the skull, as a means to effect his revenge; so, becoming like Dostoevsky's Turks, he enjoys the display of cruelty as he makes the dying Duke watch the incestuous adultery of his own wife. By contrast, it is the strength of Hamlet, not his weakness, or only superficially his weakness, that he cannot kill, that he fails to carry out his revenge. The role of Hamlet may be seen as ironically expanding from his opening lines, when he enters acting like a mourner in his customary suits of solemn black, and saying,

These indeed seem,
For they are actions that a man might play,
But I have that within which passeth show
(I, ii, 83–5)

In the action Hamlet does, in fact, reveal what is most deep within him, not, so to speak, consciously, not even in the soliloquies, but in projecting imaginatively, into art, into shows, into plays within the play, or the rhetoric of his encounters with Ophelia and Gertrude, a sense of the potential for cruelty and viciousness in himself. Shakespeare makes this art the vehicle of the moral restraint Hamlet exercises upon what is within. The combination of his full imaginative grasp of the horror of a cruelty he recognises as potentially in himself, with a moral revulsion from it of which he is unconscious, or at best obscurely aware, perhaps helps to explain why Hamlet remains both an enigma and Shakespeare's best-loved hero.

© R. A. FOAKES 1973

FROM TRAGEDY TO TRAGI-COMEDY:
'KING LEAR' AS PROLOGUE

GLYNNE WICKHAM

Credit for the definition, if not the invention, of tragi-comedy in England is normally given to John Fletcher and is firmly anchored in his preface to the printed edition of *The Faithful Shepherdess* of 1609/10:

A tragi-comedy is not so called in respect of mirth and killing, but in respect it wants deaths, which is enough to make it no tragedy, yet brings some near it, which is enough to make it no comedy, which must be a representation of familiar people, with such kind of trouble as no life be questioned; so that a god is as lawful in this as in a tragedy, and mean people as in a comedy.[1]

The Faithful Shepherdess was first performed in 1608 or 1609, and it is probable that the collaborative hand in Shakespeare's *Henry VIII* of 1612/13 was Fletcher's. Since this five-year time-span neatly embraces the period during which Shakespeare directed his primary artistic endeavour to tragi-comedy, with *Pericles*, *Cymbeline*, *The Winter's Tale* and *The Tempest* following one another in swift succession, it has been generally assumed that this sharp shift of direction was the product of Fletcher's influence, coupled with influences flowing in from Italy and France in the wake of the Counter-Reformation and those of the Masques which Ben Jonson and Inigo Jones were developing with such success at court in these years. *Hymenaei*, *The Masque of Queens*, and *The Masque of Oberon* were all presented in this period, as was Samuel Daniel's *Tethys Festival*: corporately they succeeded in focusing critical attention upon the operatic and choreographic possibilities of dramatic art as well as upon the scenic elements.

Shakespeare's preoccupation with tragi-comedy in the late period has thus frequently been explained as derived from an effort to keep up with the times; an old man doing his best with failing powers to come to terms with avant-garde taste as practised at court by John Fletcher, Ben Jonson, William Lawes, and Inigo Jones.

As the complimentary character of Jonson's masques and the romantic quality of Beaumont and Fletcher's plays provide such clear literary, musical and scenic evidence of changing tastes in Jacobean court drama between 1606 and 1616, I have no wish to accord to these practical and theoretical influences less than their due weight as contributory factors in Shakespeare's thoughts and methods at this time. They existed and are important. Jonson's strictures on Shakespeare's use of them, however, warn one that this cannot be the whole story. So does the fact that when Shakespeare started to re-work the old play of *King Leir*, his datum point was a tragi-comedy which he then deliberately restructured and transformed into a tragedy with a conclusion that is wholly dependent on circumstance for its catastrophe.

[1] The letter 'To the Reader' first appeared in Q1 which was printed by R. Bonian and H. Walley without date; but as this partnership is only traceable between 22 December 1608 and 14 January 1610, 1608 would seem to have been the date of the first performance with the printed text appearing in 1609. See E. K. Chambers, *The Elizabethan Stage* (Oxford, 1923), III, 221–2.

The ambiguity of this conclusion is only made the more obvious by Nahum Tate's redaction of Shakespeare's play in 1681 with its reversion to a tragi-comic conclusion that was destined to hold the stage for 150 years. Shakespeare was thus no stranger to tragi-comedy in 1608: nor, when he did elect to produce a sequence of tragi-comedies after that date, was he dependent on Fletcher's or Jonson's views on how to set about constructing such plays.

It thus seems to me that there are good grounds for supposing that there were other and profounder influences at work between the writing of *King Lear* and *The Tempest* which embraced all practising artists, and to which each, including Shakespeare, gave expression in the manner that best suited his own talent and personal situation. One of these, as it seems to me, was the political *Sturm und Drang* occasioned by the accession of the King of Scotland to the throne of England in 1603. Since it took the English Parliament five years of debate to decide whether or not to accept the Union of the two Crowns and on what terms – legal, and financial and religious – it would be astonishing if no trace of this revolutionary change in English life had found its way into the drama of the time; yet discussion of it scarcely figures in modern critical discussion of that drama. It is this neglected aspect of the many influences at work upon all artists in the first decade of the Jacobean era that I wish to single out therefore for closer examination in this paper.

If this idea first grew out of the speculations about the dramatic structure of *The Winter's Tale*, which I published under the title of 'A Comedy with Deaths' in *Shakespeare's Dramatic Heritage*,[1] it was powerfully reinforced by a paper read at the fourteenth international Shakespeare Conference here in Stratford by Joan Rees, 'Revenge, Retribution, and Reconciliation'. In this important paper she remarked upon the strange phenomenon of the decline of the revenge ethic in tragedy and its replacement by one of regeneration through love, mercy and forgiveness: she pinpointed this change as occurring in the first decade of the seventeenth century. This paper has since been printed in *Shakespeare Survey* 24.[2]

These interesting ideas led me to examine whether the specifically Jamesian political characteristics which had seemed to me to provide a more convincing explanation for the curious, not to say perverse, structure of *The Winter's Tale* than those which literary criticism had hitherto produced, might possess a wider application. Certainly other signposts pointed in the same direction. Not least among them was the Privy Council's attitude to acting companies in general, and James I's decision to restrict the right to act in London to companies in the service of his own family. Granted the fact that these companies were still licensed to give public performances on public stages both in London and in the provinces, their salaried status in the royal households could only increase the likelihood that commissioned work would be required of them in return for their privileged status. The Revels Office, moreover, existed to ensure that such expression as was given in plays to matters of Church and State was kept broadly in line with government policy. That such matters were of interest to King James is proved by his attitude to both the performance and publication of Chapman's 'Biron' plays, and his termination of the lease of the Blackfriars to the Children of the Revels in 1608.[3]

[1] London, 1969. See also *Times Literary Supplement*, 18 December 1969, 'Shakespeare's Investiture Play'. A much fuller version of this article was read at the 3rd Conference devoted to Elizabethan drama at the University of Waterloo, Ontario, in 1970 and is published in *Elizabethan Theatre III*, ed. David Galloway, Toronto, 1973, pp. 82–99.
[2] Cambridge, 1971, pp. 31–5.
[3] See G. Wickham, *Early English Stages*, II, Part 2 (London, 1971), pp. 135–6.

Thus, from a negative standpoint at least, the interest of the sovereign and his Council in the subject-matter of plays performed by the royal companies during the first decade of the Stuart era cannot be doubted. It was not only King Claudius who asked 'Is there no offence in't?' It is another matter, however, to go on from there to prove a more positive interest in the form of actual commissions or, at the least, the suggestion of themes which, if treated on the stage, would receive royal approval. Yet Hamlet thought it natural enough to ask the players from Wittenberg to adapt a play in their repertoire to give it an emblematic significance for those with guilty minds to recognise within the bare bones of the fable: and many critics have forestalled me in seeing compliments to James I carefully couched within the escape of Fleance in *Macbeth* and Cranmer's prophecy in the concluding scene of *Henry VIII*.[1] Two other points, however, have received less attention. The first is the deliberately complimentary character of court masques as handled by Ben Jonson and Inigo Jones after 1604, and the second is Shakespeare's personal position as a Groom of the Chamber in the service of King James himself. If masques were as influential on the late plays as many critics have claimed that they were, it is arbitrary, to say the least, to eliminate direct compliment and commission from that influence: and it is only the more irrational to do this in the case of the one and only dramatist who was himself a member of the King's Household, during the period in question.

This brings me back to *King Lear* and the antithesis between the tragi-comic conclusion of the old play and the tragic conclusion of Shakespeare's version of the story. In few of Shakespeare's plays are his intentions more ambiguous than in *King Lear*. The story or 'history' of Lear and his three daughters already existed in the Elizabethan dramatic repertoire in the form of a tragi-comedy: yet Shakespeare elected to redact it and transform it into a tragedy.[2] Nor can the Lear story itself be wholly isolated from its wider context of legendary history that stretches back to Trojan Brutus and his division of the British Isles between his three sons and forward to King Gorboduc who repeated this folly with equally disastrous results. All three stories came thus to be linked with Merlin's prophecy of a second Brutus, destined in the fullness of time to return to New Troy and reunite the Kingdom. This figure had already been recognised in the person of James I by Samuel Daniel, Thomas Dekker, and Anthony Munday in poems and pageants before Shakespeare turned his attention to the Lear story.

It is only the more tantalising, therefore, that Shakespeare should have retained something of the tragi-comic quality both of the old play and the prophecy in reuniting Lear with Cordelia, only to dismiss it in reverting to the original source of the whole story, Geoffrey of Monmouth's *Historia regum Britanniae*, in bringing catastrophe upon them both.

There is also the fascinating figure of the Duke of Albany to be accounted for. In the old play Regan was married to Camber (King of Wales) and Goneril to the King of Cornwall.[3]

---

[1] See also Peter Davison, 'The Serious Concerns of *Philaster*', *ELH*, xxx (1963), 1–15.

[2] The play was entered in the Stationers' Register in 1594 and 1605, and has been edited for the Malone Society by W. W. Greg (1907). Its publication in 1605 has been explained as an attempt to pass it off for Shakespeare's. If, as Greg supposed, the copyright in it originally rested with Queen Elizabeth's Men, I think it more probable that on James I's reorganisation of the London companies at his accession the prompt-copy, entered in the Stationers' Register as new in 1594 but not published for obvious reasons, passed into the hands of the King's Men, giving Shakespeare the chance to study it. Once he had redacted it into its new form, the company would have had no further use for it and could profit directly from its publication while retaining their copyright in the new play.

[3] In the old play King Leir's course of action is justified by one of his Nobles as follows:

Albany, as Goneril's husband, is thus a new-comer to the stage in Shakespeare's play;[1] but so was he to the English peerage in 1603 in the person of King James's younger son, Prince Charles.[2] Prince Charles's elder brother Henry, Duke of Rothesay and Prince of Scotland, was created Duke of Cornwall on James's accession to the English throne in 1603. Thus, when *King Lear* was written, James was himself possessed of three children; the Duke of Cornwall, the Duke of Albany and Princess Elizabeth.

These may be mere coincidences, but they are striking ones: and even if Shakespeare may never have 'blotted a line', it is scarcely credible that he would have made deliberate changes of this nature without pausing to think what he was doing. And here it should be recalled that Albany is the character who effects Lear's reunion with Cordelia in Shakespeare's play: it is not his fault that this reconcilement should come too late to prevent the tragic finale. Shakespeare, of course, distanced these corre-spondences by removing his characters from the Christian era of the old play and placing them in a pre-Christian world.

Another coincidence, and one no less re-markable, is the fact that at the time Shakespeare was pondering on his own and his predecessor's approach to the Lear story in terms of tragedy and tragi-comedy, the possibility of explicit antithetical contrast between the two dramatic forms was grasped and expressed by James I himself. James's use of these terms occurs in the concluding passage of his 'Discourse on the Powder-Treason', published anonymously and written in the third person, where he expressed the hope that,

the Almighty...will...put it in his Maiesties heart to make such a conclusion of this Tragedie to the Traitors, but Tragicomedie to the King and all his trew Subiects.[3]

What I wish to suggest therefore is that the drift away from revenge tragedy and towards regenerative tragi-comedy in the first decade of James's reign remarked on by Joan Rees, has its true origins in the political consciousness of the British peoples saved from foreign invasion and civil war by the peaceful accession of James I in 1603, by the timely discovery of the Gunpowder Plot in 1605, and the final ratifi-cation of the Union of the two Crowns by Act of Parliament in 1608. That these events were received, at least in London, as little short of miraculous is historically beyond dispute: that they were taken up by politicians, preachers and playwrights alike, reinforced by the disinterment of prophecies, legends, and portents that were then woven into the rhetoric and literature of a new messianic vision, with King James and his family at the centre of it, is equally well authenticated by broad-sides, homilies, and entertainments of every description. And in all of this the new King took care in his speeches from the throne to further the image of himself projected to his

Wherefore, my Leige, my censure deemes it best,
To match them with some of your neighbour Kings,
Bordering within the bounds of Albion,
By whose united friendship, this our state
May be protected 'gainst all forrayne hate.

(Sig. A 2v)

[1] In marrying Goneril to Albany and Regan to Cornwall Shakespeare deserts Holinshed who reverses the order; he also rejects the old play and *The Faerie Queene* in both of which Regan is married to the King of Wales. He reverts instead to Geoffrey of Monmouth who married Goneril to 'Maglannus, dux Albaniae' and Regan to 'Hennius, dux Cornubiae'. It is Geoffrey, too, who gives Albany the better character of the two dukes. See Wilfred Perrett, *The Story of King Lear from Geoffrey of Monmouth to Shakespeare* (Berlin, 1905), pp. 162–6.

[2] James himself had held that title between 1567 and 1587, as had his father between his marriage to Mary Queen of Scots in 1565 and his murder in 1567. Prince Charles was not created Duke of York until November 1605. See G.E.C[okayne] (ed.), *The Complete Peerage of England, Scotland, Ireland, Great Britain and the United Kingdom, Extant, Extinct, or Dormant* (London, 1887), *sub* 'Albany'.

[3] *The Workes of the Most High and Mightie Prince, Iames* (London, 1616), Sig. x3 (p. 245).

subjects in his personal motto, *Beati Pacifici:* blessed are the peace-makers.[1] The vision was itself a simple one: first to reunite the British people under a single Crown; and next to reunite divided Christendom in part by ensuring a manifestly equal and honourable disposal of the mortal remains of his Catholic mother and the Protestant Queen Elizabeth, and in part by dynastic marriages for his daughter and two sons. That this vision was not without its imperial overtones is equally apparent and a not unimportant factor in its general acceptability to Englishmen at the time: less acceptable was the fact that the King and his Parliament differed sharply on the question of Divine Right. That Shakespeare, both as a Groom of the King's Household and as principal play-maker to the King's personal company of actors, should have elected to co-operate in the active propagation of these ideas, *as far as his artistic conscience as poet and dramatist would permit*, strikes me as neither surprising nor unnatural: they were shared, one must remember, by the majority of the King's Councillors, including Sir Francis Bacon.

Whether as a genuine expression of personal belief or as a matter of political expediency, King James projected himself to the English people from the moment of his arrival in London as God's answer to prayer: a Protestant already equipped with a wife and three children, he claimed he had delivered his new subjects from decades of doubt about the succession and from the deep-rooted fears of war, foreign and domestic. His accession brought them the immediate gift of peace and the prospect of plenty in its wake: the merger of the Scottish and the English Crowns offered them not only domestic security but the promise of aggrandisement abroad. As the bringer of unity and the begetter of peace, he offered his subjects an imperial future under a British Augustus. It is from this moment that the words 'Great Britain' first became current on English lips.

These ideas he presented forcefully and in impressively figurative language in his speech from the throne to his first Parliament in 1604. Lest it be thought that a single speech to a small and select audience can only have been of temporary interest to the few, let me hasten to add that this speech was immediately printed for general circulation in a quarto edition under the imprint of Robert Barker.

After thanking his subjects for their general welcome, the King goes on to say,

mine actions of thankes, are so inseparably conioyned with my Person, as they are in a maner become individually annexed to the same.[2]

He proceeds to explain this cryptic statement:

It is the blessings which God hath in my Person bestowed upon you all, wherin I protest, I doe more glorie at the same for your weale, then for any particular respect of mine owne reputation, or advantage therein.[3]

These blessings are then enumerated:

The first then of these blessings, which God hath ioyntly with my Person sent unto you, is Outward peace.[4]

Peace abroad, he says, brings with it prosperity:

for by Peace abroad with their Neighbours the Townes florish, the Merchants become rich, the Trade

---

[1] In March 1609/10 James told his Lords and Commons that he was going to give them a 'great and rare Present'. This present was to be 'a faire and a Christall Mirror; Not such a Mirror wherein you may see your owne faces, or shadowes; but such a Mirror, or Christall, as through the transparantnesse thereof, you may see the heart of your King' – *Workes*, Sig. xx 6r (p. 527).

[2] *THE Kings Maiesties Speech, as it was delivered by him in the upper house of the Parliament to the Lords Spirituall and Temporall, and to the Knights, Citizens and Burgesses there assembled, on Munday the 19. day of March 1603, being the first day of this present Parlia-ment, and the first Parliament of his Maiesties Raigne.*

Imprinted at London by Robert Barker, Printer to the Kings most excellent Maiestie. Anno, 1604. Sig. A4.

[3] *Ibid.*   [4] *Ibid.*

doeth encrease, and the people of all sorts of the Land enioy free libertie to exercise themselves in their severall vocations without perill or disturbance.[1]

From the blessings of outward peace, James turns to those of inward peace:

the second great blessing that God hath with my Person sent unto you, is Peace within, and that in a double forme. First, by my descent lineally out of the loynes of *Henry* the seventh, is reunited and confirmed in me the Union of the two princely Roses of the two Houses of LANCASTER and YORKE, whereof that King of happy memorie was the first Uniter, as hee was also the first ground-layer of the other Peace. The lamentable and miserable events by the civill and bloody dissention betwixt these two Houses was so great and so late, as it neede not be renewed unto your memories.[2]

Shakespeare, of course, had 'renewed' it both recently and forcefully. James proceeds:

as it was first setled and united in him, so is it now reunited and confirmed in me, being iustly and lineally descended not onely of that happy coniunction, but of both the Branches thereof many times before. But the Union of these two princely Houses is nothing comparable to the Union of two ancient and famous Kingdoms, which is the other inward Peace annexed to my Person.[3]

It is this final statement, as we shall see, which gave the poets and play-makers the cue that they needed to provide the British people with a messianic vision eclipsing that which their predecessors had chosen to associate with the House of Tudor and which, as I believe, opened the way to the vogue for tragi-comedy at court and in the private theatres.

James himself, however, in projecting his message of Peace through Union and prosperity through Peace provided the poets with three figurative images which did not lie idle in their ears. Summing up on the outward and inward peace bestowed upon his subjects in his Person he declared:

What God hath co[n]ioyned then, let no man separate. I am the Husband, and all the whole Isle is my lawful Wife; I am the Head, and it is my Body; I am the Shepherd, and it is my Flocke.[4]

The second of these images was destined to find its way into the fabric of *Coriolanus*, and the first and third into the structural logic of *The Winter's Tale*.

For James, the question of the relationship between 'the head' and 'the body' was inextricably bound up with that of Divine Right, while for his English subjects, at least as represented in Parliament, it was no less firmly prescribed by the monarch's Coronation Oath. The discrepancies between these two viewpoints came into the open over the matter of 'grievances' which were to loom large in James's address to Parliament in 1609/10 and which I think Shakespeare chose to reflect on the stage in *Coriolanus*.[5] The relationship between the images of 'the husband and his wife' and between 'the shepherd and his flock' as reflected in *The Winter's Tale* will be more fully discussed later in this paper.

Immediately, however, the images in which the poets, pageanteers, and play-makers chose to project this message were culled from legend and from prophecy. 'In Troy, there lies the scene' (*Troilus and Cressida*, Prologue, line 1).

[1] *Ibid.* Sig. A3 v.
[2] *Ibid.* Sig. B. Curiously Richard Mulcaster's text of the London pageants for Queen Elizabeth's coronation in 1559, one of which was devoted to the Union of the Houses of Lancaster and York, was reprinted in 1604. See David Bergeron, *English Civic Pageantry, 1558–1642* (London, 1971), 13ff.
[3] *Ibid.*
[4] *Ibid.*, Sig. B2v. James reverted to the image of husband and wife in his speech of 1608, 'Union is a marriage...' etc., *Workes*, Sig. vu 5 (p. 513).
[5] The passage in question in this speech begins, 'Now the second generall ground whereof I am to speake, concernes the matter of *Grievances*: There are two special courses of the peoples presenting *Grievances* to their King in time of Parliament...' James then focuses his comments on 'the matter and manner' of grievances presented by the House of Commons: 'But though my speech was before directed to the whole Body of Parliament; yet in this case I must address my Speech in speciall to you of the Lower House.' *Workes*, Sig. YY4 (p. 535). See also Davison, 'The Serious Concerns of *Philaster*'.

The legend of British descent from Trojan Brutus, his founding of New Troy, or Troynovant, on the banks of Thames, his disastrous division of the Kingdom between his three sons and Merlin's later prophecy of the coming of a second Brutus who would restore what was lost, all of which had appealed so strongly to the early Tudor chroniclers, could not be bettered as a vehicle for the projection of James's message: for what better title to being the second Brutus could anyone claim than James himself?

Samuel Daniel wasted no time in making this equation in his 'Panygericke Congratulatorie' which went through four editions in London and Edinburgh in 1603.[1] One year later, James made his triumphant entry into London where he was greeted by the most spectacular pageantry ever seen in that city: it was prepared for him by Jonson, Dekker, Middleton, and Webster and centred upon the triple theme of Peace, Plenty and Regenerative Power. Troynovant, says Dekker in the first triumphal arch, has ceased to function as a city: it has become a spring garden for Jove, for the Virtues, the Graces and the Muses now that King James has arrived.[2] The following year (1605) Anthony Munday deployed the same story both at greater length and more graphically in popular iconography for the first Lord Mayor's Show of the new reign, *The Triumphs of Re-united Britania*.[3]

In Munday's pageant the first Brutus was personified by an actor 'dressed in the habite of an adventurous warlike Trojan' and seated beside his wife Britannia. Below them sat their three sons – Albanact, Camber, and Locrine. After telling the citizens how he came to build New Troy, Brutus goes on to recount how he came to divide the Kingdom between his sons. He then turns to Merlin's prophecy and says:

Albania, Scotland, where my sonne was slaine
And where my follies wretchednes began,
Hath bred another Brute, that gives againe

To *Britaine* her first name, he is the man
One whose faire birth our elder wits did scan,
    Which Prophet-like seventh Henry did forsee
    Of whose faire childe comes Britaines unitie.

And what fierce war by no meanes could effect,
To reunite those sundred lands in one,
The hand of heaven did peacefully elect
By mildest grace, to set on Britaines throne
This second Brute, than whome there else was none.
    Wales, England, Scotland, severed first by me:
    To knit againe in blessid unity.[4]

Thus James and the second Brutus were equated in the streets of London in October 1605 not only for all to see but for all to hear, whether or not they could read and write. The equation is made verbally by a character called Troynovant who incites the rivers Thames, Severn and Humber to sing '*Paeans* and songs of tryumph in honour of our second Brute, Royall King *James*'. And there the usefulness of this particular myth might have found its resting-place had it not been for the fact that within a month of the presentation of Munday's pageant the nation was shaken to its political and spiritual foundations by the discovery of the Gunpowder Plot. It is a moot point whether the nation was more disturbed by the discovery of the plot or by relief that it miscarried: what is certain is that King James wished his subjects

[1] See *Complete Works*, ed. A. B. Grosart (London, 1885), I, 143–67.

[2] See *The Dramatic Works of Thomas Dekker*, ed. Fredson Bowers (Cambridge, 1955), II, 229–309, Jonson's *Works*, ed. Herford and Simpson (Oxford, 1941), VII, 77–9, and Stephen Harrison, *The Arches of Triumph* (London, 1604). See also G. Wickham, *Early English Stages* (London, 1958), I, 82–8 and 107–8, and Bergeron, *English Civic Pageantry*, pp. 70–89.

[3] London, 1605. The text was reprinted by J. Nichols, *The Progresses of James I* (London, 1828), I, 564ff. and by R. T. D. Sayle, *Lord Mayor's Pageants of the Merchant Taylor's Company* (London, 1931), pp. 84ff. This pageant is discussed by me in *Shakespeare's Dramatic Heritage*, pp. 250ff. and by Bergeron, *English Civic Pageantry*, pp. 141–5.

[4] London, 1605, Sig. B iiij v.

to give precedence in their thoughts to their delivery from anarchy, the tragedy which Divine Providence had translated into tragicomedy. To this end he both published his 'Discourse on the Powder-Treason' and delivered another speech from the throne in Parliament which was also swiftly printed and circulated in a quarto edition.

In days when Guy Fawkes and his fellows, while still burnt in effigy on 5 November, only provide journalists with an excuse to discuss the dangers of fireworks, it is hard to re-live the feelings of horror with which the news of their original plot was received. Something of this sense of outrage survives in James's speech. As he put it,

In this great and horrible attempt, whereof the like was never either heard or read, I observe three wonderfull, or rather miraculous events.[1]

These are then enumerated:

First, in the crueltie of the Plot it selfe, wherein cannot be enough admired the horrible and fearefull crueltie of their device, which was not onely for the destruction of my Person, nor of my Wife and posteritie onely, but of the whole body of the State in generall.

The second cause for astonishment is the motive:

For if these Conspirators had only bene bankrupt persons, or discontented upon occasion of any disgraces done unto them; this might have seemed to have bene but a worke of revenge. But for my owne part, as I scarcely ever knew any of them, so cannot they alledge so much as a pretended cause of griefe: And the wretch himselfe in hands doeth confesse, That there was no cause mooving him or them, but merely and only Religion.

The third miracle is the clear intervention of Divine Providence:

Thirdly, the discovery hereof is not a little wonderfull, which would bee thought the more miraculous by you all, if you were aswell acquainted with my naturall disposition, as those are who be neere about me.

It was his own interpretation of the ambiguous anonymous letter, contrary to normal syntax and grammar, that led to Parliament being searched and the plot discovered: 'whereas', James concludes, 'if I had apprehended or interpreted it to any other sort of danger, no worldly provision or prevention could have made us escape our utter destruction'.

It was thus this third miracle which in James's own words served to translate 'this Tragedie to the Traitors' into 'Tragicomedie to the King and all his trew Subiects'.

The immediate response of dramatists was to 'the tragedy of the traitors'. From it stem directly, as I believe, Shakespeare's *Macbeth* and Jonson's *Catiline*. Thus Fleance's escape becomes much more than a generalized compliment to the House of Stuart: as a tangential reference to James's own escape and that of the Princess Elizabeth from the powder-treason, the whole of *Macbeth* provides a useful example of Shakespeare's oblique method of treating topical events. Suffice it to say here that Macbeth's crime in murdering Duncan passes, in the imagery of the play's language, beyond regicide to deicide, and that Scotland, like Hell, has to be harrowed before it can be cleansed of a monster comparable with Lucifer and Herod in his tyrannical ambition and depravity.[2]

More importantly, however, the miraculous escape of the King, the Queen and their children from the machinations of Guy Fawkes, Thomas Percy, and their fellows provided the popular imagination with vivid reinforcement of the idea of prophecy fulfilled as depicted in the story of the second Brutus preserved by

[1] This and the following quotations are taken from James I, *Workes*, Sigs. тт 5 and тт 5v (pp. 501–2). The King, the Queen and Prince Henry were to be blown up in Parliament: so, with rather less certainty was Prince Charles. Princess Elizabeth was to be surprised at her country retreat near Stratford and abducted.

[2] See Wickham, *Shakespeare's Dramatic Heritage*, pp. 214–31, and William Armstrong, 'Shakespeare's Typology: Miracle and Morality Motifs in *Macbeth*', (Westfield College, London, 1970). See also James I, *Workes*, Sigs. x2–x3.

God to return in the fullness of time to Troynovant to lead his people towards an imperial future: and there, from a poet's standpoint, lay the most convenient of correspondences with 'the tragicomedy for the King and all his true subjects'. The story of King Leir and his three daughters formed an integral part of this legend as given definitive shape by Geoffrey of Monmouth in the twelfth century and transmitted in many subsequent versions to the English prose *Brut* in the fifteenth century. This epic, compounded in part of myth and in part of more modern history, was at this very time being redacted yet again by Thomas Heywood in XVII cantos under the title of *Troia Britanica: or, Great Britaines Troy*. This work was printed by William Jaggard in 1609 and concludes with James's accession. Heywood says that

His praise is for my pen a straine too hye,
Therefore where he begins I make my pause,
and onely pray that he may still supply
Great *Brittaines* Empyre with the Lands applause,
That as he hath begun to rectifie
This Common-weale, and stablish vertuous Lawes:
  He still may inioy his Queene, and yssue Royall,
  Mongst subiects ever true, and Peeres still loyall.[1]

Troia Britanica was published a year after Parliament's final ratification of the Union and a year before the investiture of Henry Stuart as Prince of Wales. The Troy/Brutus story served to provide subject-matter for the masque commissioned from Samuel Daniel by the Queen to celebrate the investiture in the first week of June 1610, *Tethys Festival*; it was used by Ben Jonson and Inigo Jones in *The Masque at Barriers* for Prince Henry and in *The Masque of Oberon* which flanked it on the preceding Twelfth Night and the following New Year's Day. Dekker used it again for his Lord Mayor's Show, *Troia Nova Triumphans*, in 1612 when preparations were already in hand at court for the wedding of the Princess Elizabeth to the Elector Palatine.

By any reckoning this represents an extraordinary preoccupation among dramatists with a single theme. The only comparable parallel in the Elizabethan and Jacobean period is the earlier vogue for revenge tragedy. The popularity of both, and in that order, stems directly, as it seems to me, from the dominant pattern of historical event.

The eye for an eye and tooth for a tooth philosophy which governed English political life from the moment that Henry VIII divorced Catherine of Aragon and married Anne Boleyn up to the execution of Mary Queen of Scots and the defeat of the Spanish Armada, giving Catholics cause to fear Protestants and Protestants cause to suspect Catholics throughout the entire fabric of the social hierarchy, set the scene for the advent of revenge tragedy. War between England and Scotland and England and Spain in the same quarrel, culminating in the excommunication of Queen Elizabeth and the advance absolution given by the Pope to anyone who succeeded in assassinating her, had provided in real life a nauseating profusion of examples of revenge tragedy which the theatre could never hope to eclipse. What the theatre could do, and what Thomas Kyd and his successors did achieve, was to question the whole ethical basis of such conduct within a Christian society. To this extent, *Romeo and Juliet* happens to reflect relations between Tudors and Stuarts, London and Edinburgh, after the execution of Mary Queen of Scots as vividly as those between Montagues and Capulets in distant Verona; and in a climate of war and persecution in the name of religion, Hamlet's dilemma or those of the protagonists in Tourneur's tragedies, were not the exclusive concern of stage-princes. Such stage-princes served simply to focus the common experience of countless English families into theatrical prototypes which successfully mirrored the

[1] Sig. Qq 6v (p. 466). See also Perrett, *The Story of King Lear*.

bitterness of their own feelings, their own anxieties, their own grief and disillusionment. Anyone seeking an analogue today sadly need only cast his eyes as far as Northern Ireland.

James I's accession could not guarantee an end to all this, but it did offer the possibility of change. Cautious optimism about the future could become at least a viable alternative to a prospect of never-ending judicial murders, family vendettas, and massacres in the name of Christ. No-one spelt out this message more eloquently than the second Brutus himself when addressing a Parliament as sceptical about the advantages of Union as ours has proved itself to be in respect of EEC.

I quote from his speech of 1607/8. This too was immediately printed and circulated in a quarto edition.

And as for the Commodities that come by the Union of these Kingdomes, they are great and evident; Peace, Plentie, Love, free Intercourse and common Societie of two great Nations.[1]

This is not the language of revenge tragedy, but it is the language of *Cymbeline*, *The Winter's Tale* and *The Tempest*.

All foreigne Kings that have sent their Ambassadours to congratulate with me since my comming, have saluted me as Monarch of the whole Isle, and with much more respect of my greatnesse, then if I were King alone of one of these Realmes: and with what comfort doe your selves behold Irish, Scottish, Welsh, and English, divers in Nation, yet all walking as Subiects and servants within my Court, and all living under the allegeance of your King, besides the honour and lustre that the encrease of gallant men in the Court of divers Nations caries in the eyes of all strangers that repaire hither? Those confining places which were the Borders of the two Kingdomes, where heretofore much blood was shed, and many of your ancestours lost their lives; yea, that lay waste and desolate, and were habitations but for runnagates, are now become the Navell or Umbilicke of both Kingdomes, planted and peopled with civilitie and riches: their Churches begin to be planted, their doores stand now open, they feare neither robbing nor spoiling: and where there was nothing before heard nor seene in those parts but

bloodshed, oppressions, complaints and outcries, they now live every man peaceably under his owne figgetree...[2]

Fig trees in Northumberland and Berwickshire may be stretching fact towards poetic fiction; but for all that this is the unmistakable voice of the Authorised Version of the Bible and of *Beatus Pacifus* himself, the British Augustus. Within a year Parliament had committed the British people by an act of faith to the ratification of the Union. In that same year John Fletcher wrote his definition of tragi-comedy.

If I am correct in thus associating the shift towards tragi-comedy in the theatre with the changed political outlook of monarch and Parliament, this places Shakespeare's *King Lear* in a new and interesting context. Granted the fact that the Leir story as received within the Troy/Brutus/Merlin legend had a happy ending, at least for Leir himself as represented in Henslowe's old play, Shakespeare can hardly have chosen to revert, via Holinshed and *The Faerie Queene*, to Geoffrey of Monmouth's original account with its tragic catastrophe for both Lear and Cordelia unless it was planned and scripted very early in James's reign – i.e., before the Gunpowder Plot and thus before *Macbeth*. At the same time, Shakespeare's reversion to Geoffrey of Monmouth's account provides proof that he was as conversant with the whole Brutus/Troy/Merlin epic as other dramatists of the time.

In this sense Shakespeare's *King Lear* may be taken as the prologue to what he was later to do with the story *after* the Gunpowder Plot had been averted and *after* Parliament had ratified the Act of Union. At the actual time of com-

[1] *HIS MAIESTIES SPEECH TO BOTH the Houses of Parliament, in his Highnesse great Chamber at Whitehall, the day of the Adiournement of the last Session,* Which was the last day of *March 1607. IMPRINTED AT London by Robert Barker, Printer to the Kings most Excellent Maiestie.* Sig. E.
[2] *Ibid.,* E & Ev.

position, however, Shakespeare prudently chose to refrain from confusing possibilities with certainties. He thus balanced the happy reunion of father and daughter presented in the old play against Monmouth's tragic conclusion, thus combining his own artistic purposes with deliberate ambiguity in the political treatment of the story: rather than burn his boats with a public declaration that the second Brutus had finally arrived in the person of James I, he reserved judgement. The possibility is admitted through making Albany the agent of Lear's reunion with Cordelia; but Shakespeare refrains from joining Daniel, Dekker, and Munday in projections which time and events could easily prove to have been premature.

This analysis of the historical and political background to the scripting of the new play also illuminates the twin editorial problems of Lear's 'darker purpose' and 'the coronet' in act I, scene I. If, as I believe, to be the case, Shakespeare chose to sandwich the Leir legend together with that of the Brutus/Troynovant legend, and to associate both obliquely with James I and his three children, Lear's conduct in the division of the Kingdom becomes both rational and easily explicable. From the Brutus story Shakespeare takes the geographical partition of the British Isles, and from the Leir story the motivation for the division. Goneril is thus equated with Brutus's son Albanact (hence her marriage to Albany) and is to receive Scotland: Regan is equated with Camber and receives Wales and the Duchy of Cornwall: Cordelia is equated with Locrine and is to receive England. Locrine's fate was of course familiar enough to audiences from *The Lamentable Tragedy of Locrine* which had appeared in print in 1594/5.

The division is thus as equal as Lear says it is; but in this equality there is an obvious yet unstated bonus for one of the recipients, and that is the capital city – Troynovant of the Brutus story, Leicester of the Leir story. This bonus is to be the love prize; it is visually so obvious on the map on the stage for there to be no need to waste time describing it in the dialogue. When Cordelia throws away her portion, it is England, and with it the capital city of an united Britain, that is represented by the coronet which Lear then rashly tosses to Cornwall and Albany to divide between them. This is the act of folly, bordering upon madness, with which Lear in his fury prepares the way to his own ruin and the civil strife that is destined to divide the Kingdom against itself until the return of a second Brutus to New Troy restores 'Peace, Plenty, Love and Free Intercourse' – the essential prologue, within this legendary cycle of myth and prophecy, to the new deal of reconciliation and regeneration which, *if all goes well*, may well be realised as fact when Henry Frederick, Duke of Cornwall and Prince of Wales and heir-apparent to 'Great Britain' succeeded to the throne. It is to this end that at the close of act III, scene ii, Shakespeare makes the Fool turn Merlin's prophecy inside out, 'for I live before his time'.

With the Gunpowder Plot averted in 1605, the Union of the Scottish and the English Crowns achieved in 1608 and with preparations afoot for Prince Henry's Investiture, it could well be said that a new day was about to dawn for all loyal subjects of the Stuart King.

The year 1608 also marks another event of consequence in Whitehall – the coming to court of the Princess Elizabeth. Hitherto she had been secluded in the country under the tutelage of Lord Harrington at Combe Abbey in Warwickshire where, thanks to the alertness of the Lord Lieutenant of that county, she had escaped capture by the Gunpowder Plot conspirators. Now she took up residence at court, gay, intelligent, and beautiful, the most desirable bride in the Kingdom. Just such a girl appears on the stage at this time in the characters of Marina, Imogen, Perdita and Miranda.

Obviously, within the space of this paper, I

can only provide the briefest outline of how I think Shakespeare applied himself to the task of recognising and celebrating these tremendous changes in the political climate of life in Britain within the sequence of romantic tragi-comedies which, as a Groom of the Chamber in the King's Household, he wrote between 1608 and 1613, starting with *Pericles* and ending with *The Two Noble Kinsmen*.

Pericles seems to me to be a relatively simple, first experiment; it is one in which Shakespeare redacted an old play by another author in the way he had already adapted the old play of *King Leir*; but this time with a view to transforming its conclusion into a general compliment to the royal family, and to reflecting James's reunion with his daughter Elizabeth in particular.

This play, which in its revised form Brandl described as 'a chain of miracles', is conveniently summarised in Gower's epilogue.

> In Pericles, his Queen and daughter, seen,
> Although assailed with fortune fierce and keen,
> Virtue preserved from fell destruction's blast,
> Led on by heaven and crowned with joy at last.[1]

I would therefore submit that in remodelling the last three acts of George Wilkins's play, Shakespeare sought to provide Globe Playhouse audiences with a romance that corresponded in its general shape with the hardships endured by James before attaining to the succession, the escape of King, Queen and royal children from assassination, and, finally, with the reunification both of the British Isles under a single crown and of father, mother, and daughter in Whitehall. Gower continues,

> For wicked Cleon and his wife, when fame
> Had spread their cursèd deed and honoured name
> Of Pericles, to rage the city turn,
> That him and his they in his palace burn.
> The gods for murder seemèd so content
> To punish, although not done, but meant.

It does not require a sybil to decipher the reference to the Gunpowder Plot in 'murder...

although not done, but meant', nor that to the fate of the conspirators, formally executed in 1606, in that of the city's revenge on 'wicked Cleon and his wife'.

Finally Gower describes Helicanus, 'A figure of truth, of faith, of loyalty'. This, I take to correspond with that of Sir Francis Bacon, the prime architect of the Union, the Union itself being reflected in the marriage of Marina to Lysimachus. All these sophisticated correspondences are broadly sketched and only loosely dovetailed to the popular romance: but the essential images – storm, shipwreck, attempted murder, providential escape, and final reunion, with the royal children centre-stage – are there to be reworked in subsequent plays where the grafting of the new emblematic significance to the old 'tales, tempests and suchlike drolleries' is to be much more cunningly effected.

I take the first variant upon this theme to have been *Cymbeline*, a play that one might well describe as dedicated to the royal children. With Imogen and the two boys out of Wales, audiences are expected to associate the Princess Elizabeth, Prince Henry, and Prince Charles: Shakespeare signposts this message clearly in his repeated references to Milford Haven, 'blessed' because Henry VII, 'the first Uniter', landed there as Henry Tudor, Duke of Richmond, and as James and his children's claim to rule England from Troynovant was derived from the marriage of Henry's daughter Margaret to James IV of Scotland. This James had himself spelt out in the first of his speeches to Parliament quoted above, 'First, by my descent lineally out of the loynes of *Henry* the seventh ...' etc. And not for nothing had he christened his eldest son Henry, his eldest daughter Elizabeth.[2]

[1] This and the following quotations from Shakespeare are all given from *The London Shakespeare*, ed. John Munro (London, 1958).

[2] The daughter born in 1605 was christened Mary:

If Imogen and her marriage to Leonatus Posthumus are placed at the centre of *Cymbeline*, it is because Whitehall was at this very time buzzing with speculation about who the Princess Elizabeth might marry, and aware of James's intentions to supplement the 'inward peace' of domestic union with 'outward peace' that could be secured by the reunion of Britain with the continent of Europe through appropriate marriages for Elizabeth and her brothers.

> Set we forward. Let
> A Roman and a British ensign wave
> Friendly together. (*Cymbeline*, v, v, 477–9)

From the general and oblique compliment to the three children provided in *Cymbeline* in 1609 Shakespeare moved on to offer a far more specific tribute to Prince Henry in *The Winter's Tale*, motivated, as I believe, by his investiture in June 1610, as Prince of Wales. The Queen commissioned Samuel Daniel to devise a Masque for the occasion: the result was *Tethys Festival* in which she and all three children participated, the Queen herself as Tethys, Prince Charles as Zephyrus, Prince Henry as Meliadus, Lord of the Isles, and Princess Elizabeth as the River Thames.[1] Ben Jonson and Inigo Jones paid their tributes to the Prince in *The Masque at Barriers* on Twelfth Night 1610 and *The Masque of Oberon* on the following New Year's Day. Anthony Munday regaled the citizens of London with a water-pageant, *London's Love to Prince Henry*, assisted by John Rice and Richard Burbage.[2] Did Shakespeare stand aloof ignoring this occasion? I think not; for if ever an occasion demanded a commissioned work from the leading play-maker to the King's own company of players this was it.

I have argued elsewhere that Shakespeare's answer was *The Winter's Tale*.[3] In it he reworked the story of the first and the second Brutus in the person of Leontes; and in doing so he took his cue from James himself – 'I am the Husband and all the whole Isle is my lawful wife...I am the Shepherd, and it is my Flocke.' Applying these figures, which James had used to justify the Union of the Crowns, to *The Winter's Tale*, we find the play set in two countries, Sicilia and Bohemia, and further divided by a sixteen-year gap in time. Leontes,

she died in 1607. James also arranged for his own mortal remains to be buried in Henry VII's tomb in Westminster Abbey. See also the next note.

[1] All the rivers personified in this Masque

> within the goodly spacious Bay,
> Of manifold inharbouring *Milford* meete;
> The happy Port of Union, which gave way
> To that great Hero *HENRY*, and his fleete,
> To make the blest conjunction that begat
> A greater, and more glorious far than that.

Daniel clearly took the subject-matter of this passage directly from James I's speech of 1603/4: see text given on p. 38 above.

[2] London, 1610. See also Bergeron, *English Civic Pageantry*, pp. 94–6.

[3] See p. 34, n. 1. It is hard to resist the temptation to suppose that the idea of coupling the first and second Brutus in the character of Leontes was derived from *The Tragedy of Locrine* where, in the opening Dumb Show and Chorus, the first Brutus is equated emblematically with a Lion 'ruler of the woods, / of wondrous strength and great proportion'. James I, in his role as the second Brutus, could be similarly equated with a lion since the lion of Scotland had just been incorporated with the leopards of England in the royal coat-of-arms.

In the context of *The Winter's Tale* the Dumb Show has a special interest. The stage directions read: 'Enter *Atey* with thunder and lightening all in black, with a burning torch in one hand, and a bloodie swoord in the other hand, and presently let there come foorth a Lion running after a Beare or any other beast, then come forth an Archer who must kill the Lion in a dumbe show, and then depart. Remaine *Atey*.' (Ed. R. B. McKerrow, Malone Society Reprints, Oxford, 1908, Sig. A3.) A no less interesting precedent for the coupling of two commonwealths (one flourishing, the other decayed) is supplied by recourse to the figure of Time in Richard Mulcaster's pageants for Queen Elizabeth's Coronation, the texts of which were published twice, in 1559, and were then surprisingly reprinted in 1604 under the title of *The Royall Passage of Her Majesty from the Tower of London to her Palace of White-hall*. (See p. 38, n.2, above.)

as presented in part one, is the first Brutus who, figuratively speaking, by divorcing his wife divides the Kingdom: Sicilia is England. Bohemia is Scotland (hence its sea-coast) and Florizel its Prince: Florizel is Henry Stuart, created Duke of Rothesay and Prince of Scotland at his baptism, Duke of Cornwall in 1603, and now newly-created Prince of Wales as well. It is he, therefore, who will thus truly reunite in his own person Scotland, Wales, and Cornwall with England and Ireland as heir-apparent, thus coupling (as Doricles) the image of 'husband and wife' to that of 'Shepherd and flock'.

The Leontes of part two is the second Brutus whose deeds of atonement as a bringer of peace and the provider of tombs and painted statues in the King Henry VII Chapel in Westminster Abbey for Queen Elizabeth I and Mary Queen of Scots have prepared the way for a double reunion – the return of Hermione to Leontes himself, and the marriage of the heir-apparent to Great Britain, alias Perdita, lost by the first Brutus but restored in the fullness of time by Divine Providence to become Prince Henry's bride. Polixenes, King of Bohemia, thus begins where Goneril's husband, the Duke of Albany, left off, and serves to translate the tragic finale of *King Lear* into the 'exultation' of 'precious winners all' that concludes *The Winter's Tale*. The legend has come full cycle and the play could as appropriately be sub-titled 'The Triumph of Re-united Britannia' as Robert Greene's novel *Pandosto* was sub-titled 'The Triumph of Time'.

Following the investiture the focus of interest in royal affairs at court passed swiftly from James's efforts to reunify the British Isles to his no less forceful efforts to reunite divided Christendom by dynastic marriages, a policy pursued just as vigorously on the domestic front in James's attempts to make British Protestants at court marry into Catholic families and *vice-versa*. It is this objective which Shakespeare took up next in *The Tempest*.

Diplomatic activity in the quest for an appropriate husband for Princess Elizabeth and a suitable wife for Prince Henry had begun in 1609. James cast his eyes south to Catholic Spain and east to Protestant Germany: the Duke of Savoy tried to grab both children; but Henry and Elizabeth had ideas of their own. In 1611 these delicate negotiations lost whatever cover of secrecy may have been desired for them when the proposal to marry Elizabeth to Philip of Spain became public knowledge and was openly denounced by Prince Henry. Such was the public outcry that this plan although supported by Queen Anne was finally dropped on Lord Salisbury's advice. Whether or not Shakespeare took sides in this affair is beside the point: that he sympathised with the general objective that informed this and other marriage plans for the royal children seems patently clear from the dramatic structure of *The Tempest*.

Unlike *Pericles*, its three successors seem to me to bear the unmistakable hall-mark of court commission, with the Blackfriars in mind by way of hard-cash earnings from a wider public, and with transfer to the Globe as a subsequent possibility rather than a certainty. Not only is the compliment in each case far more specific and recognisable within court circles, but the stylistic qualities both of the writing and the scenic representation are more carefully tailored to meet the changing literary and aesthetic tastes of court audiences. Finally, within the limits of the new tragi-comic genre, the fusion between exposition of patron's policies and artist's fable becomes progressively more expert and professionally polished. All four plays are linked by a father figure wracked by adversity, brought near to death and disaster, but steadfast in his faith, constant in his purpose and protected by providence to bring his policies to a successful and joyous conclusion.

If this figure is not the poet's patron, given a patron as prolific and explicit in his public pronouncements as James I, I am the proverbial Dutchman: no less obvious is the correspondence between the idealised bride for all four romances and the real-life Princess who came to court in 1608 and was finally married to the future King of Bohemia in 1613.

A word requires to be said about *Henry VIII* and *The Two Noble Kinsmen*. The former, like *Pericles*, is a collaborative work and planned for public playhouse audiences in the first instance. Cranmer deputises for Merlin as prophet in pointing the way ahead to an imperial future under a British Augustus.

> peace, plenty, love, truth, terror,
> That were the servants to this chosen infant,
> Shall then be his, and like a vine grow to him:
> Wherever the bright sun of heaven shall shine
> His honour and the greatness of his name
> Shall be, and make new nations: he shall flourish,
> And like a mountain cedar, reach his branches
> To all the plains about him: our children's children
> Shall see this and bless heaven.   (v, iv, 47–55)

Alas, 'the bright sun of heaven' was soon to be clouded over: for the year 1613 saw not only the destruction of the first Globe by fire during a performance of this play, but the death of the flower of chivalry, Prince Henry, just as the preparations for the wedding of the Princess Elizabeth to the Elector Palatine were approaching their peak. It is this situation which, as Professor Bradbrook demonstrated in a paper read to the World Shakespeare Congress in Vancouver last year, finds its mirror image in *The Two Noble Kinsmen* where 'with an auspicious and a dropping eye, / In equal scale weighing delight and dole' the collaborating poets contrive to respect court mourning for the dead heir-apparent while celebrating simultaneously his sister's nuptials.[1]

The final submission, therefore, to emerge from a paper which must at times have seemed rambling and discursive, is this. In the course of transforming the old tragi-comedy of *King Leir* into a tragedy, Shakespeare came face to face with the sources of the Brutus/New Troy stories to which James I's accession had given new life in the minds of other poets. He chose at first to use this material guardedly and not to interpret it as explicitly as Samuel Daniel or Thomas Dekker or Anthony Munday had done. However, he clearly read and digested his patron's speeches; and, following the abortive Gunpowder Plot and the ratification of the Act of Union, he returned to it again and adopted James's own belief that what was, in the minds of traitors, to have been a real-life tragedy, had been miraculously transformed by divine providence into a tragi-comedy for the royal family and all loyal subjects. There followed from his pen a succession of plays which, if obliquely and *en passant* rather than directly, reflected the fulfilment of prophecy in the advent of a second Brutus in New Troy: these plays all dwell lovingly on children whose ages and qualities closely resembled those of his patron's daughter and sons.

In *Pericles* Shakespeare celebrated,

> Virtue preserved from fell destruction's blast
> Led on by heaven and crowned with joy at last.
>   (Epilogue, lines 5–6)

In *Cymbeline* he celebrated the lopped branches who were 'for many years thought dead' but who 'are now revived' and

> To the majestic cedar joined, whose issue
> Promises Britain peace and plenty.   (v, v, 457–9)

It is of this same majestic cedar that Cranmer prophesies in *Henry VIII*, whose branches are to reach 'to all the plains about us': and this of course includes 'the remote Bermoothes' and Virginia.

In *The Winter's Tale* it is the re-unification

[1] 'Shakespeare and his Collaborators', *Shakespeare 1971*, ed. C. Leech and J. M. R. Margeson (Toronto, 1972), pp. 29–34.

of those lands which the first Brutus so rashly gave to his sons Albanact, Camber, and Locrine, and which Lear in his turn divided between Goneril and Regan, that is celebrated. This subject is handled under the twin figures of the husband reunited with his wife and the shepherd with his flock: to it is added the deed of atonement for past wrongs, symbolised in real life by the burial of the Protestant Queen Elizabeth and the Catholic Mary Queen of Scots surmounted by painted alabaster effigies in the Henry VII Chapel at Westminster Abbey, and figured in the play by the resurrection of the statue of Hermione in Leontes' chapel. As Leontes himself observes, 'Our Perdita is found.' *The Winter's Tale*, as it seems to me, was the only play of the four romances in which Shakespeare found himself trapped by the uniqueness of the occasion celebrated into providing a wholly explicit and consistent allegory within the frame of tragi-comic romance: and even in this he did no more than Jonson and Daniel found it artistically legitimate to do in *The Masque at Barriers* and *Tethys Festival* at that same time.[1]

Moving outwards from the domestic to the foreign scene, *The Tempest* bodies forth the beatific vision of the reunification of divided Christendom through royal weddings.

> Their understanding
> Begins to swell; and the approaching tide
> Will shortly fill the reasonable shore,
> That now looks foul and muddy.
>
> (v, i, 79–82)

The patron's vision, like the insubstantial pageant of the stage itself, was punctured first by the death of Prince Henry and then by the outbreak of the Thirty Years' War. Being of mortal coinage it could scarcely have fared otherwise. But that does not deny it its own grandeur: nor does it diminish the artistic treatment accorded to it by our own, and that patron's, greatest poet, who, like Lear's fool, could be loyal to the end, while offering compliments where they were due and strictures when they seemed warranted.

[1] The mystical character of the Union, expounded by James in his speeches and figured by Shakespeare in the Chapel scene of *The Winter's Tale*, was no less elegantly treated by Ben Johnson in Epigram v.

> When was there contract better driven by Fate,
> Or celebrated with more truth of state?
> The world the temple was, the priest a King,
> The spoused pair two realms, the sea the ring,

© GLYNNE WICKHAM 1973

JACOBEAN TRAGEDY AND THE MANNERIST STYLE

CYRUS HOY

The imaginative vision that produced Shakespeare's Jacobean tragedies was conditioned by that crisis of the Renaissance – that counter-Renaissance, as it is sometimes termed – brought on by those innovations in science and religion, political and moral philosophy that are associated with the names of Copernicus and Luther, Machiavelli and Montaigne. The effects of these have been often described. They issue in the recognition that truth is not absolute and completely objective but relative, that morality has a double standard (one for rulers, the other for the ruled), that the intellect is of no avail in scrutinizing the wisdom of God, that the earth is not the centre of the universe. It would be odd if so thorough-going a revolution in man's conception of himself, his world, and his relation to deity – all accomplished within the limits of a single century – had not left its impact on the art of the sixteenth and early seventeenth centuries and of course it has done so, both on the art of literature, and on the arts of painting, architecture and sculpture.

In attempting to draw some analogies between the anti-classical movement in sixteenth-century painting and Jacobean tragedy, my purpose is to examine the drama of Shakespeare and his contemporary playwrights in the context of a post-Renaissance movement in the arts which by the beginning of the seventeenth century had spread across all of Europe, and to try and isolate some of the features which Jacobean drama shares with the style of continental mannerism. The term 'mannerism'

has been troublesome in the past, for one reason because it has not always been properly differentiated from the baroque (a point on which I will have something to say later), and for another because the term has too often been understood as a synonym for 'mannered', and so been taken as a term of disparagement. Since the publication of Arnold Hauser's definitive account of Mannerism in 1965 there is no reason why misconceptions about the term should any longer obtain, and I raise the matter simply to reassure anyone who is shocked at the suggestion that Shakespearian tragedy should be associated with it; since mannerism, properly understood, can claim Tintoretto, Bruegel, and El Greco among painters, and Cervantes among writers, the term is not to be thought of as demeaning.

It may be reassuring for me to say at once that in this paper I am not attempting to transfer the formal principles of the visual arts to literature, and so will not be analyzing Jacobean dramatic speech and plotting in the language – for example – of Wölfflin's categories ('linear', 'painterly', and the rest). I am concerned with the tragedies of Shakespeare and his contemporary dramatists as expressions of the intellectual crisis that obtains throughout Europe at the end of the Renaissance, and I turn to sixteenth-century painting (chiefly Italian) as the artistic medium in which this crisis makes itself felt most fully and explicitly. Certain ways of representing reality – certain assumptions about the nature of reality – that are present in the work of sixteenth-century painters such as Rosso and Pontormo, Parmigianino and Bronzino, Tintoretto and El Greco, have not been present in the art of the high Renaissance; they are to be taken, I think, as legitimate responses to the contemporary intellectual and emotional climate, which is the climate of the counter-Renaissance; and I am here concerned with investigating the extent to which Jacobean tragedy exhibits comparable ways of representing reality, comparable assumptions about the nature of reality.

Mannerist art, says Hauser, is 'impregnated with the mentality of Crisis'.[1]

One of the fictions of the Renaissance, [he declares] was that mind and body, man's moral demands and the demands of his senses, formed a harmonious unity, or were at any rate reconcilable as such without any grave conflict...The crisis of the Renaissance began with the doubt whether it were possible to reconcile the spiritual with the physical, the pursuit of salvation with the pursuit of terrestrial happiness.[2]

The artistic style which gives expression to this mentality of crisis is above all things paradoxical; it is obsessed with the contradictory quality of things; it is the product of the tension between the spiritual and sensual impulses of the age; it reflects a world which has become – in every sense of the word – problematic. Over the years, Jacobean tragic dramatists have come in for some hard treatment by critics who have censured them for their inability to differentiate between real and unrealistic dramatic conventions, for their confusion of different stylistic levels, their fumbling efforts to achieve a dramatic form adequate to the vision of experience they wished to convey. As concerns this last, what Hauser says about the 'supersensible nature' of the vision with which mannerism is continually at grips is of particular interest: the vision is never (says Hauser) 'completely absorbed in form, never completely mastered, but is always hinted at', and it produces a spiritual tension which partakes of 'an essenti-

ally religious unrest'.[3] This accounts for 'the distortion of form and the disruption of boundaries'[4] so characteristic of the art of Parmigianino or El Greco or Tintoretto, and I do not think it is fanciful to find a comparable tension issuing in a comparable quality of formal distortion in the tragedies of Shakespeare and his contemporaries.

Nothing is more characteristic of mannerist painting than the representation of different kinds and levels of reality in the same picture. The practice is evident in one of the earliest of distinctly mannerist works, Pontormo's *Joseph in Egypt* (painted *c.* 1518; National Gallery, London), where the figures on pedestals have the effect of calling into question the reality of the living forms that swirl about them. Sometimes different details of reality are represented with different degrees of realism. This may be achieved by a radical disproportion in the scale of figures represented in different parts of the picture, as in Parmigianino's famous *Madonna del collo lungo* (begun 1535 and left uncompleted; Uffizi, Florence), where the towering madonna and her spectacularly-elongated child quite dwarf the tiny prophet with the scroll in the lower right-hand corner. The greatest of all Italian mannerists, Tintoretto, renders different levels of reality by means of different techniques of painting: one (in Hauser's words) plastic, realistic, substantial, the other sketchy and flat, fleeting and shadowy.[5] Hauser says of them: 'The two different methods of representation seem primarily intended to indicate that we live simultaneously in a world of spirit and another of tangible fact without ever knowing exactly where the boundary between them lies.'[6] The juxtaposition of figures modelled in their full substantiality and ghostly images that

[1] Arnold Hauser, *Mannerism: The Crisis of the Renaissance and the Origin of Modern Art* (London, 1965), p. 7. [2] *Ibid.*, p. 10.
[3] *Ibid.*, pp. 16–17. [4] *Ibid.*, p. 10.
[5] *Ibid.*, pp. 222–3, 228–9. [6] *Ibid.*, p. 222.

look as if they were sketched in with chalk make for some impressive – and celebrated – effects in Tintoretto's work: the wraith-like figures fleeing toward the colonnade that encloses the left-hand side of the square across which the body of St Mark is being carried in the painting in the Accademia in Venice; the insubstantial on-lookers who line the shore behind the kneeling Christ in the *Baptism* in the Scuola di S. Rocco, Venice; the virtually translucent figures of the two prophets in the background of the S. Rocco *Ascension*; the horsemen in the retinue of the Magi, seen glimmering in an unearthly light through a door at the back of the stable in the S. Rocco *Adoration*.

The tendency in mannerism to combine things from different spheres of reality is most evident in the increasing naturalism brought to the representation of sacred subjects. Here it is not simply a question of the combination – and juxtaposition – of things, but of the combination of the effects to which the things juxtaposed give rise: the emotional with the spiritual, the grotesque with the sublime, the mundane with the eternal; and always any tendency toward naturalism itself is managed with a high degree of formalism. One of the most important of early mannerist paintings, Rosso Fiorentino's *Descent from the Cross* (1521; Pinacotecca, Volterra – see Plate I) is one of the most deeply-felt representations of the subject in all of art, but it is also one of the most grotesque, and a principal source of its grotesquerie lies in its disconcerting combination of profound passion and formal – not to say abstract – design. Against an acid blue sky is imposed a latticework of forms inanimate and human: the great cross itself; a pair of ladders on either side but in reversed positions to the picture plane, with the spidery figures of three men outlined against the sky engaged in the work of lowering Christ's livid-green body to the ground, while a fourth, a wildly-bearded,

grim-faced figure in a red tunic, leans on the top of the cross, one bony bare arm and elbow thrust out at a sharp angle, watching over the scene like a praying mantis. Among his contemporaries, Rosso had a reputation for eccentricity in his art that has persisted. Sir Kenneth Clark refers to Rosso and Pontormo as 'those two neurotics with whom the anti-classical movement of the sixteenth century begins',[1] and mannerism is essentially an anti-classical style, just as is the style of Jacobean tragedy, a fact that many critics of the plays of Shakespeare and his contemporary dramatists have found troublesome. Eliot's strictures on the 'impure art' of the Elizabethans are familiar: their aim, he said, 'was to attain complete realism without surrendering any of the advantages which as artists they observed in unrealistic conventions'.[2] By this measure, mannerist painting is as impure an art as Elizabethan (or Jacobean) tragedy; in his pursuit of realism, a Tintoretto is no more prepared than a Shakespeare to surrender any of the advantages available to him in unrealistic conventions. In any case, terms such as 'realistic' and 'unrealistic' have a way of turning back on themselves when applied to the work of a great mannerist artist. The point can be made from Tintoretto's several treatments of the Last Supper. He painted no less than seven versions of this subject in the course of his long career, the first in 1547 (in San Marcuola, Venice), when he was twenty-nine years old. Its representational manner is simplicity itself: a table stretched horizontally across the front of the picture, with Christ in the centre, à la Leonardo. There is a woman personifying Faith at the left, and another at the right representing Charity with an infant in her arms and a small child at her feet. There is a flagon on the floor at the left, balanced by a

[1] *The Nude* (New York, 1959), p. 343.
[2] T. S. Eliot, *Selected Essays* (New York, 1950) pp. 96, 97.

cat on the floor at the right, and that is all. The back wall is closed, so that the sense of space is distinctly shallow. When Tintoretto returned to the subject at the age of forty-two for the church of San Trovaso, Venice, he produced a picture that is very much more realistic but also more mysterious. The table has now been given a characteristic mannerist turn so that one corner juts out of the picture plane, toward the viewer. The apostles are no longer sitting sedately round the table, but are leaning on it, or pushed back from it; Judas has left it and stands in shadow at the back, behind the figure of Christ, leaving his chair over-turned; two of the figures in the front are reaching behind them – one to grasp the neck of a wine flask, the other to lift the lid from a dish into which a cat is getting ready to thrust a paw. Neither is looking in the direction where he is reaching, both having their gaze firmly fixed on Christ, who sits opposite them; there is a Michaelangelesque quality about their elaborately-contorted postures, rather as if two of the nude youths had descended from the Sistine ceiling with their clothes on, but the turns which their twisting bodies are in process of executing have the effect of flinging the whole picture into motion. The most remarkable thing about the San Trovaso *Last Supper*, however, is its treatment of space. The scene is no longer enclosed with a blank wall; instead, an oblique staircase ends in a mysterious darkness at the left, while to the right of centre, behind the seated figure of Christ, the picture takes a typical mannerist plunge into the depth by means of an emphasized recession: a long, narrow colonnade opens, flooded with light, and occupied by two chalky, almost disembodied figures. It is a simple but movingly effective way of suggesting the interpenetration of a spiritual world with our mundane one.

All Tintoretto's later versions of the Last Supper might be said to strive toward a form that will fully infuse naturalistic detail with supernatural implication, and he achieves it in his final version (in San Giorgio Maggiore, Venice – see Plate IV), which he painted just before his death in 1594. It is a memorable example of how the materials of reality can be incorporated into a work of art whose ultimate effect is transcendent, visionary. Here the table is thrust diagonally back into the picture by means of some violent foreshortening. The apostles – with the exception of Judas, who sits alone – are all gathered on the far side of the table, engaged in heated discussion; the room is aswarm with servants; the floor is littered with containers of food and drink, and domestic animals. But the air above this commonplace scene is thick with angelic shapes: ghostly forms like figures seen in clouds or in wisps of smoke like those that surround the blazing oil lamp from which at first they seem to emanate. The whole initial impression of realism is in fact delusory. The plethora of naturalistic detail lacks clarity upon inspection, and the radiance which surrounds the figure of Christ is as blinding as the smoky flare which comes from the aforementioned lamp is ambiguous. The world of spirit is descending on the world of physical matter, and while it transforms, it also calls into question.

A final mannerist technique for combining different levels of reality is the construction of those soaring, two-storey compositions wherein an earthly event depicted in the lower half of the canvas is watched over or commented on or given its apotheosis by a heavenly host which occupies the picture's upper half. The technique is not, strictly speaking, a mannerist one; it is, for example, a common Renaissance method of representing Ascensions, or the Assumption of the Virgin, as in Titian's famous *Assuntà* in the church of the Frari, Venice. But it comes to have particular value for the mannerist artist in his search for formal means of combining opposing realities, opposing worlds. Tintoretto employs the structural technique frequently in the paintings done for the Scuola di San Rocco: e.g. in *The Brazen Serpent*, *Moses Bringing forth Water from the Rock*, and the *Ascension*. Sometimes both upper and lower halves of the picture represent aspects of a single earthly event, but with the upper half representing those aspects which have their reference to a world beyond the earthly one in which the event has transpired, as in *The Agony in the Garden*, or *The Raising of Lazarus*, or *The Miracle of the Loaves and Fishes*. There is nothing simplistic about Tintoretto's lines of demarcation in these cases; the poles of spiritual energy – and of dramatic interest – are precisely if somewhat perilously balanced between the two halves. Lazarus is lifted out of his tomb at the top of the San Rocco painting while the figure of Christ, the instrument of the miracle, half reclines in the lower right-hand corner, amid a company of mortal spectators. In both the San Rocco *Agony in the Garden* and the nearly contemporary and closely related one in the church of Santo Stefano, Venice, Christ rests and a ministering angel attends him in the upper half, while in the lower half the apostles sleep and through the dark foliage at the left, their figures picked out in Tintoretto's sketchy, chalky manner, come Judas and the informers.

The most spectacular use, however, to which this method of combining different orders of reality is put in mannerist painting comes in the work of El Greco. Beginning with the *Dream of Phillip II* (c. 1579; Escorial), El Greco represents events on earth crowned – in every sense of the word – with explosions of activity in heaven, where events on earth are, in effect, completed and given their significance. Hauser has commented on the pronounced differentiation between earthly and heavenly events in the famous painting of the *Burial of the Count of Orgaz* (1586–8, Santo Tomé, Toledo – see Plate II), where El Greco has endowed them with different degrees of realism.[1] In the lower

half, all is meticulous definition; the row of heads of the aristocratic mourners who look on while the body of the Count is lowered into its tomb are rendered with the utmost psychological precision. Above them, and unseen by all but a priest and a boy who points to the miraculous scene, the clouds open to reveal a resplendent vision of all the hosts of heaven. The vision amounts to a dream, and one that is passionately entertained. It satisfies the imagination's need to express itself in forms more rhythmic, colors more brilliant, volumes and masses freer and more buoyant than any that the world affords.

The representation of different levels of reality by way of different levels of style is a familiar feature of Jacobean tragedy in general, and of Shakespearian tragedy in particular. Auerbach, in *Mimesis*, has commented of Shakespeare's tragedies that 'there is none in which a single level of style is maintained from beginning to end';[2] and he cites the example of 'the grotesque scene with the porter in *Macbeth*'. The combination of the tragic and the comic, the sublime and the low, has long been recognized as one of the most characteristic features of Jacobean tragedy, and I would suggest that the large, basic dichotomy that is here points directly to the essentially mannerist nature of Jacobean tragic style. The dichotomy has reference to both form and matter, inevitably so since tragic form in the Renaissance implies a certain level of seriousness with regard to tragic story and a certain greatness of spirit with regard to tragic personages, while comic form implies a quality of the commonplace and the vulgar with reference to both. Since sixteenth-century English drama produced nothing comparable to the separation of comic and tragic form that obtained, for example, on the Renaissance Italian stage, the

[1] Hauser, *Mannerism*, p. 262.
[2] Erich Auerbach, *Mimesis* (New York, 1957), p. 278.

tendency to fuse comic and tragic elements – evident from the outset in Elizabethan tragedy and fully established on the Jacobean stage – is not always recognized for the sign of the times that in fact it is. Faced with the combination of a comic sub-plot which parodies a serious main one, as in plays such as Marlowe's *Faustus* or Middleton and Rowley's *Changeling*, critics have too often been content to trot forth the example of the Wakefield *Second Shepherd's Play* and announce that this sort of thing had been a feature of English drama since medieval times, which of course it had; but this fails to recognize that a traditional device of dramatic plotting now has its place in a distinctly different dramatic idiom. Nothing in the *Second Shepherd's Play* prepares us for the grotesque discontinuities achieved by Marlowe and by Middleton and Rowley in the articulation of their tragic action with its zany counterpart.

Outside Italy, there was in fact a close connection between mannerism and the gothic. Mannerism had its origins in a reaction against the classicism of the Renaissance, but this can only be fully understood with reference to the art that produced the style, painting, and the land in which it developed, Italy. The classicism of Italian Renaissance painting is sufficiently well defined – in the art of Fra Bartolommeo and Perugino and Raphael and Andrea del Sarto – as to make quite clear in what ways and to what degrees a Pontormo or a Rosso or a Parmigianino is departing from its stylistic tenets. Despite the freedom with which the term is used, the Renaissance never extended far outside Italy; as Hauser says, 'only in its state of disintegration, in the form of courtly mannerism, did it become a general European movement';[1] but this does not preclude the development of mannerism in countries where there was no classic style to react against or depart from; Hauser stresses the fact that 'mannerism was international from the first', springing as it did 'from a spiritual crisis that affected the whole of Europe'.[2] In countries such as France and the Netherlands where it came to flourish in the arts of painting and sculpture, it developed directly out of surviving gothic traditions; contemporary Italian influences were brought to bear upon these in due course, as at the court of Fontainebleau, and in the case of one of the greatest of mannerist artists, Bruegel. The sophisticated art of Fontainebleau ended by superseding the gothic in France, while in the Low Countries Bruegel, who was as much affected by the spiritual crisis of the age as Shakespeare was, remains as faithful as does Shakespeare to the native traditions of his art. To term Elizabethan and Jacobean tragedy 'mannerist' is not then to deny the medieval heritage of either. The medieval elements that survive into both are familiar: the parodic sub-plots, the *De Casibus* thematic tradition and the goddess Fortuna, the hierarchical world order, the contempt of the world and all the rest. They now contribute to the artist's sense of living in divided worlds that is such a characteristic feature of the mannerist style: a division that opposes the sense that human suffering is due to irrational chance against the sense that it is the result of the human propensity to sin and error; a division that opposes the ideal of hierarchy to the reality of threatening chaos; a division that opposes the contempt of the world over against the lust for life.

For the Jacobean dramatist, the dichotomy of tragic and comic, sublime and low, encloses a subtly-graded sequence of opposing realities, opposing worlds, together with the distinctly mannerist tendency to invert their usual signification. One small sign of this last practise is evident when prose assumes the function of verse as the appropriate language of tragedy. In *Hamlet* or *Lear*, for example, tragic utterance frequently finds expression in

[1] Hauser, *Mannerism*, p. 241.
[2] *Ibid.*, p. 251.

the cadence of prose, not verse, and the effect, instead of rendering the speaker commonplace, makes him more mysterious. Language for Shakespeare, like color and form for El Greco or Tintoretto, yields different kinds of reality. *Lear* abounds in them, and they join together in a vast, intricate design in which the grotesque is inseparable from the tragic. The shallow complacency of Gloucester introducing his bastard son to Kent in the opening scene joins many scenes later, after shallow Gloucester has been so readily duped by that son, with the resonance of Edgar's address to the bastard: 'The dark and vicious place where thee he got / Cost him his eyes' (v, iii, 173–4). One kind of reality is constantly being replaced by another in the play: Goneril and Regan's cajolery with Goneril and Regan's viciousness; Cordelia's banishment with Cordelia's reconciliation to her father, replaced in turn by a final reality which embraces the deaths of both; Lear's pride with Lear's humility. The most sublime and the most loathsome imaginings inhere in the language of the play, from one scene to the next. The difference in kinds of reality that I am pointing to is the difference between, on the one hand, Lear's obscene reflections on women viewed in the image of Goneril and Regan ('But to the girdle do the gods inherit' – iv, vi, 125) and, on the other, the eager appeal to Cordelia ('Come, let's away to prison' – v, iii, 8).[1] The kinds of reality that are dramatized in the last part of the play exhibit a distinct, not to say grotesque, disparity, with the chaste simplicity of Lear's reconciliation with Cordelia clashing fiercely with the lurid sexual tangle in which all the degenerate children – Goneril, Regan, Edmund – are involved. But this is only the final example of an artistic principle that has been even more memorably exhibited in the great central scenes of the play with their alternation between two worlds: the hard, rational, brutal one from which Lear is driven and where

Gloucester is blinded, and the large, empty universe where the victims of the rational world's bland duplicity take refuge. In their outcast state, stripped of their identities, Lear, Kent, the Fool, Edgar, Gloucester are the dramatic equivalents of those wraith-like figures in Tintoretto: the ghosts of their worldly selves, alienated from each other and from themselves, wandering under a lightning-torn sky like the one Tintoretto has provided for the *Removal of the Body of St Mark*, or the apocalyptic heavens of El Greco under which Toledo lies in its bone-grey stillness, and Laocoon and his sons writhe in their agony.

II

The outcasts in *Lear* comprise Shakespeare's most comprehensive emblem for the condition – alienated and dispossessed – which all his tragic personages share. The subject of inheritance and disinheritance is treated everywhere one looks in Jacobean drama. There are dukes deprived of their dukedoms, like Marston's Malevole and Shakespeare's Prospero; there are sons foully done out of their inheritance, like Hamlet or Marston's Antonio or Charlemont in Tourneur's *Atheist's Tragedy* or Beaumont and Fletcher's Philaster. What, in one way or another, the state of the disinherited always has reference to is the fate of fallen man, dispossessed of the condition that was originally his. When on the Jacobean stage disinheritance is not being dealt with in the literal terms of the world's goods, it is treated with reference to the loss of moral properties which imply even more directly the loss of man's pre-lapsarian condition. The subject may be treated in a number of ways: from Chapman's analysis of the loss of man's native

[1] Quotations from Shakespeare are based on the text of the Pelican edition, of *The Complete Works*, general editor, Alfred Harbage (Baltimore, Maryland, 1969).

virtue, whereby the innocence that once inhered in Bussy D'Ambois and Byron is betrayed by the world's politic scheming, to Middleton's Beatrice in *The Changeling*, turned out from her 'first condition' by 'peace and innocency' and now claimed by her instrument of murder, her tempter, with whom she is at one in her corruption. Othello's murder of Desdemona issues in a paradise lost, its loss brought to pass by a 'demi-devil' who has ensnared his victim 'soul and body' (v, ii, 301). The world of Jacobean tragedy is thoroughly secular, but it adumbrates a world of sacred mystery which artists like Shakespeare and the most gifted of his contemporaries can trace out in the actions of men; the result is that tension between a world of absolute injunctions and a world of moral relativism that gives to plays like *Hamlet* and *Othello* and *King Lear* and *The Revenger's Tragedy* and *The Changeling* one of their most distinctive mannerist features.

If the typically dispossessed, disinherited condition of characters in Jacobean drama reflects the common lot of post-lapsarian man, what characters in this drama do by way of remedying their lot is even more revealing of man's condition after the fall. Jacobean comedy is notoriously full of men and women out to improve their fortunes, like the legacy-hunters in Jonson's *Volpone* or the seekers after the philosopher's stone in *The Alchemist*, or the throngs of would-be but impoverished gallants who populate Jacobean city comedy. Disinheritance, in Jacobean drama, always leads to efforts to regain one's fortune, and the efforts are at best unscrupulous and at worst downright villainous. They can only succeed with a certain amount of deception, which always implies a disguise, either a literal one or the invisible mask of hypocrisy. And so we have a virtual paradigm of human kind's readiness to improve on its common condition by whatever politic means are at hand – a paradigm, in effect, for a crucial theme of Jacobean tragedy.

Everybody is engaged in double-dealing, in playing the game of appearances, and everybody is wearing a mask of one kind or another. This accounts for the air of secrecy that is so pronounced a feature of all those Jacobean plays set in courts where the air is heavy with rival ambitions and clandestine lusts. The real self – what it plans to do and how it plans to do it – must be concealed from others, and the self that is presented to the world is a model of seeming indifference: cool, poised, utterly self-absorbed – though in fact, of course, never so self-absorbed that it does not have an eye ready to detect any betrayal of intention or motive from others. Jonson's two Roman tragedies are particularly effective in conveying this quality of isolated watchfulness in an atmosphere of high political tension. In this respect, Jonson might be termed the Bronzino of Jacobean mannerism. Bronzino worked at the Medicean court of Cosimo I, so that the subjects of his many portraits knew what life was like under a violent and capricious tyrant. Bronzino paints them in attitudes of surpassing haughtiness; they are cold, detached, guarded; in them, the need to repress emotion has resulted in an impenetrable reserve. Hauser has said of Bronzino that 'with him the face is obviously not the mirror of the soul, but its mask, and the portrait is an art form that conceals as well as reveals',[1] and the same might be said of Jonson's portrayal of all the principal personages in *Sejanus* and *Catiline*, with the obvious qualification, of course, that the dramatist can avail himself of the opportunity to go behind the mask and reveal the inner man, as in soliloquy.

Jonson is linked to Bronzino in another way, and that concerns the quality of courtly eroticism so prominent in later mannerism. Its most celebrated example is Bronzino's *Venus, Cupid and Time*, which Cosimo I sent to

[1] Hauser, *Mannerism*, p. 199.

Francis I, and which is now in the National Gallery in London (see Plate III). It is a remarkable picture, and it makes its impression in a typically mannerist way, by bringing together – and not necessarily reconciling – opposites: it is distinctly erotic but also frigid, an effect that is altogether in keeping with its subject, which has been fully explicated by Panofsky[1] and which concerns the ambiguous delights of love. The suave, nude Venus who is being caressed in no maternal way by her adolescent and equally nude son is surrounded by equivocal figures: Pleasure on the right is counter-balanced by Jealousy on the left, and behind Pleasure is a sweet-faced girl in a green dress who, though woman all above, is, as Lear would say, inherited by the gods only to the girdle: beneath is all the fiend's; her body ends in a coiled cluster of monstrous appendages: fish scales, animal claws, a serpent's tail. The two masks in front of her clearly label her the figure of Deceit. Though an edifying moral could be – and presumably was – claimed for the allegory, it is hardly to be supposed that the fame of Bronzino's painting ever rested on this. Its fame rests firmly on its lascivious detail, but sixteenth-century courtly etiquette was coming to require that lascivious detail be camouflaged, and this Bronzino managed to do with a steely technical elegance and a formidable sophistication. It is one of the most knowing, least innocent, pictures in the world. The manner in which the taste for the erotic found satisfaction in fashionable circles interested Jonson almost from the outset of his career. He dealt with it tentatively in *Cynthia's Revels* and in the character of Livia in *Sejanus*; returned to the subject on a much fuller scale in his treatment of the Collegiate Ladies and their ambiguous erotic tastes in *Epicoene*, and then proceeded to his definitive portrait of courtly and secret eroticism in the character of Fulvia in *Catiline*. Fulvia is a figure of controlled lust: so controlled that she is able to make her lover

reveal Catiline's conspiracy to her, and then at the advantageous moment betray it as well to Cicero, thereby winning fortune and fame as the saviour of Rome. Jacobean dramatists revel in the portrayal of the sort of sleek, self-possessed lasciviousness that is able fully to sate its erotic appetite while imperturbably maintaining the façade of courtly decorum, and Marston (in the figure of the Duchess Aurelia and in the Maquerelle scenes in *The Malcontent*), the creator of Lussurioso and his panders in *The Revenger's Tragedy*, Tourneur's Levidulcia in *The Atheist's Tragedy*, Webster in the Julia scenes of *The Duchess of Malfi*, Middleton in the character of Livia in *Women Beware Women*, have all depicted the sundry devices by means of which lust masks itself in high places. It is one of the subtler ironies of the period that Jonson, the most perceptive of all contemporary viewers of this sort of thing, should have devoted the last half of his career to devising masques that would permit the members of courtly society to disguise themselves as something differnt from – and usually better than – what in truth they were. Viewed with the knowledge of hindsight, masques like *Hymenaei* and *A Challenge at Tilt* – wherein all the powers of virtuous love are invoked to celebrate the two marriages of Lady Frances Howard – seem almost too blatant examples of idealism come unhooked from the occasions it was intended to inform. The spectacle of a court whose moral tone was not high witnessing and enacting the grave and learned and indeed often sublime philosophic fables which Jonson provided for its ritual occasions brings sharply into focus the tension between spiritualism and sensualism, rationalism and irrationalism, which is at the heart of the crisis of the Renaissance, and of the mannerist style. Jonson's quarrel with Inigo Jones was inevitable, and inevitably couched in a dualistic

[1] Erwin Panofsky, *Studies in Iconology* (New York, 1962), pp. 86–91.

metaphor: would scenic spectacle (the body of the masque) be allowed to overwhelm the graceful beauty and wisdom of poetry (its soul)? The answer was 'yes', and Jones's triumph marks a clear stage in the decline of mannerism and the advent of the baroque.

III

In no major body of tragic drama have deceptions, disguises, the manipulation of appearances loomed so large as in that of Shakespeare and his Jacobean contemporaries. Their concern with masks is directly related to the fact that long before the end of the sixteenth century the question of what is real and what is not had become a problem; reality had become, in a word, problematic, which is what the crisis of the Renaissance is about. The issue is central to all Shakespeare's mature tragedies, but it presents itself in two distinctly different aspects in the earlier and the later of these. Tragic personages such as Hamlet, Othello, Lear and Timon must pick their way through a maze of conflicting appearances that have been wilfully erected by the unscrupulous to confound the image of truth, and the contradictions that encompass them are their undoing. This may be true in a sense of Macbeth as well, but only in a superficial sense, for in that play and in Shakespeare's other two later, fully Jacobean tragedies (*Coriolanus* and *Antony and Cleopatra*) the tragic issue has shifted profoundly. The contradiction of appearance and truth in these plays is no longer really a problem; and in saying as much I am in effect dismissing the supernatural machinery of *Macbeth*, which exists to give visible shape and impetus to invisible and unacknowledged longings. In these late tragedies, there is no Claudius, no Iago, no false daughters, no false friends. Macbeth, Coriolanus, Antony and Cleopatra are not the victims of deceptive appearances; they are beyond appearances,

they cannot be other than they are even if they wished to be which they don't, they are obsessed with being themselves, and appearances have no effect upon them except when (as in the case of Macbeth) they confirm them in their inclination to follow the dictates of their own inner will. In their tragic fates, Macbeth, Coriolanus, Antony and Cleopatra are victims to their own self-absorption. Self-absorption is a form of narcissism, and narcissism and its consequent alienation are distinctly mannerist subjects.

Hamlet's shocked recognition that a man could smile and smile and be a villain was a truism that nonetheless propelled the dramatist's imagination through the next two tragedies, where Iago engineered the fall of Othello, and Goneril and Regan exploited the folly of Lear. It may also have propelled the dramatist's imagination at least half-way through a third tragedy if (as I would like to assume) *Timon of Athens* followed *Lear*. Timon's betrayal by his flattering friends follows the familiar example of Othello betrayed by Iago, and Lear by his false daughters, but the play continues (in its last two acts), as it examines what betrayal has done to Timon, into regions of the soul that the dramatist had not explored before, but which – in the figures of Macbeth and Coriolanus – he would shortly be exploring again. Lear, even in his outcast state, is never without attendant and beneficent spirits: Kent, the Fool, later Cordelia. Timon in his exile is alone with his hate for mankind, and his periodic shouting matches with Apemantus or Alcibiades but confirm the finality of his alienation, of which he is indeed an archetypal figure. Hauser has termed alienation 'the key to mannerism',[1] and has

[1] Alienation, Hauser affirms, appeared for the first time in conscious form as the crisis of the Renaissance; concerning its process, he writes: 'Man created objects, forms, and values, and became their slave and servant instead of their master. The works of his hand and mind assumed an autonomy of their own, and became independent of him while he became depen-

gone on to declare that the psychology of alienation is narcissism;[1] and there is something distinctly narcissistic about Timon's misanthropy. This accounts for the complete stasis of the figure of Timon himself throughout the last half of the play where he is frozen into an immobility that permits him only to go on staring relentlessly into the image of his hate as this turns into a passion for universal ruin on a scale sufficient to satisfy his outrage at the fact of human ingratitude.

Shakespeare had dealt with narcissistic types before, notably in the person of Hamlet. What is new about the psychological condition that is being explored in the last two acts of *Timon of Athens* is its depiction of a figure bent on making his actions square with his words, and both actions and words square with his inner desire, regardless of how destructive this may be: in effect, the unfulfilled ideal so basic to the tragedy of *Hamlet*. Early in the play Timon has commended the Painter for his art whose 'pencilled figures are / Even such as they give out' (I, i, 159–160), which is more than can be said for the figures of human nature which, stained with dishonor, are too often 'but outside'. And much later in the play he commends the bandits for frankly professing to be what in truth they are: 'Yet thanks I must you con / That you are thieves professed, that you work not / In holier shapes' (IV, iii, 421–3). Timon, with his huge invective against mankind, is acting on the injunction of Edgar at the close of *Lear*, speaking what he feels, not what he ought to say, and achieving thereby a rare coherence of intention and word whose only precedent hitherto in Shakespearian tragedy has been Cordelia, with her refusal to speak other than as she feels. But the

assumes a nature completely different from the self, becomes alien and hostile to it, and threatens to diminish and destroy it. Meanwhile the self loses itself in its objectifications, faces an alienated form of itself in them' (pp. 95–6). Hauser stresses the importance of economic factors in the process of alienation in the sixteenth century, where 'the concept of commodities became the fundamental category of social life and reshaped and refashioned every field of human endeavour' (p. 101). The effect of this is to turn the worker and his work alike into a saleable object. The middle of the sixteenth century, Hauser notes, 'saw the real birth of the art trade' (p. 102); and the sense of artists as dealers in commodities is clearly evident in the figures of the poet and the painter in *Timon of Athens*. 'Nothing', says Hauser (p. 102) 'illustrates the process of alienation in economic and social life more strikingly and significantly than the part played by money in modern capitalism'; *Timon of Athens*, where everything turns on the power of money, is Shakespeare's demonstration of this.

[1] 'Alienation is an essentially sociological concept, the real meaning of which is lost, or restricted and falsified, when it is simply transferred to the psychological plane. It has scientific value only as long as it means a crisis in human relations and loss of roots in the social soil. The psychological phenomena accompanying alienation are most striking and impressive, which makes it tempting to be led astray into describing them for their own sake, but they offer too wide a field for purely impressionistic, literary descriptions, and objectively they are as a rule not particularly revealing. In this inappropriately used psychological aspect of the word, alienation becomes a mere synonym for a sense of unrest and discomfort. A more genuinely psychological concomitant of alienation, and one better adapted to scientific investigation, is a phenomenon *sui generis* that is closely connected but by no means identical with it. It is the more or less pathological condition which Freud calls by the borrowed term of narcissism and is an illness of the individual mind, just as alienation is an illness of the social body. A narcissistic character in Freud's sense of the term has withdrawn his libido – his love and affect-charged interest – from the outer or objective world, from persons and things, and has concentrated it on the self. He is able to love no one but himself, and in reality not even himself, for anyone able to love only himself would be bound to despise and hate himself. The psychoanalytic description of this dialectical process is that the narcissist identifies himself with the object from which he has withdrawn his love, and develops a hate-love of himself (sometimes associated with suicidal impulses) which bears all the marks of the attitude known as ambivalence' (Hauser, pp. 115–16).

dent on them...In the classical meaning of the term ...alienation means divestiture of the self, the loss of subjectivity; a turning inside out of the personality, exteriorising and driving out what ought to remain within, with the result that what is ejected in this way

achievement is totally self-destructive, and Timon ends as some monstrous parody of Christ: one who dies for hate of mankind. He is in every way a paradoxical creation: broken by suffering but uninstructed by it, a sorrowing figure whose sorrows only the mind – and not the heart – responds to. With its tragic sense of the contradictory nature of things, of the appalling chasm that separates appearance from truth, the play is in fact one of Shakespeare's most mannerist performances, and its mannerist features extend to the different degrees of reality which it exhibits: Timon's rage is far more fully rendered than Timon in prosperity, and the periphery of the play is populated by wraith-like figures who are hardly more than sketched in. The play is a mannerist work in the way that Michelangelo's *Pietà Rondanini* is mannerist: the mode of representation is irrational, anti-natural, but informed with a profound spiritual vision which both Michelangelo and Shakespeare seem ultimately to have despaired of translating adequately into material form. The *Pietà Rondanini* is unfinished, and so, I suspect, is *Timon of Athens*.

The coherence of intention and word which Timon so extravagantly achieves makes for the psychological congruence whose moral and immoral implications are explored in *Macbeth* and *Coriolanus*, two other narcissists and so – in the present context – highly mannerist figures.[1] 'Art thou afeard / To be the same in thine own act and valour / As thou art in desire?' Lady Macbeth demands of her husband (I, vii, 39–41). In fact he is, as she well knows; her question is designed to shame him into a more manly – which is to say more murderous – disposition, and Macbeth's tragedy is the monument to her success. He has begun by frankly recognizing that his desires will not bear scrutiny; he cannot imagine doing the deed that would satisfy them, though he wishes that he could, or that somebody would. His aside when he realizes that to gain the throne he

must not only kill Duncan but murder Duncan's son Malcolm as well contains a characteristic equivocation: 'Stars, hide your fires; / Let not light see my black and deep desires. / The eye wink at the hand; yet let that be / Which the eye fears, when it is done, to see' (I, iv, 50–3). Under his wife's urging, he is prepared, for the moment, to adopt a mask to the end of accomplishing his desire, and so on the evening of the murder he accepts the need to 'mock the time with fairest show'. After he has killed Duncan he is afraid to think what he has done (II, ii, 50), and he voices one last despairing impulse to divorce himself from the act he has so fervently wished might be performed without himself performing it and which without quite knowing how he has managed to commit: 'To know my deed, 'twere best not know myself' (II, ii, 72). But this is another equivocation, and it is promptly branded as such by the entrance of the Porter, muttering drunkenly of equivocators and the hell-gate to which in the end they come. What the Porter says concerning drink as an equivocator with lechery can be applied to Duncan's murder and the equivocal effects it works on the murderer: 'it makes him, and it mars him; it sets him on, and it takes him off; it persuades him and disheartens him; makes

---

[1] Cf. Hauser's account of the institutionalization of society and the resultant depersonalization and dehumanization as factors in alienation: 'The first thing to be sacrificed to an institution is spontaneity, not merely in those who administer it, but also in most of those who come into contact with it from the outside. It leads a life of its own, as if driven by an internal mechanism. Every mannerist style, and every mannerist vision of life, either bears marks of this deadening of spontaneity and mechanisation of reactions, or shows signs of struggle against it by the development of exaggerated forms of individualism, sensibility, and arbitrariness' (p. 107). A deadening of spontaneous emotion and a tendency to mechanisation of reaction are prominent in the characters of Macbeth and Coriolanus *vis-à-vis* their respective 'institutions': in the case of Macbeth, the institution of kingship (embodied, ironically enough, in himself); in the case of Coriolanus, the institution of the Roman state.

him stand to, and not stand to; in conclusion, equivocates him in a sleep, and, giving him the lie, leaves him' (II, iii, 29–33). This in fact is an accurate description of what happens in the rest of the play, down to the moment when Macbeth begins 'To doubt th' equivocation of the fiend, / That lies like truth' (v, v, 43–4).

In the last part of the play, Macbeth is virtually sealed off from reality, walled up in the identity and the fate which, in more ways than one, he has made for himself. Not content to go on indefinitely mocking the time with fairest show, he has yearned to give over dissimulation, and the means to this end has been the murder of Banquo. Banquo has had to die, among other reasons, in order that Macbeth and his wife might be delivered from the necessity – as he has put it to her – to 'lave / Our honours in these flattering streams / And make our faces vizards to our hearts, / Disguising what they are' (III, ii, 32–5). But if their hearts are not disguised, then they must appear in their true guiltiness, and by the time the play enters its final stage, Macbeth is prepared that this should be so. He decrees the murder of Macduff's family and thereby provides himself with a model of alacrity in matching thought with act. Then, resigned to be what his sundry bloody deeds have made him, he withdraws into the ambivalencies of the Witches' prophecies. Hauser has noted that the complexity of narcissistic characters 'lies in the often extraordinarily involved and elaborate technique by which they maintain their identity, their infinite resourcefulness in devising fictions and stratagems, like Don Quixote, to evade reality and truth'.[1] And he continues: 'The inner conflict of their nature lies in the fact that, while they have completely withdrawn their love and sympathy from the world of men, they still need them as their partners, public, or victims.'[2] The need is evident in such figures as Timon, Macbeth, Coriolanus, and Antony and Cleopatra.

Coriolanus is another study in tragic dedication – on the part of the protagonist – to a principle of behavior or a line of action that defines the protagonist's self-integrity even as it alienates him from the rest of the world. For Timon, for Macbeth, for Coriolanus, to be himself is to be at odds with the world, and they are prepared to be at odds for the sake of their own integrity, which is to say, for the sake of their own wholeness, for the sake of that condition of self-consistency where thought and act, intention and word are at one. It is the tragedy of each that the drive for wholeness brings about a collision between the private inner man where the impulse to action originates, and the outer public world where action must fulfill itself; and in the collision the impulse is subtly warped, distorted, rendered either futile or vicious. Timon's impulse to an indiscriminate love for mankind turns to an indiscriminate hate; Macbeth's impulse to kingly greatness turns him into a kingly butcher; Coriolanus' passion for honor makes him infamous. The great tragic impression which is common to all three of these plays, and which is unlike anything else in Shakespearian tragedy, is of the three protagonists presiding to the end over – not so much the collapse of – but the perversion of their aims. They persist to the end in their determination to be true to themselves in thought and word and act, without ever seeming to realize that their efforts to be true to themselves made them traitors to themselves. Coriolanus possesses from the beginning that congruity of thought and word which Timon (like Hamlet before him) has found to be so notably lacking in the world, and which Macbeth aspires to in his warped way. Menenius describes him as one whose 'heart's his mouth. / What his breast forges, that his tongue must vent' (III, i, 257–8). His aversion to flattery makes him seem a kind of

[1] Hauser, *Mannerism*, p. 121.
[2] *Ibid.*, pp. 121–2.

older brother to Cordelia. But in fact we learn that Coriolanus' sense of honor is not so absolute as it might seem. The play joins the issue between the double standards of morality that obtain in private and public life – and obtain as well in different spheres of public life – in a way that has particular relevance to the whole question of moral relativism and its crucial place in the intellectual crisis of the Renaissance. Volumnia addresses her son:

> I have heard you say,
> Honour and policy, like unsevered friends,
> I'th' war do grow together. Grant this, and tell me,
> In peace what each of them by th' other lose,
> That they combine not there. (III, ii, 41–5)

Coriolanus would turn the question aside with an impatient 'Tush!' but Menenius from the sidelines pronounces it 'A good demand' and the mother continues:

> If it be honour in your wars to seem
> The same you are not – which, for your best ends,
> You adopt your policy – how is it less or worse,
> That it shall hold companionship in peace
> With honour, as in war; since that to both
> It stands in like request?

Coriolanus has no defense against this line of attack and Volumnia presses her advantage: for him to address the people 'with such words that are but roted in / [His] tongue, though but bastards and syllables / Of no allowance to [his] bosom's truth' no more dishonors him 'Than to take in a town with gentle words, / Which else would put you to your fortune and /The hazard of much blood.' 'I would', she announces, 'dissemble with my nature where / My fortunes and my friends at stake required / I should do so in honour.' What is to be noted here is Volumnia's bold assurance that one can dissemble in honor. But the combination of dissemblance and honor is of a piece with the combination of honor and policy which, as Volumnia has already said on Coriolanus' authority, grow together in time of war like unsevered friends. Nothing could be more characteristic of counter-Renaissance moral and ethical dilemmas than this.

Coriolanus is usually regarded as Shakespeare's final tragedy, but the evidence is by no means conclusive, and I prefer to view *Antony and Cleopatra* in this light. It is a summing up of the dramatist's work in the tragic form, and the imaginative vision contained in its close leads straight on to the final plays; this highly romantic tragedy is the link between the tragedies and the romantic tragi-comedies which close Shakespeare's career. By now the dramatist has fully explored the resources of tragedy as a means for expressing the mystery of suffering and the reality of evil, the disasters that overtake the person who does not know himself or who allows his passions to go unchecked by reason. *Antony and Cleopatra* touches on all these issues, but to view the play in any such terms as these alone is sadly simplistic. What the play shows us are two people who from the time we see them first, until they breathe their last, manage to be exactly what – when everything else is said – they want to be, namely lovers. To be the triple pillar of the world or the queen of Egypt is secondary to this. The play, in typically mannerist fashion, sets before us opposing worlds, opposing realities – Rome v. Alexandria, public duty v. private passion, etc. – but there is no real sense in which Antony is found vacillating between the two. In I, ii he tells himself that he must break his 'strong Egyptian fetters' or lose himself in dotage (I, ii, 113–14); he never does break them, and I think it is not unfair to say that he does lose himself in dotage. That he should be taken in by the false report of Cleopatra's death is one of the play's more wicked ironies; Enorbarbus has told him in the beginning about her 'celerity in dying' (I, ii, 141). And the details of his death are rich in signs of dotage, starting with the bungled suicide attempt. Trust none about Caesar but

Proculeius, he tells Cleopatra (IV, xv, 48), and as usual he is wrong, for it is Proculeius who supervises her seizure by Roman soldiers two scenes later. His dying words invoke his former greatness, as he has been prone to do increasingly in the latter part of the play, and he clutches the comforting fiction that he dies 'A Roman, by a Roman / Valiantly vanquished' (IV, xv, 57–8). The role Cleopatra has played in bringing about his death goes unnoticed.

In Shakespeare's play, the reality of Antony's heroic young manhood is now but a memory of the past, though it is vividly invoked from time to time; the play gives us the reality of Antony's middle-age wherein he lurches from crisis to crisis, often parodying his previous heroism, but finally providing an example of a new kind of heroics as he doggedly continues on to the end in the way that passion has led. The result of this is to match up words with deeds to a degree that he may not originally have intended. His rapturous address to Cleopatra at the beginning of the play – 'Let Rome in Tiber melt,' etc. – may sound at the time like so much splendid rhetoric; Cleopatra terms it 'Excellent falsehood'; but at last, his share in Rome and the ranged empire gone smash, he does in fact die in her embrace in a stage tableau that re-enacts the embrace in which the lovers have engaged in the earlier speech.

The manner in which glamorous but seemingly empty rhetoric comes in the course of the play to be informed with equally glamorous acts has been the cause of much critical gaping. *Antony and Cleopatra* is like nothing so much as one of those soaring, two-storey mannerist paintings wherein the bottom half is occupied with events on what Antony would call 'our dungy earth' (I, i, 35), above which the heavens open in a transfiguring blaze that begins with the death of Antony at the end of act IV and keeps ascending to the death of Cleopatra at

the end of act V. The plays open indeed with a distinctly mannerist device; Philo's injunction to Demetrius – and by implication to the audience ('Look, where they come: / Take but good note, and you shall see in him / The triple pillar of the world transform'd / Into a strumpet's fool: behold and see') – is to the play what the foreground figure of the small boy who points to the burial of the Count of Orgaz is to El Greco's painting. Hauser speaks of these 'foreground figures whose role in mannerism is to connect the domain of art with the world of the spectator, linking fiction with reality, the picture space with real space'.[1] 'Their purpose', he continues, 'is not the creation of illusion, as it is in the baroque, but the opposite. They make play with illusion, point to the existence of the two worlds that are entered upon in entering the world of art, and emphasise the narrow edge between imagination and reality, poetry and truth, dream and real life, on which mannerism moves.' The narrowness of this edge is nowhere more impressively demonstrated than in the final act of *Antony and Cleopatra*, where we are witnesses to the process whereby reality is transformed by the power of feeling. 'My desolation does begin to make / A better life', Cleopatra says to her women at the beginning of V, ii, the play's last scene; reality has been replaced by imagination in the dream-like vision of Antony as colossus which she shares with Dolabella. In her final apotheosis, the narrow edge between imagination and reality, dream and waking has been obliterated in the glazed rapture of her embrace with death. But it is characteristic of the style of this highly mannerist play – with its delight in paradox, in bringing together irreconcilable elements – that the apotheosis itself is the product of sublime imaginings and vulgar resources; the erotic implications of the figs and the asps have not

[1] *Ibid.*, p. 263.

escaped comment; they are the sensuous and very mortal means to fulfilling Cleopatra's immortal longings.

Shakespeare orchestrates the contradictory qualities of the play with ever-increasing bravura as the tragedy enters its finale. We are constantly being shuttled back and forth between ecstatic heights and lowly depths, between poetic visions and the prosaic common-place. Cleopatra, upon finishing her epic delineation of Antony, asks Dolabella if he thinks 'there was, or might be, such a man / As this I dream'd of?' and he replies as kindly as possible, 'no'. Though she has announced her scorn for this world, she does not scorn it so greatly that she has failed to make provision for going on living in it, as the embarrassing episode with Seleucus reveals. Then Dolabella returns with the news that Caesar, despite his blandishments, intends to parade her in his triumphs, and her royal thoughts are in the ascendant again, and the tragic finale is back on its sublime track, though not before the Clown has come on and we have been treated to his innuendoes about the worm and dying. Her immolation is as eloquent in its vocal utterance as its motives are equivocal. Both lovers are prepared to die, as they have lived, by love, and their tragic stature consists in their readiness to accept their fate, but they do not accept their fate without a certain amount of imaginative re-adjustment of the realities that have overtaken them. Antony expires in the flattering conviction that he has conquered himself, and Cleopatra can only be absolute for death when desolation has functioned as a stimulant to her imagination. When the imagination has done its work – when the vision of 'a better life' that will replace this one which has proved unsatisfactory has become sufficiently vivid – she can then stage the last of her many death scenes. The art of dying as she practices it is a heady compound of im-mortal longing and erotic fantasying.

The transformation of reality that is going forth throughout the last act of *Antony and Cleopatra* becomes the whole impulse to Shakespeare's final artistic style, a style that is intimately bound up with mannerism, which may indeed be viewed as the ultimate expression of mannerist principles in Shakespeare's art. To consider Shakespeare's last plays in any detail is beyond the strictly appropriate limits of a paper dealing with his Jacobean tragedies, though one could argue that the final plays are, in effect, tragedies with happy endings. They cannot, however, be altogether ignored in a paper dealing with mannerism and Jacobean dramatic style. Mannerism, with its tendency to combine different levels of reality, variant modes of vision, may be said to come into its own on the Jacobean stage with the advent of tragi-comedy, which is the mannerist dramatic form *par excellence*. *Pericles*, *Cymbeline*, *The Winter's Tale*, and *The Tempest* are all, in their several ways, extensions of that imaginative endeavor to make out of desolation 'a better life' which Cleopatra manages in the closing scene of her tragedy. The dramatic impulse in these last plays is to sanctify human suffering, to turn desolation into rejoicing, to represent the whole of earthly reality touched with an unearthly radiance. Shakespeare's final artistic manner is as distinct as that of Tintoretto or El Greco, and it tends in the same direction. Hauser speaks of Tintoretto's 'spiritualisation of form' and of space[1] as crucial ingredients in the final style which produced the great 'fantasy landscapes' in the Scuola di San Rocco: the *Flight into Egypt*, the *St Mary of Egypt*, the *St Mary Magdalen*. The details of these night scenes are partly lost in obscurity and partly outlined with an unearthly brilliance; what is not deep in shadow is drenched in light that does not so much illuminate as it trans-figures the world on which it falls. The style of

[1] *Ibid.*, p. 225.

the late El Greco – though entirely characteristic of that highly individual artist – tends in the direction of a similar abstraction from reality. Hauser writes of such paintings as the *Baptism* and the *Resurrection of Christ* (both in the Prado, Madrid), the *Annunciation* (Thyssen–Bornemisza Collection, Lugano), the *Immaculate Conception* (Museo de Santa Cruz, Toledo):

The bodies that he paints are transfigured; they have lost their substance as well as their form, and have been turned into weightless, lambent flames. Their solid, tangible corporeality has been transformed into pure colour and life; they are absorbed in light, become embodiments of light, light is the medium in which they take shape. El Greco abolishes their earthly form and material being and turns them into astral bodies.[1]

In a like way, the figures in Tintoretto's *Paradise* (in the Doges' Palace) 'are transformed into the revolving planets of a solar system'.[2] Over the desolate scenes of *Pericles* and *Cymbeline*, the heavens open – as in some mannerist painting – to reveal a vision of Diana, or of Jupiter on his eagle. These are Shakespeare's early, tentative efforts to secure the artistic means for conveying the vision which all the final plays are concerned with dramatizing. They are crude by comparison with what is to follow, but they serve the purpose, which is to bring the influence of heaven to bear upon earth.

The mannerist features of *The Winter's Tale* are particularly prominent. The process of temporal foreshortening, whereby Leontes' jealousy springs into being and is full grown within the space of some sixty lines, is as violent as any spatial foreshortening in Tintoretto. The Chorus of Time which bridges the two halves of the play and makes for the transition from the world of Sicilia to the world of Bohemia fulfills its purpose by the familiar mannerist device of directly signalling to the audience; Time here is the Shakespearian equivalent to El Greco's pointing boy in the

Burial of the Count of Orgaz. What by all the traditions governing classical dramatic structure ought to be one of the great scenes in *The Winter's Tale* – the one in which Leontes recognizes his long-lost and presumably dead daughter – is left out: an anti-classic feature of the play that has its analogy in the tendency in mannerist painting to relegate the principal scene or figure from the foreground or centre to the background or side; Tintoretto's *Presentation of the Virgin* (Madonna dell'Orto, Venice) is a famous example. Then we come to the scene in which Hermione's statue is revealed. The mannerist fondness for securing bizarre and somewhat equivocal effects from mixing figures on pedestals with living figures has already been mentioned in connection with Pontormo's *Joseph in Egypt*. That the statue should be the reputed work of one of the most celebrated of mannerist painters and sculptors, Giulio Romano (v, ii, 105) is the sort of detail which it is doubtless rash to attach too much importance to, but perverse to pass over in silence.[3]

---

[1] *Ibid.*, pp. 264–5.   [2] *Ibid.*, pp. 230–1.

[3] A pupil of Raphael's, Giulio (1499?–1546) was a master of painted but seemingly statuary forms set forth in equivocal surroundings. His frescoes in the *Sala di Costantino* in the Vatican (painted between 1520 and 1524) are virtuoso examples of art imitating not only nature but other forms of art. Painted to simulate tapestry, the figures in the frescoes are remarkable for their sculptured shapes. The supposed tapestries hang between papal thrones which are also painted on a flat surface, but rendered with such a degree of verisimilitude as to appear architectural volumes thrusting into the room. S. J. Freedberg thus describes the effect of the whole: 'In Giulio's pseudo-tapestries there is... aggressive excavation of a depth of space and, in the figures, a plasticity of nearly violent insistence. In contradiction of the look of tapestries, the figures here suggest an almost tangible existence; but this existence seems to be less of human than of statuary forms. The painting, which counterfeits one genre of art in its frame, counterfeits an antithetic genre, that of sculpture, in its contents; further, there is pretense to counterfeit, simultaneously, of both art and actuality. The whole intellectual and visual situation given us to

In *The Winter's Tale*, the spiritual vision is no longer confined to a single spectacular epiphany (as in *Pericles* and *Cymbeline*), though it still occupies, as it were, the upper half of the canvas; however, this upper half – deriving out of and quite transfiguring the havoc wrought by Leontes' jealousy – is resplendent with the figures of the young Perdita and Florizel, and the resurrected Hermione. With *The Tempest*, we are no longer presented with a divided canvas; the scene of desolation – Prospero's betrayal and exile – is left completely out of the picture, and the human scene that we are shown, though like Tintoretto's fantasy landscapes it has its areas of darkness labelled Antonio and Sebastian, Stephano and Trinculo and Caliban, is in process of transfiguration as we watch it unfold: a process managed by a figure (Prospero) who occupies a highly ambiguous position somewhere between human and spiritual form, and his assistant (Ariel) who might well qualify as one of El Greco's astral bodies.

Shakespeare's last plays represent the culmination of the mannerist style in Jacobean drama; thereafter, the style disintegrates, though it never completely disappears from the stage until the closing of the theatres; it is found in the Middleton of *Women Beware Women* and *The Changeling*, and fitfully in Ford. Typically in the history of styles, by the time one has reached its apogee, another which will eventually replace it is already in process of formation; so it was with Jacobean mannerism; by the time it received its ultimate stylistic expression in Shakespeare's tragi-comic romances at the end of the first decade of the seventeenth century, the elements of a new style – also cast in a tragi-comic mold – had begun to appear in the Beaumont and Fletcher plays. These have often been compared to Shakespeare's last plays, but whatever qualities they may have in common, they are in fact products of two quite distinct modes of vision

expressed in the vocabulary of two quite distinct stylistic canons: mannerism and the baroque. The distinction is immediately apparent when one notes that reality in the Beaumont and Fletcher tragi-comedies has ceased to be problematic. They are, to be sure, full of problems, but problems that always admit of a solution. Where mannerism is the expression of the conflict between the spiritual and the sensual, the baroque resolves that conflict by affirming the primacy of emotion. The air of the irrational, the paradoxical, the ambiguous, the uncertain hovering between different worlds or contradictory realities so characteristic of mannerism is replaced in the baroque with a highly rational power of assertiveness; the loyalties of the baroque hero may be strenuously divided, but there is never any doubt as to where his true allegiance lies. The appeal of a mannerist work is essentially intellectual; the baroque, with its cultivation

comprehend within these scenes is of more than an ambivalence; it is a calculated and emphatic multivalence. This effect is compounded by that of the adjacent papal groups, where the invasion is of yet another medium of art: that of an architecture, which works to excavate the wall and, even more strongly, to project out of it' (*Painting of the High Renaissance in Rome and Florence*, Cambridge, Mass., 1961, p. 571). A decade later, Giulio created an even more spectacular example of *trompe-l'oeil* in his decorations for the Gonzaga Palazzo del Tè at Mantua (1532–4), where the walls of one whole room are covered with a fresco depicting the Fall of the Giants. Massive columns buckle and crumble – as it seems – right out of the picture plane, into the viewer's space; wild-eyed figures writhe and flee under heaps of falling masonry; in the midst of all which, the Gonzaga guests disported themselves, their sports presumably given a pleasant titillation by the impression that the room was collapsing about their ears. Though ambiguity is virtually an artistic principle with Giulio, it is ambiguity of a kind that derives from his illusionistic expertise. The words spoken in his praise by Shakespeare's Third Gentleman ('that rare Italian master... who, had he himself eternity and could put breath into his work, would beguile Nature of her custom, so perfectly he is her ape' – v, ii, 91–4) are entirely in accord with his contemporary reputation.

of emotion and sentiment, the premium that it places on pain and suffering, wounds and tears, makes its effect in a more directly sensuous way. The difference between *Hamlet* and Beaumont and Fletcher's *Philaster* – appearing respectively at the beginning and the end of the first decade of the century – epitomizes the difference between mannerism and the baroque. The heroes of both plays have been dispossessed of their fathers' kingdoms by a usurper, and both disinherited princes haunt the courts that are rightfully theirs, but Philaster, far from biding his time for revenge on the usurper, occupies it by falling in love with the usurper's daughter. Eventually he marries her and thereby regains his own, certainly a rational – and an emotionally gratifying – way of setting right the time that has been out of joint, but not a way that deals seriously with the questions of justice and honor that are supposedly at issue in the play. The baroque style which dominated the English stage from Beaumont and Fletcher through Dryden to the end of the century was productive of a number of glories, but intellectual seriousness was not one of them.

'KING LEAR' AND DOOMSDAY

MARY LASCELLES

There are numerous references to Doomsday (the Day of Judgement, the Last Day) in Shakespeare's plays. Many, at one end of the scale, amount to little more than casual profanity. Some, at the other, are (I believe) significant. By calling these *allusions*, I hope to designate their character and function. Allusion rests on analogy: it cites a correspondence, in respect of some property or attribute, between *this* and *that*. Like metaphor, it has no use for mere similarity: this is a correspondence rather between a pair of shoes than a pair of socks. It will, however, hardly speak home to the imaginative response of an audience if it is too abstruse or too personal: it touches the known, in an unfamiliar way. It should flatter the hearers' quickness of apprehension, not their patient ingenuity.

Somewhere between mere casual references and allusions heavily charged with significance come passages in which the correspondence between a particular situation and Doomsday denotes a measure of degree or extent. This can be bluntly paraphrased as 'I can't say worse than that, can I?' – or 'You can't see further than that, can you?' Thus, in I *Henry IV*, I, i, 29–30,[1] Winchester's tribute to the dead King –

> Unto the French the dreadful judgement-day
> So dreadful will not be as was his sight

– is a simple rhetorical figure measuring degree of dreadfulness. The Second Murderer's observation on the sleeping Clarence, 'Why, he

shall never wake until the great judgement-day' (*Richard III*, I, iv, 104), though offered as a simple figure of extent – the furthest conceivable point in time – presently discovers unsuspected implications: a prospect of damnation.

A denser and more complex texture of allusion is discernible in Young Clifford's exclamation when he finds the dead body of his father:

> O, let the vile world end
> And the premised flames of the last day
> Knit earth and heaven together!
> Now let the general trumpet blow his blast...
>
> (2 *Henry VI*, v, ii, 40)

In his New Arden edition, 1957, A. S. Cairncross comments: 'A regular Shakespearean group of images, compounded from various sources, and centring on the Last Judgement, as presented in mediaeval art and thought. The situation is always one of horror aroused by the death of a dear friend or relative, and the effect on the bereaved that of chaos come again.' And he cites, as analogues, 'the great doom's image' in *Macbeth* and 'the promis'd end' in *Lear*. To this I should like to add that the context – Young Clifford's reflections on civil war – brings the passage markedly nearer to those in *Lear* and *Macbeth*, and that the emphasis on spectacle – flames and trumpet – fully justifies the reference to medieval *art*. On this account, I welcome A. S. Cairncross's

[1] References throughout to Peter Alexander's one-volume Shakespeare (London, 1951).

suggestion that *promis'd* in *Lear* might be emended to *premis'd*: the *premised end* being the end we have been taught to expect, taught, not only by precept but also by pictorial demonstration.

There remains, however, a wide divergence between these two Doomsday passages (in *Lear* and *Macbeth*) and every other Shakespearian reference to the event. In these alone the allusion is intrinsic, it chimes with tones which have been audible throughout either play. That the theme of judgement runs through *Macbeth* needs no demonstration. I hope to demonstrate that it is no less pervasive in *King Lear*. It is moreover my contention that, in order to understand this fully, we must consider the impact of certain pictorial representations of the Last Judgement on the imagination of those who formed Shakespeare's first audience. Furthermore, to recognise not only that this is a play burdened with a vision of Doomsday but also that its allusions to that vision were once able to recall a particular visual experience may help to explain impressions of waywardness made, here and there, upon a generation to which this experience is unknown.

I begin with objections which Edgar's course of action may prompt. From the outset, it defies probability – not, I admit, a major consideration in *King Lear*, but this instance of disregard for it deserves analysis. Edgar is first established by his own reaction to his brother's intrigue and that brother's characterisation of him, as simple almost to fatuity. But, on discovering his own predicament, he proposes to himself a stratagem requiring resource and cunning (II, iii); and on his next appearance embarks effortlessly on what will prove to be the first of a series of sophisticated impersonations: the Bedlam beggar – a virtuoso performance (III, iv). It is surely strange that he should sustain subsequent improvised parts with unflagging fertility of invention; even stranger that he, a man of indubitable good

will, should so employ this cunning as to drive the King further into insanity, and deprive his father of the only comfort he craves.

Disguise is so patent a convention on the stage, and so diverse in its uses – varying from the mere make-believe of masks (as in *Much Ado*) to effectual deception by means of stolen dress (as in *Cymbeline*) – that we should be able to accept the taking-off of clothes as equally effective with putting them on, for the concealment of identity. And, in an age when dress proclaimed a man's place in society, to be divested of it was to be signalised as an outcast from the social order of that age; if an outcast, a mendicant and probably a vagrant. Should it appear that a vagrant will best serve the dramatist's purpose, then we may assume that this purpose – here, surely, to meet a structural need of the play – governs the course undertaken and pursued by Edgar. Alike in play or novel,[1] a vagrant has one inalienable attribute: mobility. In Shakespearian practice, mobility is most often the Fool's contribution to a play's resilience. Feste, for example, passes unchallenged between one group of characters and another, altering his tone to suit each. I am not now referring to his deliberate impersonation, which will require attention presently, but only to his adaptability as he moves to and fro. This mobility is denied to Lear's Fool, by reason of his helpless dependence upon, and close attachment to, his master. Edgar, once he has established his disguise as impenetrable, enjoys the Fool's customary freedom of movement and association. But if this choice of role, the vagrant's, is thus far explicable, there remains one further question to be asked: why, among the diversity of vagrants generated by the disturbed economy of the times, this particular sort? Why the Bedlam beggar, the Abram man, poor Tom? This was a type familiar to readers of the popular vagabond

[1] Scott seems to have learnt from Shakespeare how to use this type for purposes not simply comic.

literature of the age;[1] all too familiar to frightened women in lonely farmhouses. Released from Bedlam with a licence to beg, he was by definition insane, and, according to the prevailing conception of insanity, possessed. Edgar describes the condition and behaviour of this particular type of social outcast in a soliloquy which gives him the whole stage and our undivided attention:

I...am bethought
To take the basest and most poorest shape
That ever penury in contempt of man
Brought near to beast...   (II, iii, 6–9)

He will deface his own image,

And with presented nakedness outface
The winds and persecutions of the sky.
The country gives me proof and precedent
Of Bedlam beggars, who, with roaring voices,
Strike in their numb'd and mortified bare arms
Pins, wooden pricks, nails, sprigs of rosemary;
And with this horrible object, from low farms,
Poor pelting villages, sheep-cotes, and mills,
Sometimes with lunatic bans, sometime with prayers,
Enforce their charity.   (II, iii, 11–20)

This is notably different from Kent's disguise, for which the livery of a rough serving-man and a moderate degree of self-caricature will suffice. It is, moreover, sharply distinguishable from Hamlet's 'antic disposition'. Again and again, Edgar makes it clear that he is assuming an established pattern of behaviour, from which he remains in himself wholly detached.

With the emergence of Edgar/Tom as the ostensibly possessed man in III, iv, it becomes evident that the devils which infest him have names and that these names would convey certain associations amongst Shakespeare's first audience. Nearly all of them, together with some of the phrases in which they are embedded, are to be found in Samuel Harsnet's *Declaration of Egregious Popish Impostures* (1603). This, it should be borne in mind, was Harsnet's second exercise in exposure of alleged possession and pretended exorcism.

It was Lewis Theobald who first drew attention to the correspondence between the names of devils in Harsnet's *Declaration* and *King Lear*. The influence of his discovery on editorial practice has been considerable. Malone's text is studded with notes on this or that particular correspondence; and from 1790[2] to the present editors have followed suit. In our day, Professor Muir has made the most thorough and systematic study of the parallel: first in an article, 'Samuel Harsnett and *King Lear*',[3] then in his edition of the play;[4] last, in his book *Shakespeare's Sources*.[5] Each of these amplifies its predecessor.

It was acute of Theobald to recognise that Shakespeare had used some of Harsnet's devil-names. It was, I believe, obtuse of him to call Harsnet's share of the *Declaration* 'a smart narrative', and to infer that Shakespeare was exploiting a contemporary scandal for the sake of its notoriety – but he cannot be held accountable for the consequences of his interpretation. It is strange that, far removed as we now are from his jovial scepticism, only one critic has (to my knowledge) asked the crucial question 'Why?'

Robert Stevenson's article, 'Shakespeare's Interest in Harsnett's *Declaration*'[6] gives cogent reasons for asking this question. There is, he argues, nothing in Shakespeare comparable with this full and exact recall of a piece of polemical theology. Other tracts on demonology would have served his purpose; why did he choose Harsnet? He proffers an answer, but it is one which raises difficulties of its own:

[1] See A. V. Judges, *The Elizabethan Underworld* (London, 1930), pp. 372–8.
[2] Johnson had mentioned the work casually when he suggested that IV, i, 59–63, lines absent from the folio, were omitted 'because I suppose the story was forgotten, the jest was lost'.
[3] *RES*, N.S. II (1951), 11–21.
[4] New Arden, 1952.
[5] London, 1957, vol. I.
[6] *PMLA*, LXVII (1952), 898–902.

among the Jesuits arraigned in this case some could have been personally known to Shakespeare. This would indeed account for his reading Harsnet's recital of it with close attention; but not, surely, for his making this very use of what he found there. A personal relationship, of whatever kind or degree, would hardly prompt a man to exhibit particulars of the charges in the framework of Edgar's grotesque impersonation.

Samuel Harsnet's[1] *Declaration of Egregious Popish Impostures* is composed of an account (narrative interspersed with denunciation) of a case which began in 1585, but dragged on into 1602 – this occupies 171 pages – together with examinations of witnesses and confessions of accused – a further 103 pages. The Jesuit 'Edmunds *alias* Weston', with a number of associates, was accused of inducing a sense of possession in certain persons, notably three maidservants, and proceeding to practise pretended exorcism on them. It appears that the bodies as well as the minds of the women were abused. This disgusting case is investigated without repugnance by a man who was to rise high under James I – regrettably, in the Church. Harsnet's cart-horse irony, his ostentatious learning, and that knowledge of the theatre which enabled him to present the affair in terms of play-acting, must have gained him enough readers to account for two further editions (1604 and 1605).

Before accepting unreservedly the position that Harsnet's *Declaration* is a major factor in the interpretation of *King Lear*, we should bring into focus for comparison his earlier (and in many ways similar) pamphlet: *A Discovery of the Fraudulent Practises of J. Darrel* (1599). Here he arraigned John Darrel, designated a Puritan, maintaining that he induced a youth, William Somers, with some others,[2] to feign possession, in order that he might seem to exorcise the evil spirit infesting them. As in the *Declaration*, such doings are likened to a

theatrical performance: here, the reader is promised, in the prefatory Epistle, a 'puppet-show'. The matter and tone are indeed by so much the less distressing as the throes of the puppet are, than those of a living actor: the aim being exposure for the purpose of derision, not a criminal charge. It therefore seems likely that allusions to the *Discovery* should be carried by that mirthless jest, Feste's gulling of Malvolio under the pretence that he, as Sir Topas, is practising exorcism on the imprisoned 'madman'.[3]

The principal difference, however, between *Discovery* and *Declaration* is the virtual absence of devil-names from the earlier work. (One *Roofey* is mentioned, but there is nothing to match the legions called by name in the *Declaration*.)

In 1950, F. P. Wilson wrote: 'It is to be observed how little use he [Shakespeare] made in his plays of some of the books he looked at. We catch him dipping into that spirited piece of anti-Catholic propaganda, Samuel Harsnett's *Declaration of egregious Popish Impostures*, and coming up with the names of Edgar's fiends – Flibbertigibbet and the rest – and a few phrases.'[4] Would he have altered this if he had been able to revise the essay after the publication of Professor Muir's findings? Perhaps, but (I believe) not much. I suggest that we begin afresh, from this position – hypothetical, but not untenable: Shakespeare, wanting devils and devil-names, for a reason still to be determined, found his memory furnished with them. He had read the *Declaration* through –

[1] Harsnet on both title-pages (and of course in S.T.C.). Elsewhere (except in Peter Alexander's *Shakespeare*, 1964) Harsnett.

[2] Will Somers's case occupies 264 pages, the rest are summarily dismissed in the remaining 60.

[3] See, for example, introduction by Morton Luce to the 1937 Arden edition of *Twelfth Night*, p. xxi.

[4] 'Shakespeare's Reading', first printed in *Shakespeare Survey 3* (Cambridge, 1950); reprinted posthumously in *Shakespearian and Other Studies* (Oxford, 1969), p. 136.

Robert Stevenson's explanation is the only one hitherto advanced – and remembered, or perhaps found himself unable to forget, some of the names contained in it. Has the process by which names are lodged in the memory been sufficiently considered? Unprecedented and outlandish names are explored *as though* by the tongue. It is not necessarily a pleasurable experience, any more than the exploration of a decaying tooth is pleasurable; but it can, like that, be compulsive. I do not question Theobald's characterisation of the *Declaration* as 'this popular piece of satire'.[1] I do call in question any inference which supposes Shakespeare to have exploited this satire, and to that end foisted Harsnet's devils into his play. I am therefore obliged to offer an alternative explanation for what G. S. Gordon calls the demon-haunted world of *Lear*.[2]

The source of that emotional response upon which this and kindred suggestions work, in this play, is fear; and it is a fear whose onset is sudden. Whereas *Hamlet* and many of the histories had opened in a mood of foreboding, the ostensible occasion of the opening of *Lear* is as festive as a royal birthday. The King's own mood, for all his talk of age and death, is overweening self-confidence, and confidence in the willingness of others to play out the play according to his design. Only knowledge of the story tells us that his assurance is misplaced; and we have no such reason for distrusting Gloucester's complacency. Hence we have to be *precipitated* into fear; and – unlike the apprehension and despondency of Leir and Perillus in the old play – this pervasive fear exceeds altogether the sum of its circumstantial causes.

Fear is a passion which, more powerfully than any other, works upon us by evocation: it obeys the prompting of allusion rather than statement. The disproportion between cause and effect cannot be explained in rational terms. Lear on the heath is suffering more than the anguish of outraged fatherhood – the storm within. Those who are apprehensive on his account fear something more than the exposure of an old man to the storm without. All this we must be brought to understand with uncommon rapidity. Between the glib references of Regan and Cornwall to the inconvenience of remaining out of doors on such a night, and Cordelia's heart-broken lament for the harm it has done her father,[3] something has happened to Lear which transcends the event and even her compassionate understanding – and it goes on happening, to the end. Critics (always so much more moral than Shakespeare, as Walter Raleigh pointed out) affirm that Lear has come to a sense of his own misdoing. How then should his experience penetrate us? – *as it does*. We have not all lost a kingdom through our own fault, nor even wronged a daughter. How is this deep perturbation evoked in us? How was it evoked in that first audience?

It is to the second of these questions that (I believe) a circumstantial answer can be offered. Too much emphasis has been laid, in the interpretation of this play, on verbal allusions. I propose, as I have intimated, to consider a visual allusion: the Doomsday paintings, especially those over the chancel arch in so many English churches.[4] Superseding the more allusive, earlier representations of Christ in Majesty, these Dooms established in the late fourteenth and early fifteenth centuries, what may be called a stereotype – determined (I sup-

1 *The Works of Shakespeare* (London, 1733), V, 164.
2 'A Note on the World of *King Lear*' in *Shakespearian Comedy and Other Studies* (Oxford, 1944), pp. 116–28. 3 II, iv, 303–6; IV, vii, 30–42.
4 See A. Caiger-Smith, *English Mediaeval Mural Paintings* (Oxford, 1963); M. D. Anderson, *History and Imagery in British Churches* (1971). 'Except for the image of St. Christopher, the Judgement was by far the most frequent of the themes of wall-paintings; it almost always occupied the most arresting position in churches, the space over the chancel arch' (Caiger-Smith, p. 31, where seventy-eight are enumerated). More are still being uncovered – e.g., Kidlington.

pose) in part by the space allotted them. They were explicit, even to crudity; and, taking into account this characteristic and the resemblance among them, we may perhaps liken them to posters, which, reproduced and displayed in many places, can be resented but not easily forgotten. They must, in the fifteenth and early sixteenth centuries, have been familiar to numberless church-goers. But how many of them survived the first phase of Tudor icono-clasm, and the subsequent sporadic 'deface-ment of images'?

To this question of survival, I can reply only with an estimate of probability.[1] It should, in the first place, be remembered that the oppro-brious term 'images' included statues, wall-paintings, and the embellishment of shrines. Of these, the paintings were least likely to give offence, being seldom if ever associated with superstitious practices or claims to miraculous effects; and Doomsday paintings – subject to one provision – would not be obnoxious to a sixteenth-century congregation, however they may affect us. St Michael might be shown weighing souls, provided there were no intercession on behalf of any soul in the scales.[2]

Although information available to visitors in parish churches can tell when these paintings were first discovered – and sometimes covered again, so horrifying were their implications – it seems impossible to ascertain when they had first been covered with lime-wash; and it is doubtful whether access to original records would yield certainty. The chapel of the Trinity in Stratford-upon-Avon is a case in point. It belonged to the Guild of the Holy Cross; and, since it is variously named in references, it will be convenient to call it the Guild Chapel. The tremendous Doomsday painting over its chancel arch was first released from its obliter-ating, and protective, coat of lime-wash in 1804. Thomas Fisher, the antiquary, made drawings of this and the paintings on the walls of the

nave, which were published with a descriptive account by John Gough Nichols in 1838.[3] These drawings, as reproduced by lithography, are crude but clear and vigorous. The paintings were then covered afresh. When they were once more uncovered, E. W. Tristram made a drawing of the Doom[4] – now much fainter – which illustrates the artistic merit he claims for it. Unfortunately, the belief that it must have been familiar to Shakespeare[5] was shaken by the entry in the Chamberlains' Accounts for 1562–3: 'Item payd for defaysing Ymages in ye chappell ijs.'[6] The man charged with this operation was John Shakespeare. It is therefore a generally-accepted view that this Doom was covered with lime-wash before John's son William was born.

Nevertheless, I would regard the obliteration of the Stratford Doom in 1562–3 as probable rather than proven: urging that 'images' is a term of diverse connotations at that date; and that, even supposing it to have signified mural paintings in this entry, those on the walls of the nave were far more likely to provoke

[1] See Caiger-Smith, *English Medieval Mural Paintings*, chapter VIII, 'The Destruction of Images'.

[2] This transaction was obliterated from the Dooms-day painting at Penn in Buckinghamshire. See Caiger-Smith, *ibid.*, p. 35.

[3] Thomas Fisher and John Gough Nichols, *Ancient Allegorical, Historical and Legendary Paintings on the walls of the chapel of the Trinity, belonging to the Gilde of the Holy Cross at Stratford-upon-Avon in Warwick-shire* (London, 1838). Fisher had returned for a further inspection in 1807.

[4] Published with a descriptive account in *The Illustrated London News*, 27 April 1929. The original drawing is in the Victoria and Albert Museum. There is also an article in *The Burlington Magazine*, May 1930, by E. T. Long, 'Some Recently Discovered English Wall Paintings'.

[5] Lional Cust, in *Shakespeare's England* (Oxford, 1916), II, 4.

[6] *Minutes and Accounts of the Corporation and Other Records*, ed. R. Savage and E. Fripp, Publications of the Dugdale Society (Stratford-upon-Avon, 1921–9), I, 128. Cited by E. K. Chambers, *William Shakespeare* (Oxford, 1930), I, 9.

iconoclasm, including as they did the death of Thomas à Becket and the Finding of the True Cross. They were besides more easily accessible than that over the chancel arch. They are now in worse case. Even should these arguments be disallowed in respect of the Stratford Doom, there remains the very strong probability that many other Doomsday paintings of this type had survived into the second half of the sixteenth century: the Puritans of that time complained that iconoclasm was half-hearted and white-wash insufficient to conceal wall-paintings; and enough 'images' seem to have been left to occupy the zeal of their successors under the Commonwealth.[1]

The similarity among these Dooms, conditioned as they were by the space available,[2] allows a generic description to be offered. The design is vertical, there is no near and far, only higher and lower. In the apex of the arch, Christ sits in judgement. Around and below him are ranged angels, apostles, saints; close to his knees often appear the Virgin Mary and St John – usually the Evangelist, but sometimes (as at Stratford – see Plate v) the Baptist.[3] In the lowest part of the painting the figures shown in motion are sharply divided: on the Judge's right hand – that is, to the left of the picture as we see it – the blessed are conducted towards a heavenly gate, at which St Peter usually receives them; on our right (and it will be convenient to continue the description in these terms) the lost are driven or drawn into the mouth of hell, marshalled by fiends; a little lower, on this side, they are tormented. These are not the only figures to occupy the lowest parts of the painting; there are also souls emerging from their graves, and looking upwards. I say *parts* because the left and right of its lowest level are separated by the aperture of the arch; and this causes a sort of imbalance in the distribution of the graves: since the blessed are in an ascending and the lost in a descending train, there is more room at the left than at the

right foot of the picture, and this is usually filled by graves and emerging figures. One particular should be borne in mind, because it is an almost constant[4] visual impression: the nakedness of all these souls, both those awaiting judgement and those who have been judged. As an indication of their state, this is not remarkable; but it does heighten the terror and pity of their predicament.[5]

The dominant theme of these paintings is that account of the Judgement propounded in the Athanasian Creed: 'At whose coming all men shall rise again with their bodies and shall give account for their own works. And they that have done good shall go into life everlasting and they that have done evil into everlasting fire.' It is, however, given an extension of meaning by the message of St Matthew's Gospel, chapters 24 and 25 – especially 25 – as both the authorities I have already cited affirm:[6] 'Inasmuch as ye have done it unto one of the least of these my brethren, ye have done it unto me' (25.40) – with its terrible complement: 'Then shall he answer them, saying, Verily I say unto you, Inasmuch as ye did it not to one of the least of these, ye did it not to me' (25.45).

[1] Caiger-Smith, *English Medieval Mural Paintings*, pp. 113, 115–16.

[2] The spring of the arch, and the pitch of the roof, varying from church to church, may influence arrangement; and perhaps the craftsman sometimes found the space they allowed insufficient for his needs: at South Leigh the picture has spread on to adjacent walls.

[3] See E. W. Tristram, *English Wall Painting in the Fourteenth Century*, ed. Eileen Tristram (London, 1955), p. 19.

[4] The wall-paintings at Chalgrove seem to be the only representation of souls emerging fully clothed from their graves. In the Doom over the chancel arch in St Thomas's Church, Salisbury, the dishonest ale-wife alone is clothed – an anomalous comic figure.

[5] At Cliffe-at-Hoo the blessed retain vestiges of grave-clothes, as do figures emerging from graves in some paintings.

[6] Caiger-Smith, *English Medieval Mural Paintings*, pp. 6–7 and 31; Anderson, *History and Imagery in British Churches*, pp. 115, 125 and 145.

It should be evident that, in these Doomsday paintings, the part most visible to the congregation, indeed, inescapable, was the lowest area: that which showed bodies – naked or with vestiges of shrouds – emerging from graves, and naked bodies herded together and driven into hell. Moreover, this latter subject invited a dreadful inventiveness on the part of the craftsman, in the representation of fiends and their activities. If this was, as I believe, a familiar spectacle, it must have been hard to forget.

There would thus be at Shakespeare's disposal, when he needed to evoke overmastering fear, a common visual experience readily recalled by allusion. The dominant impression in this visual pattern is nakedness – signifying defencelessness, but with a further suggestion of suddenly-realised equality. Emblematic head-dress – crown or mitre – suggests a former differentiation, now meaningless.

Among Elizabethan vagrants, the Bedlam beggar seems to have been marked out by his nearly naked plight; and it is clear that Edgar as originally played presented this condition, so far as stage decency allowed. This, I surmise, prompts the Fool's insistence that the strange figure lurking in the hovel is a *spirit* (III, iv, 39 and 42). It certainly gives point to Lear's question, when he supposes Poor Tom to have been reduced to this state by his daughters – 'Could'st thou save nothing? Would'st thou give them all?' – with the Fool's rejoinder, 'Nay, he reserv'd a blanket, else we had all been sham'd' (63–5). This particular will recur, with curious insistence, not only in Lear's 'Thou wert better in a grave than to answer with thy uncover'd body the extremity of the skies' (100–3), but also in Gloucester's recollection of 'the naked fellow' (IV, i, 41 and 50), and his plea to the Old Man: 'Bring some covering for this naked soul' (*ibid.*, 45).

And so the ambiguous figure of the Bedlam beggar, sufferer or sinner or both, victim or impostor, with his 'presented nakedness' and his infestation by fiends, has much in common with those beings in Doomsday paintings. United thus, the two images wake a deep and powerful fear. Lear, who will be drawn into the world of Tom's fiend-haunted imagination, has himself projected the theme of nakedness, with its concomitant equality, into *our* imagination in a strange and sudden way. Left to his own thoughts outside the hovel, he has uttered that memorable invocation:

Poor naked wretches, wheresoe'er you are,
That bide the pelting of this pitiless storm,
How shall your houseless heads and unfed sides,
Your loop'd and window'd raggedness, defend
    you
From seasons such as these? O, I have ta'en
Too little care of this!   (III, iv, 28–33)

and he proceeds to the medieval doctrine, itself familiar from exposition in wall-paintings, that the poor man is the direct responsibility of the man who has it in his power to relieve him.[1] Edwin Muir and Professor L. C. Knights have both argued persuasively[2] that the play expresses a conflict between the old, time-honoured pieties and loyalties and a new policy of ruthless self-advancement. Certainly Lear, for all his impulsive errors, pays heartfelt if incomplete tribute to an older, more stable order in terms of

The offices of nature, bond of childhood,
Effects of courtesy, dues of gratitude...
    (II, iv, 177–8)

[1] E.g., in the Works of Mercy and Seven Deadly Sins at Trotton (Anderson, *History and Imagery in British Churches*, Plate 46) the souls of the man who has relieved want, and the man who has denied help, are shown naked at the Judgement Seat; thereafter, the just man is clothed, and the niggard naked and tormented. See also G. R. Owst, *Literature and Pulpit in Mediaeval England* (Oxford, 1966), pp. 560–2.

[2] Edwin Muir, *The Politics of 'King Lear'*, W. P. Ker Lecture for 1946 reprinted in *Essays on Literature and Society* (London, 1949); L. C. Knights, *Shakespeare's Politics: with some Reflections on the Nature of Tradition*, Annual Shakespeare Lecture of the British Academy for 1957.

And all the well-disposed characters sub-scribe, each in his own way; the Fool, by his bitter insistence that it is Lear himself who has untied these bonds and let loose dis-order.

Lear's vision, contemplated in its entirety – and this will not be easy – must surely lie very close to the meaning of the play. In such Judgement plays as survive among the Guild cycles,[1] the kings and other potentates may be regarded as spokesmen for the assembled souls. Lear is evidently much more than this. 'Bad'[2] kings in the Guild plays confess to a bewilder-ing variety of sins – debasing the currency, for example – as they move towards a culmination clearly intended to recall Matthew 25. Lear's self-arraignment follows a course which, despite the vagaries of madness, seems to be charged, perhaps over-charged, with a meaning integral to the play.

The first intimation of Lear's preoccupation with Judgement comes with the rising storm: he calls on the gods, whom he still regards as allies, to make this an occasion of Judgement by disclosing undivulged guilt (III, ii, 49–59). I avoid the term Judgement Day on account of its conventional associations, although, in a Britain where floods may threaten *steeples* and *weathercocks*, anachronistic references to Christ-ian usage matter very little. There is nothing to perplex, and therefore nothing to require specific comment, in the likening of the thunder to 'dreadful summoners'; but neither is there any reason why this metaphor should not recall the angelic summons, by trumpet or other wind instrument, shown in all the paintings. (It is part of the horror of these representations that the devils are allowed to join in with their horns.)

It is while Lear is still fighting to retain his sanity that he invokes those 'poor naked wretches' whose misery is a rebuke to him (III, iv, 28–37). I must ask leave to defer con-sideration of this passage and its relevance to

my argument until that, in its course, reaches the point of his return to sanity.

In his madness, Lear is obsessed with ideas of human justice. He passes from a doubt of its sufficiency to a conviction of its impossibility. The first impulse, the mock trial of his daughters (III, vi, 20, *passim* to 78), is a direct reaction to his own situation. But whereas, on reverting to the theme of human justice in IV, vi, he is still in the judgement-seat – 'I pardon that man's life' (109) – he is coming to question the worth of pardon or validity of sentence. From social satire such as can be found in many sorts of contemporary literature he passes to these images: the figure on the bench which might well change places with that in the dock, the farmer's dog in authority, the big and little plunderers of their fellows – and so to the idea of Justice itself as an imposture, concealing our common guilt. Therefore he will himself override this perverted justice with a gesture of amnesty. The underlying despair of 'None does offend, none, I say, none' (168) is a world away from Cymbeline's easy 'Pardon's the word to all' (V, v, 422). It is the distance between tragi-comedy and tragedy.

Although these judgement fantasies of Lear's madness are interspersed with references to hell and devils, they imply no appeal to, nor shrinking from, any concept of divine Justice.

Before returning to Lear's last sane utterance, and considering its relation to the words which will mark his restoration to sanity (IV, vii, 45–9), I find myself obliged to offer a personal impression, which is (of course) quite insignifi-cant – unless it prompts others to look at the object and note their own reactions to it. In the English mural-paintings I have seen, the souls rising from graves and the souls consigned to hell form a conspicuous part of the most

---

[1] E.g., York, Chester, the incomplete Towneley and the fragmentary *Ludus Coventriae*.

[2] All have sinned; these have sought mercy tardily and ineffectually.

clearly visible portion of the composition; they are nearly all facing towards us, and I can see in their faces hardly any intimation of the painter's wish to signalise evil.[1] Yet there were established conventions for depicting the faces not only of devils but also of human adversaries of the saints. Among possible explanations, I suggest one which must rest on an appeal to common experience. According to Matthew 25.45, they stand convicted of the sin of omission; and sins of omission are those that most trouble the conscience: opportunities for them are far more numerous, and they make less immediate impact on the consciousness. This does not mean that the look of simple dismay on the faces of these paintings – so different from the expressions of the lost in the Judgements of great masters[2] – is meant to extenuate the guilt of those who, in denying human need, have denied Christ: nothing so unedifying. Rather is it intended to convey the truth that this is our common predicament.

This may help us to understand something which is surely surprising, certainly precipitate, in Lear's cry to the poor naked wretches: still in command of his thoughts, he is himself facing judgement – the challenge of his own former life as ruler. But, suppose he were answering in this capacity Malcolm's interrogatory, how many of the 'king-becoming graces' (*Macbeth*, IV, iii, 91–4) would he be able to claim? Justice, temperance, lowliness, patience? Why should he so promptly single out care of the poor as the obligation in which he has come short? Solely because he is himself now destitute, or for a deeper cause, one which touches us all as this threat of reversal cannot? It may have been the intention of the Guild plays to bring this sin of omission home to everyone through the verdict on the bad ruler; but, even granted the benefit of better texts than we possess, the exigencies of stage presentation would forbid it. The souls cannot be shown rising from their graves[3] – we miss the

impact of an awakening: the full recognition of a truth long known but never accepted. This surely was what gave point, in those minds familiar with the Doom paintings, to Lear's forlorn admission:

> O, I have ta'en
> Too little care of this!

There remain two more significant allusions, on my reckoning, to be considered. When Lear comes to himself, in all the agony this entails, he expostulates with those who stand round: 'You do me wrong to take me out o' th' grave' (IV, vii, 45), and then singles out Cordelia: 'Thou art a soul in bliss.' It is to the saints ranged above them that the souls who rise from their graves in the Doom paintings look up, and sometimes stretch their arms. That Lear continues

> but I am bound
> Upon a wheel of fire, that mine own tears
> Do scald like molten lead –

and that no wheel of fire appears, among the torments of hell, in any chancel painting that I have seen or heard of, is of small consequence. Literary analogues have been proposed by editors; and a common cut, used in *The Kalender of Shepherdes*,[4] shows the torture of the wheel as punishment of pride. But the correspondence seems to me neither close[5] nor necessary. The image has surely been conceived expressly for its purpose, to convey poignantly Lear's conviction that what he has done separates him for ever from Cordelia. Furthermore, if the

---

[1] Very seldom a single figure standing apart, like the ale-wife of Salisbury, shows a different intention.

[2] See for example Robert Hughes, *Heaven and Hell in Western Art* (London, 1968).

[3] In the York Judgement, there are explicit references to a reunion of soul and body which has taken place elsewhere.

[4] *The Kalender of Shepherdes*, ed. H. O. Sommer (London, 1892). The cut here reproduced, on p. 68, illustrates the account given by Lazarus of the pains of hell as revealed to him by death.

[5] There are no souls in bliss, for this is hell.

whole passage once derived some of its power from the evocation of a familiar visual experience, the sight of a Doomsday painting over a chancel arch, then the Folio reading for Lear's next question –

You are a spirit, I know. Where did you die? –

becomes at once clear and appropriate, these pictures representing, not any particular place, but the whole globe revealed as a graveyard at the Last Day. The souls depicted stand as tokens for all those assembled in an instant – as Donne was to represent them:

At the round world's imagin'd corners, blow
Your trumpets, Angells, and arise, arise
From death, you numberlesse infinities
Of soules, and to your scattred bodies goe...[1]

In such a context, it is natural enough to ask: Where did you die?

Last of all, there is the explicit, but still enigmatic, allusion to a pictured Doomsday, in that response of Albany, Kent and Edgar to the sight of Lear with Cordelia dead in his arms:

Kent. Is this the promis'd end?
Edgar.
　　　　Or image of that horror?　　(v, iii, 263–4)

This promised – or, as I would prefer to suppose, premised – end, with Albany's ensuing prayer for a termination, can refer only to Doomsday. Not, however, as a purely intellectual concept. Regarded so, the exchange between Kent and Edgar would fall into anticlimax – as though one should say (for example) 'Is this Armageddon, or merely a spectacle intended to represent it?' Admittedly, the order in which choric utterances are delivered need not be logical; but these lines establish themselves as choric mainly because we recognise them as allusive, their allusion framed to evoke traditional recollections: that inescapable consciousness of *the thing seen* which I have here tried to reconstruct.

[1] John Donne, *The Divine Poems*, ed. Helen Gardner (Oxford, 1952), p. 8.

I acknowledge gratefully suggestions from Mr and Mrs Emrys Jones.

MACBETH ON HORSEBACK

LEAH SCRAGG

Since the authenticity of Simon Forman's *Bocke of Plaies* was finally established in 1947,[1] its famous record of the author's visit to a performance of *Macbeth* in 1611[2] has been the subject of careful scrutiny by both textual and theatrical historians. In the same year that Professor Dover Wilson and Dr R. W. Hunt published their refutation of Tannenbaum's attack on the manuscript,[3] J. M. Nosworthy[4] attempted to reconstruct elements of a longer version of the play than that which has come down to us by collating Forman's account with the 'Argument' to Davenant's adapted text of 1674, arguing that where these agreed with Shakespeare's source we might well suppose that portions of Holinshed used by Shakespeare had been preserved by Forman and Davenant though lost to us in the process of transmission. Though Nosworthy subsequently discovered a source for Davenant's 'Argument' other than *Macbeth*,[5] he saw no reason to retreat from his original position that careful analysis of Forman's account, used in conjunction with Holinshed, might supply us with words, phrases and even entire passages that have subsequently disappeared from Shakespeare's play. More recently, Dennis Bartholomeusz,[6] approaching Forman's notes with an eye to the stage business they imply, has discussed the four major spectacles with which they present us and the way in which these may have been produced, making no mention, however, of the occasional discrepancies between the action narrated by Forman and

Holinshed and the dramatised version by Shakespeare.

It has been noticed for some considerable time that Forman's recollections of what he saw at the Globe not only diverge from the folio version of the play but are oddly interspersed with elements which seem to derive directly from Shakespeare's source. Collier himself, introducing the *Bocke of Plaies* to the world in 1836, noted that 'Forman's memory seems to have failed him upon particular points', citing the description of the Witches as 'feiries or Nimphes'; the hailing of Macbeth as king, not

[1] J. Dover Wilson and R. W. Hunt, 'The Authenticity of Simon Forman's *Bocke of Plaies*', *RES*, XXIII (1947), 193–200.

[2] Forman notes that his visit took place on Saturday, 20 April 1610, but as 20 April fell on a Friday, not a Saturday, in that year, it has generally been assumed that 1610 was written in error and that the visit took place one year later; cf. E. K. Chambers, *William Shakespeare* (Oxford, 1930), II, 337.

[3] Samuel A. Tannenbaum, *Shaksperian Scraps and other Elizabethan Fragments* (New York, 1933).

[4] '*Macbeth* at the Globe', *The Library*, II (1947–8), 108–18. Nosworthy's transcript of Forman's manuscript (a corrected version of Chamber's) is used below.

[5] Viz. Peter Heylyn's *Microcosmus; a little description of the great world* (second edition, 1625). Nosworthy suggests in the postscript to his article that Heylyn based his account of Macbeth's reign on Shakespeare's play (and thus that Davenant's 'Argument' does derive, indirectly, from Shakespeare) but as the historian rejects both Stowe and Holinshed as 'full of confusion and commixture of vnworthy relations' it seems unlikely that he would draw on a dramatist.

[6] *Macbeth and the Players* (Cambridge, 1969).

thane, of Cawdor; the elevation of Macbeth to 'Prince of Northumberland'; and the 'mob accordant incident' involving Macbeth and his wife failing to cleanse their hands of the blood of their victim.[1] Though the authenticity of the manuscript remained undisputed for many years after Collier's death, further 'lapses of memory' on Forman's part continued to be noted, and by 1903 a caveat had been entered against placing too much reliance on the evidence afforded by the synopsis: 'In reading this description it is to be noted that Forman is writing from memory, and that he is only setting down "moral conclusions" from the play... Too much importance, therefore must not be attached to his description.'[2] Early doubts about the reliability of the document were succeeded by misgivings concerning its authenticity – misgivings generated in part by the discovery of extensive verbal parallels between Forman's version of incidents in Macbeth's career and comparable passages of Holinshed. J. Q. Adams, in his 1931 edition of the play, presented a formidable list of echoes of this kind, together with evidence of 'misrepresentation' of Shakespeare's Banquet scene, concluding that 'Forman's' account could not have been the work of a man who had 'actually witnessed' the play.[3] The same conclusion, supported by 'bibliotic' evidence, was reached two years later by S. A. Tannenbaum in his full-scale attack on the manuscript as a Collier forgery,[4] and though Professor Dover Wilson and Dr R. W. Hunt effectively demolished his 'bibliotic' arguments in the article cited above, they made no attempt to account for either the puzzling 'lapses of memory' or the apparent dependence on the *Chronicles*. In view of this somewhat inconclusive position, J. M. Nosworthy's hypothesis that Forman's résumé preserves vestiges of a longer version of Shakespeare's play than that which has come down to us seems at first sight to provide both a welcome and an acceptable means of reconciling

the *prima facie* debt to Shakespeare's source with an authentic record of a specific production of the play.

Nosworthy puts forward eight suggestions in all concerning possible discrepancies between the *Macbeth*s of 1611 and 1623 but as one relates to the pronunciation of a name (an unprofitable area of speculation at the best of times) and another is dismissed by the author himself as improbable, only six will be discussed below. The first concerns the location of the initial encounter between Macbeth and the Witches. Forman describes the meeting as taking place as Macbeth was 'Ridinge thorowe a wod', thus agreeing (in part at least) with Holinshed's 'passing thorough the woods and fields'.[5] Chambers, discussing Forman's account in 1930, remarked that 'there is nothing in the text or stage-directions to confirm or refute his statement that Macbeth and Banquo came riding through a wood'[6] but, in fact, as a succession of scholars[7] (including Mr Nosworthy) have pointed out, Macbeth very pointedly designates the scene 'this blasted heath' (I, iii, 77)[8] – clearly not a chance reference since the Witches have already announced their intention to meet 'upon the

[1] J. Payne Collier, *New Particulars regarding the Works of Shakespeare* (London, 1836), pp. 25–6.

[2] *The Tragedie of Macbeth*, ed. Mark Harvey Liddell, The Elizabethan Shakspere (New York, 1903), p. 122.

[3] *Macbeth*, ed. Joseph Quincy Adams (Boston, 1931), pp. 294ff.

[4] Tannenbaum argues that Collier used Holinshed in order 'to give his narrative an Elizabethan flavour' (*Shaksperian Scraps*, p. 25).

[5] W. G. Boswell-Stone, *Shakspere's Holinshed* (London, 1896). All quotations are from pages 23–5 with the exception of the passages relating to the promptings of Donwald's wife and Fleance's flight into Wales which occur on pages 27 and 33 respectively.

[6] *William Shakespeare*, I, 473.

[7] Cf. Adams, *Macbeth*, p. 295; Tannenbaum, *Shaksperian Scraps*, p. 24.

[8] Quotations from *Macbeth* are from the Arden edition, ed. Kenneth Muir (London, 1962).

heath' (I, i, 6). Nevertheless, though recognising the lack of supporting evidence, Nosworthy proceeds to deduce from the conjunction of woods in Forman and Holinshed that some 'specific allusion to a wood or forest' may have dropped out of the play, thus substituting confusion in the mind of the dramatist for the 'lapses of memory' and 'fabricator's' obsession 'with the notion of a forest'[1] which satisfied earlier commentators. The second point relates to the description of the weird sisters themselves. Forman refers to them as '3 women feiries or Nimphes', agreeing with Holinshed's 'nymphs or feiries' but disagreeing radically, as Nosworthy again remarks, with Shakespeare's 'secret, black, and midnight hags' (IV, i, 48) with their 'choppy' fingers and 'skinny lips' (I, iii, 44–5). But again, though finding the phrase 'inconsistent with the general presentation of the Witches', Nosworthy accounts for its presence in Forman's résumé by suggesting that either Macbeth, or Banquo, may have referred to the Witches at some stage in the action as fairies or nymphs – a deduction which implies a kind of uncertainty on Shakespeare's part over the nature of his supernatural solicitors which is not borne out by the play as a whole. The third and fourth significant points concern Banquo's interchange with the weird sisters. Forman recounts the scene as follows: 'then said Bancko, What all to mackbeth And nothing to me. yes, said the nimphes, Haille to thee Banko,' which is remarkably similar to Holinshed's:

Then Banquho: 'What manner of women' (saith he) 'are you, that seeme so little fauourable vnto me, whereas to my fellow heere, besides high offices, ye assigne also the kingdome, appointing foorth nothing for me at all?' 'Yes' (saith the first of them) 'we promise greater benefits vnto thee, than vnto him.'

Nosworthy discusses this exchange in two separate points, noting the 'world of difference' between the 'envious utterances' recorded by Forman and Holinshed and the 'courteous

speech' of Banquo in the folio, and pointing out that the 'yes' in Forman's account is not supported by Shakespeare's text. The additions he postulates to the folio version on the basis of this evidence are 'an abrupt and envious question or ejaculation from Banquo' (possibly in the form of an aside) and a new line for the First Witch 'roughly as Forman reports it'. Objections here are two-fold. Not only would 'an abrupt and envious question or ejaculation' be out of accord with the character of Banquo as presented throughout the rest of the play, but the proposed additions fail to take into account the extent of the similarities between Forman and Holinshed in the passage as a whole – similarities initially pointed out by Adams and subsequently schematised by Tannenbaum:[2]

F: There stood before them [Macbeth and Banquo] three women.
H: There met them three women.
F: Feiries or nimphes.   H: nymphs or feiries.[3]
F: And saluted Macbeth, saying. H: The first of them spake and said.
F: Then said Bancko.   H: Then Banqho.
F: Yes, said the nimphes.   H: Yes, saith the first witch. [sic]
F: And nothing to me?   H: Nothing for me?

An abrupt and envious exclamation in Shakespeare's text would not explain the parallel organisation of the material at this point, nor could it account for the striking similarities in the presentation of direct speech: 'Then said Bancko' / 'Then Banquho': 'yes, said the nimphes' / 'Yes (saith the first)'.

Nosworthy's final points relate to Forman's evident confusion over people and places.

[1] Tannenbaum, *Shaksperian Scraps*, p. 17.
[2] *Ibid.*, p. 25.
[3] Though Tannenbaum's summary selects from both accounts, only in the case of Holinshed's 'nymphs or feiries' is the order of either narrative disturbed. The phrase occurs several lines after the interchange between Banquo and the Witches.

Forman states that after the encounter with the Witches Macbeth 'cam to the Courte of Scotland' where Duncan made him 'forth with Prince of Northumberland', while he reports that subsequent to the murder 'Dunkin's 2 sonns fled, the on to England, the [other to] Walles'. The first departure from Shakespeare's text Nosworthy attributes to simple error on Forman's part (i.e. he wrote Macbeth for Malcolm) though the sentence structure does not support this,[1] while he suggests that the Cumberland/Northumberland confusion may spring from Forman's jumbled recollections of 'an allusion to Malcolm's lineage in I, iv' based on the comparable passage in Holinshed: 'But shortlie after it chanced that King Duncane, hauing two sonnes by his wife which was the daughter of Siward earle of Northumberland, he made the elder of them, called Malcolme, prince of Cumberland.' Since, however, the play is concerned to stress the line of descent *from* Banquo rather than *to* Malcolm, an account of the latter's lineage (which receives no further mention in the play) would be difficult to justify at this point, particularly in view of the fact that attention is focused here not upon Malcolm himself but upon Macbeth's response to his preferment. The substitution of 'Walles' for Ireland Nosworthy explains in a similar manner. Holinshed reports that after the murder of Banquo Fleance 'fled into Wales', supplying the dramatist, it is suggested, with a specific destination for the fugitive which Forman later confused with that of another of the play's runaways. But again, an allusion to Fleance as 'a refugee in Wales' would be extraneous to the central action and might possibly draw attention to his subsequent (disreputable) career – a subject Shakespeare is careful to avoid. In both these cases the discrepancies between Forman's account of the play and the text which has come down to us seem more likely to derive from the reporter's own conflation of drama and chronicle than

from some process of textual revision. In brief, in all six instances in which Forman and Holinshed agree in disagreeing with Shakespeare, the additions Nosworthy postulates either run counter to Shakespeare's intention as exemplified in the play as a whole or fail to take into account the extent of the verbal parallels involved.[2] While the argument that the folio text is the work of a reviser who has cut material that 'seemed to him to be digressive, inconsistent, or merely redundant' might have explained the first objection had Forman been present at an earlier performance of the play (it is hard to believe that Shakespeare[3] would have allowed the hodge-podge of heaths and woods, hags and nymphs to stand until after the performance of 1611 before undertaking the task of revision), it fails to explain the textual parallels between the *Chronicles* and Forman's synopsis. There must therefore continue to be doubt about the reliability of much of the evidence afforded by Forman's manuscript, and hence about the validity of any attempt at reconstruction founded upon it.

In the light of this conclusion, Dr Bartholomeusz's deductions concerning what took place on stage at the Globe in 1611 assume a dubious

[1] Forman's text reads: 'Dunkin bad them both [Macbeth and Banquo] kindly wellcom, And made Mackbeth forth with Prince of Northumberland, and sent him hom to his own castell, and appointed mackbeth to prouid for him, for he wold Sup with him the next dai at night'.

[2] Other parallels between Holinshed and Forman not noted by Nosworthy and inimical to his position are in the use of the phrase 'through setting on of his wife' (Forman: 'thorowe the persuasion of his wife'), the implied personal involvement of Macbeth in the murder of Lady Macduff and her children, and the appearance of the Witches to Macbeth and Banquo (discussed below).

[3] I assume that the reviser could not have been anyone else since he appears to have had a more profound understanding of the action of the play than the author of the undeniably Shakespearian first version.

aspect from the outset.[1] Bartholomeusz suggests that it is 'very likely that Shakespeare had instructed the actors'[2] for the 1611 performance of *Macbeth* and consequently that Forman's notes on the production give us 'glimpses of what possibly was the result of creative collaboration between actor and playwright'. Forman describes four scenes in sufficient detail to convey something of the way in which this 'creative collaboration' might have functioned – the initial entrance of Macbeth, including the encounter with the Witches; the scene between Macbeth and Lady Macbeth following the murder of Duncan; the appearance of Banquo's ghost; and the sleepwalking scene. Of these, Bartholomeusz dismisses the last fairly cursorily in a general discussion of the boy-actor tradition, devoting most of his attention to the three principal spectacles which seem to have caught the imagination of the spectator – the first appearance of Macbeth, Forman's description of which, Bartholomeusz maintains, can be accepted 'in its literal sense'; the hand-washing scene after the murder which, by contrast, 'one cannot afford to take literally'; and the 'second'[3] appearance of Banquo's ghost. Though commentators from Liddell onwards have consistently remarked upon the extent to which Forman's version of the production of the third diverges from both Shakespeare's text and theatrical tradition,[4] in this instance Bartholomeusz largely overlooks the contentious aspects of the stage business described, concentrating instead upon the method of acting implied. Since his observations are based here upon dubious but unverifiable evidence (no source for this incident existing outside the play) only the hand-washing scene and the entrance with Banquo will be discussed below.

Forman reports that after the murder of the King: 'the blod on his [Macbeth's] hands could not be washed of by Any meanes, nor from his wiues handes, which handled the bloddi daggers in hiding them, By which means they became both moch amazed & Affronted'. The passage, if taken at face value, clearly suggests some kind of stage business (Collier's 'mob accordant incident') no longer implicit in the action of the play,[5] but in this case Bartholo-

[1] Dr Bartholomeusz is not the only commentator who has attempted to reconstruct what took place at the Globe in 1611 now that the authenticity of Forman's manuscript has been proved beyond dispute. Henry N. Paul in *The Royal Play of 'Macbeth'* (New York, 1950) has used the account as a basis for arguing that what Forman witnessed was 'a play powerfully portraying the workings of a guilty conscience and showing how easily they may betray the murderer' (p. 410). Unlike Bartholomeusz, Paul acknowledges Forman's debt to Holinshed but dismisses it with a glibness that robs his subsequent discussion of any value: 'He did not remember what had happened near the beginning of the play (perhaps he was a little late getting to the Globe that afternoon), and therefore took down his Holinshed to help him to piece out his account; but what he records after the first scenes is what he saw on the stage, except for one or two unimportant slips' (p. 409). These 'unimportant slips' include the notorious 'mob accordant incident', the flight into Wales, and the appearance of Banquo's ghost (see below).

[2] All quotations from *Macbeth and the Players* are from pages 3–7.

[3] Forman mentions only one appearance of the apparition.

[4] Cf. Liddell, *Macbeth*, p. 122; Adams, *Macbeth*, p. 296; Tannenbaum, *Shaksperian Scraps*, p. 23. Though Dr Bartholomeusz quotes (p. 8) from J. Dover Wilson's edition of the play (Cambridge, 1947) in support of his contention that theatrical tradition coincides with Forman's account, in fact, the passage in question (from C. B. Young's postscript to the Introduction on the stage-history of the play) precedes an explicit statement to the contrary: 'the detail, if Forman was an accurate observer, shows a different original staging of Banquo's ghost from the traditional plan, represented by Rowe's S.D. (1709) at 4.3.92' (p. lxx).

[5] J. M. Nosworthy, while rejecting the possibility that Shakespeare might have authorised the kind of sensational incident suggested by the passage, proposes that 'the properties for II, ii [may have] included a bowl of water and a towel' and that 'use was made of a simplified dumb-show'. Alternatively, 'the ablution may have accompanied the dialogue in the second half of the scene'. Bartholomeusz, however,

meusz rejects the need for literal interpretation:

Commentators from Collier onwards have argued that Forman's account of Duncan's murder points to a scene which the Folio omits, because they have taken his statement that the blood could not be washed off by any means in its literal sense. If we accept their view, then on April 20, 1611, Shakespeare and his actors were using spectacle of an unbelievably sensational kind.

Bartholomeusz's alternative to this unattractive hypothesis is a more liberal interpretation of the manuscript than has hitherto been proposed:

Forman appears to have been thinking and writing metaphorically. . . . [He] could not have read the play before he saw the production of *Macbeth* at the Globe, but the actors seem to have communicated one of Shakespeare's themes to him: the sensitiveness of the murderers to the evil in which they are caught.

In other words, it would seem that, in some places at least, Forman's résumé of the action of the play cannot be used as a basis for either textual or theatrical reconstruction because its author has unconsciously translated ideas or images into events.

With Forman's three likely areas of obligation (to Shakespeare, Holinshed and his own imagination) in mind, it is possible to turn to Bartholomeusz's reconstruction of what, if it actually took place, must have been one of the most striking scenes in a play notable for its spectacular effects – the initial entrance of Macbeth. Forman plunges to the heart of it with characteristic brevity: 'ther was to be obserued, firste, howe Mackbeth and Bancko, 2 noble men of Scotland, Ridinge thorowe a wod, the[r] stode before them 3 women feiries or Nimphes'. Unlike Mr Nosworthy, Bartholomeusz is concerned with neither the un-Shakespearian location nor the curious description of the Witches. His attention is focused exclusively upon the theatrical significance of the capitalised 'Ridinge': 'The observation made by Forman is, if true, slightly startling in

its implications. The actor playing Macbeth appears to have made his first entrance at the Globe on horseback.' Startling as the deduction may be, it is by no means a novel one. As early as 1931, J. Q. Adams, having canvassed the implications of the whole passage, discounted not merely its reliability but contemporary attempts to justify it: 'Not only is there no textual indication that Macbeth and Banquo entered on horseback, but the appearance of horses on the Globe stage is almost inconceivable, and the use of hobby-horses, suggested by some scholars, would render the situation absurd;'[1] while S. A. Tannenbaum, also scorning the hobby-horse hypothesis, went to considerable lengths, two years later, to demonstrate the care with which Shakespeare avoids the necessity of bringing horses on stage.[2] Though he makes no mention of previous discussion of the subject, Bartholomeusz counters both objections by inference, suggesting that 'there was a long tradition of entrances on horseback' from the Middle Ages to the Restoration and that the absence of a supporting stage direction in the folio text is capable of practical explanation:

Stage business in the theatre frequently goes unrecorded because it is often the result of creative, spontaneous discoveries made during rehearsals. While there is no explicit stage direction in the Folio, it is possible to argue that the rhythm of the scene and the imagery of the play justify an entrance on horseback, that it is theatrically arresting and is dramatically right.

But even granting that the concept of Macbeth (and Banquo) cantering onto the stage at the Globe in 1611 is both feasible and defensible, did such a perilous exhibition of thespian creativity actually occur? Unfortunately, Dr Bartholomeusz fails to point out that, if Shakespeare did overcome his apparent reluct-

rejects even these tentative suggestions as showing 'a disturbing literalness'.

[1] *Macbeth*, p. 295.
[2] *Shaksperian Scraps*, pp. 26–7.

ance to make use of this particular piece of stage business, he did so not once, but twice, for less than 300 words later in Forman's manuscript the verb 'ride' (in its past tense) recurs: 'Then was Mackbeth Crowned kinge, and then he for feare of Banko, his old Companion, that he should beget kings but be no kinge him selfe, he contriued the death of Banko, and caused him to be Murdred on the way as he Rode.' Two explanations offer themselves. Either Shakespeare's actors overplayed the 'spontaneous discoveries' they made during rehearsals, or Forman, regarding horses as the obvious mode of locomotion, has translated the concept of travelling into concrete terms, aided in this instance not merely by the 'rhythm of the scene and the imagery of the play' but by the murderers' explicit references to their victim's horses (cf. his 'translation' of the thematic imagery of the hand-washing scene). The folio text, which provides incontrovertible evidence that Forman's account is unreliable here, lends support to the latter explanation:

3 Murderer.   Hark! I hear horses.
Banquo. [*Within.*] Give us a light there, ho!
2 Murderer.   Then 'tis he: the rest
    That are within the note of expectation,
    Already are i' th' court.
1 Murderer.   His horses go about.
3 Murderer.
    Almost a mile; but he does usually,
    So all men do, from hence to the palace gate
    Make it their *walk*. [my italics]

(III, iii, 8–14)

Other doubts, however, cluster about Forman's version of Macbeth's first appearance. The location of the scene and the description of the Witches (as noted above) both seem closer to Holinshed than to Shakespeare, while Macbeth and Banquo enter to the Witches in the drama, whereas in Forman and Holinshed the weird sisters appear to the travellers (Holinshed: 'there met them three women in strange and wild apparell' / Forman: 'the[r] stode before

them 3 women feiries or Nimphes'). Moreover, it is possible that the word 'Ridinge' may itself have been suggested by the *Chronicles*. Though both the 1577 and 1587 editions agree that the encounter took place as Macbeth and Banquo were 'passing thorough [1577: through] the woods and fields', the earlier version supplements the narrative with a wood-cut which shows Macbeth and Banquo, on horseback, confronting three very respectable-looking ladies who bear very little resemblance to Shakespeare's 'hags' but have some affinity with 'feiries or Nimphes'. Though it is generally accepted that Shakespeare used the 1587 rather than the 1577 edition of Holinshed,[1] it is not inconceivable that he was familiar with the wood-cut and that it stimulated the spectacular entrance the synopsis implies, but in view of the very suspect nature of Forman's recollections at this point, together with his apparent inability to distinguish between what he saw on the printed page and what he witnessed on the stage, it seems more likely that, if any impact was made by the wood-cut, it was upon the imagination of the diarist rather than the dramatist. In short, Forman's readiness to substitute visual for verbal imagery, together with his extensive dependence on Shakespeare's source, must militate against the reliability of his testimony in this scene as elsewhere. Another hobby-horse, it seems, must be forgot.

The precise nature of the relationship between play, history, and synopsis remains, of course, unresolved. By what process of composition Forman arrived at an account which is faithful to Holinshed's phraseology in one instance and garbles people and places in the next, which carefully records some scenes of Shakespeare's play and yet omits whole areas of action (the Cavern scene provides an obvious example) which seem particularly relevant to

1 Cf. Boswell-Stone, *Shakspere's Holinshed*, pp. ix–x.

the author's interests, defies explanation. That Forman saw a performance of *Macbeth* in 1611 seems indisputable, but it seems equally certain that the numerous discrepancies between his summary of the play and the folio text derive, not from the activities of an unknown reviser, but from the haphazard workings of an agglutinative memory. Thus, though the authenticity of the manuscript remains beyond dispute, there can be very little assurance that in its terse memorandum on Macbeth's sylvan entrance upon horseback we have unassailable evidence of the kind of spectacle to be seen at the Globe when the dramatist turned producer.

© LEAH SCRAGG 1973

SHAKESPEARE'S MISANTHROPE

HARRY LEVIN

We do not need Herman Melville to warn us that *Timon of Athens* is an ambush for critics. Yet, in his nondescript edition of Shakespeare now at Harvard University, it is one of the plays most heavily marked. Marginal annotations are rare but pithy. Thus, when Timon urges the Bandits to plunder the shops of Athens, two of them are almost dissuaded from banditry. The third, an opportunist, tells his colleagues that it would be better to reform when less plunder is available: 'There is no time so miserable but a man may be true' (IV, iii, 459–60). This has been didactically paraphrased by the anonymous editor: 'There is no hour in a man's life so wretched, but he always has it in his power to become *true*, i.e. honest.' And Melville, in the margin, has glossed the comment, after crossing it out: 'Peace, peace! Thou ass of a commentator!' His own feelings come to the surface when Timon drives his false friends out of the banquet hall, and Melville comments with Yankee succinctness: 'Served 'em right.' In his other reading he would frequently return to his misanthropic touchstone. Where La Bruyère wrote skeptically about friendship, Melville commented: 'True, Shakespeare goes further: None die but somebody spurns them into the grave.' Melville's misquotation is even more absolute than the words of Shakespeare's Apemantus: 'Who dies that bears not one spurn to the grave / Of their friends' gift?' (I, ii, 136–7).

Timon of Athens provided a moral backdrop for Melville's *Confidence-Man*, as *Hamlet* had for *Pierre* and *King Lear* for *Moby Dick*. His literary career bogged down at the stage that his biographers would call Timonism, and *The Confidence-Man* – with its masquerade of Emersonian ideals and Hawthornesque doubts, its dialectic between a self-deluding optimism and an ever-deepening mistrust – was the last work of fiction he published. But from first to last he worshipped at the Shakespearian pantheon, and ranked Timon with Lear and Hamlet as a spokesman for those bitter truths to which he felt the American public was deaf. Shakespeare's more professional interpreters, with the emphatic exception of Wilson Knight, have been less inclined to inflate the evaluation so subjectively. Some of the others, such as Una Ellis-Fermor, Willard Farnham, and Terence Spencer, have used classical precedent and textual scrutiny to frame the play in critical perspective. A substantial consensus, locating it somewhere in the sequence through Shakespeare's later tragedies to his romances, would regard it as an unpolished draft, probably set aside before it reached actual performance. This assumption might allow us a glimpse into the playwright's workshop, accounting for the rough spots and the obvious inconsistencies. Yet there are brilliantly finished scenes and powerful speeches: the diatribe on universal thievery, for example, from which Vladimir Nabokov stole his title *Pale Fire*.

Why then, we shall find ourselves asking, should the tragedy have been shelved? We can discern its limits as a tragedy by recalling Edmond Malone's observation: 'Of all the works of Shakespeare, *Timon of Athens* possesses most the character of a satire.' Now *satura* is traditionally a mixed mode, closer perhaps to the comic than to the tragic, and not always combining successfully with drama. Ben Jonson failed in his trilogy of so-called 'comical satires', though *Volpone* would fully live up to that specification. Its effectiveness can be measured by comparing the savage indignation of Timon's speech on gold (iv, iii, 384–95), with the controlled irony of Volpone's opening hymn to his treasure. Shakespeare's principal source is the *Timon* of Lucian, who is there and elsewhere the arch-satirist of gold. Lucian's Timon is presented as a poor labourer who, after the gods restore his lost riches, beats off the parasitical types that besiege him again. The Lucianic dialogue has dramatic elements, but it shows no development of character or conflict. It has no beginning, nothing more than a backward glance at former fortunes, and no ending, simply a hostile stance toward all other men. This is the figure that crystallized in popular mythology, the 'critic Timon' mentioned in *Love's Labour's Lost*, the archetypal 'Timonist' of Elizabethan allusion. The misanthrope's role was as clearly laid out for him as the pandar's was for Pandarus in *Troilus and Cressida*.

Hence he could self-consciously announce: 'I am *Misanthropos*, and hate mankind' (iv, iii, 54). But that is scarcely more than the application of a label, and it is inadequately dramatized when Lucian's Timon stones his interlocutors – let alone when Shakespeare's Timon bribes his visitors to go away. In 'Some Thoughts on Playwriting' Thornton Wilder remarked: 'The exposition of the nature of misanthropy…in Shakespeare's *Timon of Athens* has never been a success.'[1] Solitude, after all, is antisocial by definition, and anchorites can express their distaste for society by undramati-

cally avoiding it. Molière's *Misanthrope*, on the other hand, takes place in a highly social setting. To be sure, its hero is constantly contemplating a retirement to some desert island: 'Trop de perversité règne au siècle où nous sommes, / Et je veux me tirer du commerce des hommes.' Yet it takes the mundanity of the court to bring out the misanthropy of Alceste; his intransigent sincerity has its foil in the worldly hypocrisy of the courtiers; and we end by wondering which has been the more sharply satirized. *Timon of Athens*, by contrast, moves in the direction of a monodrama which is unresolved. The isolated protagonist is subject to successive interrogations. If he is being tested like Job, he does not survive the ordeal. If he is being punished like Prometheus, he retaliates by verbal castigations and assumes the final responsibility for his own victimization.

He can be brought nearer to his Jacobean context if we view him as a malcontent. But malcontents, while cursing their lot, undertake to set things right: to retrieve a princely heritage or avenge a sister's rape. Hamlet wears his antic disposition as a cloak to mask his vengeance. The ingrained malignity of Iago, or of Webster's disgruntled adventurers, seeks to vent itself in action. A closer prototype would be the melancholy Jaques, who cultivates melancholia for its own sake, and whom Hazlitt has described as the sole contemplative personage among the Shakespearian *dramatis personae*. When he retires to a house of convertites, one can imagine him finding matter for raillery there. He is not likely to be put out of his humor; nor, on a cruder level, is the low-minded and single-minded Thersites. In comparison, we must remember that Timon did not begin as a Timonist. He was, as one Senator puts it, a phoenix before he became a gull (ii, i, 31). Legend has preserved him in the posture of

[1] In Augusto Centeno (ed.), *The Intent of the Artist* (Princeton, 1941), p. 92.

a reclusive curmudgeon; in his prime he had personified the image of a gregarious prodigal. The problem of recreating that earlier personality, and registering the stages of alienation and decline, was one to overtax the flexibility and resourcefulness of Shakespeare himself. His philanthropist is one man, his misanthropist another, and the transition between them is a sudden recoil rather than a gradual disillusionment.

All this, in bald outline, corresponds well enough with the basic patterns of medieval or Renaissance tragedy. Seldom indeed has a downfall been so precipitate from such lavish prosperity to such crouching adversity. But, whereas the traditional sacrifice was a throne, a high office, or a beloved partner, here the loss is reckoned in financial terms. Fortune still is the presiding goddess, although her precipitating symbol is not a wheel but a hill, which the competitive crowd is climbing up or sliding down. The venal allegory of the Poet, which serves as an expository device, is rounded out by his reappearance with a moralistic satire. The barometric references to Timon's *fortune* indicate both his destiny and his affluence. Romeo is 'fortune's fool' because he is crossed by fate; Timon's 'trencher-friends' are 'fools of fortune' because they would do anything for wealth (III, vi, 92). The key-words of the play, employed more often than anywhere else in Shakespeare, *friend* and *gold*, almost seem to cancel each other out. Timon learns, from his painful experience with his selfish following, to equate them. Love between the sexes plays no part in either of his two worlds. In the first, though it is Cupid who presents the masque, the dancing ladies are Amazons quickly dismissed. In the second Alcibiades introduces the only two feminine characters, courtesans ungallantly encouraged by Timon to infect mankind with their alleged diseases.

His relations with his fellow men have been predicated upon 'a dream of friendship', from which – his steward Flavius perceives – he was bound to be rudely wakened (IV, ii, 34). Much of what we hear about his nobility is attested by those who have something to gain from their flattery. While they profit literally from his patronage, he accounts himself metaphorically wealthy in his friends (II, ii, 188). However, the arrangement is not reciprocal. His ideal is 'to have so many like brothers commanding one another's fortunes' (I, ii, 102–3). But he proves to be the lone member of such a brotherhood; as a benefactor he has been a spendthrift. The test of magnanimity on both sides, the process of debasement and undeception, comprises a three-act drama in itself. The opening act is a veritable blaze of overdone hospitality and exploited munificence. The monetary tensions behind this extravagant pageantry come out swiftly in the series of confrontations that follows: the servants shuttling back and forth between debtors and creditors; the sycophants tried and found wanting, each of them fumbling for excuses and disavowals; and, in the dim background, the usurers pulling the ultimate strings. The last scene of the third act, where the fair-weather flatterers are invited to a mock-banquet and told off, is a kind of dénouement. We may well then feel, as Melville apparently did, that the curtain of poetic justice has fallen at last. 'Served 'em right.'

The first three acts attempt to trace, so to speak, the etiology of Timon's malaise. The treatment is somewhat diagrammatic, as in a morality play. Instead of the psychological insight that revealed, step by step, how a Macbeth could become steeped in blood or an Othello corrupted by unworthy suspicions, we are confronted with the overt theatricalism of a Leontes overcome by jealousy in a single instantaneous seizure. As in *The Winter's Tale* likewise, there is a sharp disjunction between the first three acts and acts IV and V. Yet, insofar as the characterization of Timon is concerned, the real break occurs in act III. During his absence from the stage, bills have been accumulating and loans put off. One of the servants alerts the others to the fact that an identity crisis is brewing: 'my lord leans wondrously to discontent' (III, iv, 69). When Timon reappears soon afterward, he is – as the stage direction specifies – '*in a rage*'. No longer the easy-going host of act I or the bewildered patron of act II, he is abruptly ready to denounce his duns, summon his ever-greedy *clientèle* to an anti-feast, and emerge as a full-fledged misanthrope: 'Henceforth hated be / Of Timon, man and all humanity!' (III, vi, 100–1). This lightning change from one state of mind to its polar opposite merits the criticism that Apemantus will lodge against Timon himself: 'The middle of humanity thou never knewest, but the extremity of both ends' (IV, iii, 301–2).

Timon, the man-hater of the last two acts, has hardened into his monolithic attitude. If his prior self seems in retrospect shallow, it is attributable to his thoroughly extroverted disposition. But how much deeper does his embitterment go? In the 'better days' of lordly innocence, he held no mental reservations (IV, ii, 27); hence he needed no asides or soliloquies. In his 'latter spirits' he continues to speak out directly (V, iv, 74). But he cannot be said to have moved from the one extreme to the other through the medium of introspection; nor does he, as an ascetic hermit, engage his thoughts in spiritual meditation. The first scene of act IV constitutes a soliloquy merely because, for the first time it would seem, he stands alone. This has its counterpart in the climactic episode of *Coriolanus*, where at the gates of Rome the exiled general pronounces his personal decree of banishment against his fellow citizens. Henceforth the speeches of Timon extend and intensify the acrid rhetoric of Coriolanus: the invective vein, the serried style, the pregnant imagery. Timon's farewell

to Athens is a baneful prayer that the laws of nature reverse themselves, a litany of curses, 'multiplying bans' (IV, i, 34). Since obligations to him have not been met, let all sanctions be broken: 'Degrees, observances, customs and laws, / Decline to your confounding contraries' (IV, i, 19–20). Timon prays for everything that Ulysses warned the Greek generals against. No wonder Karl Marx relished Shakespeare's imprecation against gold.

The discontinuity between the first and second halves of the play is widened further by the shift in locale. A young and lyrical Shakespeare, in *A Midsummer Night's Dream*, had conveyed his characters from Athens to the neighboring woods, where their problems were solved by magical charms. Protagonists of Shakespearian comedy had often found their happiness in one or another part of the forest. Oedipus, on leaving Thebes for Colonus after a much more terrible catastrophe, had found at least a mood of resignation. Timon gives way to his fury even as he relinquishes his Athenian mansion for a cave. The titular epithet, Timon of Athens, has an ironic ring, echoing his bitterness against the Athenians and underscoring his gesture of self-exile. Like Lear, he exposes man's ingratitude by exposing himself to the barren countryside, by reducing himself to the condition of 'unaccommodated man'. When he looks back to the city from his arboreal retreat, he can accept the paradox of Apemantus: 'the commonwealth of Athens is become a forest of beasts' (IV, iii, 350). It is an additional paradox that, when Timon digs for roots, he discovers gold – now meaningless to him or, rather, fraught with the evil meaning of civic corruption. 'The hundredheaded rabble of the cathedral close'. Such was Athens for Swift, as characterized by Joyce. 'A hater of his kind ran from them to the wood of madness, his mane foaming in the moon, his eyeballs stars. Houyhnhnm, horsenostrilled.'

Apemantus performs a unifying function by

prefiguring the second part during the first, eating roots while the others are banqueting, recognized by them as being 'opposite to humanity' (I, i, 272). He strikes the morose note that prepares us for future dissonances: 'Who lives that's not depraved or depraves?' (I, ii, 136). As a Cynic philosopher, in the historical and the etymological sense, he seems to welcome the association with dogs by which he is continually saluted. Timon at one point is constrained to remind him, since his preference for animals is so pronounced, that they are quite as predatory as men (IV, iii, 328–47). The reunion of these two caitiffs is worthy of Samuel Beckett in its mutual vexation and name-calling, its surly interchange of taunts and gibes. Apemantus seems understandably suspicious – and slightly jealous – of Timon in his new role as a carper. Can it be authentic if he has assumed it 'enforceably', if he had no choice but to put on 'this sour cold habit' as a response to misfortune (IV, iii, 243, 241)? Timon, in his turn, feels better qualified to scorn the world because he has known its amenities. 'Why shouldst thou hate men?' he asks Apemantus. 'They never flatter'd thee' (IV, iii, 271–2). Apemantus, the natural misanthrope, for whom the grapes have never been anything but sour, is put down and driven off by Timon, the conditioned misanthrope, for whom life is all the sourer because he has tasted its sweetness.

The scene that reunites them temporarily and disjoins them forever (IV, iii), one of the longest in Shakespeare, is completed by the first scene of act v, wherein Timon makes his last appearance. Having delivered his curse against gold, and thereupon discovered and renounced it, he alternates between solitary monologue and denunciation of his old Athenian companions, seeking him out to be rebuffed again, in a quick succession of what might be termed non-recognition scenes. Having been more or less continuously on-stage, from one encounter to the next, he withdraws and dies offstage. The moribund moment, which figures so importantly in most of Shakespeare's tragedies, is evaded here. This does not even seem to be a suicide, but rather an expected dissolution. After so vocal and long-drawn-out a rejection of existence, what would be left to say? Why should Timon, having learned to abominate his contemporaries, care for the good opinion of posterity? Instead of a rousing death-speech, three different epitaphs are reported. Each of them is a sullen and stilted couplet in rhymed fourteeners, and two of them are transcribed from North's Plutarch, one of which is translated from Callimachus: 'Here lie I, Timon, who, alive, all living men did hate. / Pass by and curse thy fill, but pass and stay not here thy gait' (v, iv, 72–3). Whatever the inscription on his grave, it will soon be washed away by the sea – a quiet consummation and a static conclusion.

As contrasted with this slackening quiescence, into which his lamentations and agonies subside, the under-plot has been loudly kept astir by the drum and fife of Alcibiades' army. Alcibiades has his own reasons for looking back in anger at the Athenians. 'To be in anger is impiety', he has confessed before the Senators. 'But who is man that is not angry?' (III, v, 57–8). Hardly Alcibiades, any more than Timon, and the unwanted gold of the passive angry man backs the revenge of his active brother-in-arms. The Senate has ignored his plea for a fellow soldier's life and, when Alcibiades has pressed it, has responded by banishing him. Therefore he has turned against the City–State, which he re-enters in military triumph at the end. He is a more attractive, if no more reliable, figure than his Plutarchian parallel, Coriolanus. Shakespeare has individualized Alcibiades, along with Apemantus and Flavius, because they sustain a degree of affinity with Timon himself. All the other members of the cast are merely typified, as if to suggest that these are the sort of men to whom his cynical generalizations apply. As for Flavius, he is the nonpareil, the *raisonneur* whose head-shaking asides give us an early clue to the situation, the faithful servitor whose continuing honesty forces his master to recognize one exception – 'but one' – to the general rule of bad faith. 'How fain would I have hated all mankind, / And thou redeem'st thyself' (IV, 501, 503–4).

The redeeming virtue of Flavius modifies the scope, if not the intensity, of Timon's hatred. Diogenes the Cynic might have been happy to have encountered a single honest man – might have become, in Melville's phrase, 'a genial misanthrope'. And Melville, who on occasion could out-Timon Shakespeare, sharpens a nice distinction in *The Confidence-Man*: 'tell me, was not that humor, of Diogenes, which led him to live, a merry-andrew, in the flower-market, better than that of the less wise Athenian, which made him a skulking scare-crow in pine-barrens? An injudicious gentle-man, Lord Timon.' It remains an open question whether Timon's experience should be viewed as one man's hard-luck story or as an indict-ment of the human race. Other tragic heroes have undergone worse tribulations than bank-ruptcy, and have not arrived at so wholesale a condemnation of their fellow men. Since Timon is the victim of callousness rather than cruelty, his sufferings are not to be compared with those of King Lear. Grief, which has a humanizing effect on Lear, dehumanizes Timon. Should the limitation be ascribed to the character or to the playwright? Could it be that Shakespeare, so adept and far-ranging in his sympathy, was balked at the portrayal of anti-pathy? It seems clear that he, who empathized with such numerous and varied themes, found this an uncongenial one. It would be significant if his uncertainties over *Timon of Athens* marked his transition from tragedy to romance.

Not that there is much romance about *Timon*. Its subject-matter would, by neo-classical standards, relegate it to the bourgeois sphere of comedy, where parasites and moneylenders flourish and rich men like Trimalchio entertain. Actually it has few comic moments, if any, and its Fool is Shakespeare's dimmest and dullest. Molière's misanthrope has his laughable aspects, which were sorely resented by Rousseau. Timon himself had been a laughing-stock of the Old Comedy; he would be mocked again in an eighteenth-century harlequinade. Shakespeare, taking him seriously, focused attention on the object of his grim mockery: not on money itself, but on the colluding attributes of greed and guile. These, of course, are the mainsprings of Jonson's comedies and of many others – though not, on the whole, of Shakespeare's. Living in the same society at its hour of capitalistic emergence, he cannot have been less aware than they were of acquisition and dispossession as a timely theme. They em-bodied it in the coney-catching of the London underworld. He conceived it as a cosmic pro-jection, when Timon assures the thieves that sun and moon and sea and earth are bent on pilfering and pillaging. This is darker than those occasional glimpses of anarchy which rift the chain of being from play to play. Possibly it is intended to estrange us, like the sardonic harshness of Bertolt Brecht, and unlike the brighter and warmer vistas that we think of as more characteristically Shakespearian. Shake-speare himself was so far from being *Misanthro-pos*, so very far from hating all mankind, that for once his negative capability got in the way of his dramaturgy.

'ANTONY AND CLEOPATRA' AND 'CORIOLANUS', SHAKESPEARE'S HEROIC TRAGEDIES: A JACOBEAN ADJUSTMENT

J. L. SIMMONS

Shakespeare wrote many plays about heroes, but only *Antony and Cleopatra* and *Coriolanus* are distinguished by heroic appeals that are exclusively and definitively aristocratic. Coriolanus and Cleopatra make strange bedfellows; yet despite their different life styles they share an unyielding horror of being scrutinized and judged by a vulgar audience. When the Queen of Egypt contemplates her dishonor at the hands of Octavius, her most terrifying thought is the vulgarization of her nobility in a dramatic representation for a popular Roman audience:

Cleopatra.   Now, Iras, what think'st thou?
    Thou an Egyptian puppet shall be shown
    In Rome as well as I. Mechanic slaves,
    With greasy aprons, rules, and hammers, shall
    Uplift us to the view; in their thick breaths,
    Rank of gross diet, shall we be enclouded,
    And forc'd to drink their vapour.
Iras.   The gods forbid!
Cleopatra.
       Nay, 'tis most certain, Iras. Saucy lictors
    Will catch at us like strumpets, and scald
       rhymers
    Ballad us out o' tune; the quick comedians
    Extemporally will stage us, and present
    Our Alexandrian revels; Antony
    Shall be brought drunken forth, and I shall see
    Some squeaking Cleopatra boy my greatness
    I' th' posture of a whore.   (v, ii, 206–20)[1]

Cleopatra dazzlingly holds up a mirror to the world of the Globe playhouse. Her speculation about a Roman play reflects the actual dramatic event of Shakespeare's Roman play: the Roman populace looks exactly like the London populace crowded around her open stage; Cleopatra is in fact being boyed by some incredible young master and often, no doubt, in the exaggerated posture of a whore; the Alexandrian revels have already generated the laughter to encloud the Globe with the vapor of garlic. In other words, the heroic couple have already been exposed to the dramatic humiliation which the noble Cleopatra dreads; and they have deserved it to the extent that their aspiration has been punctured comically by the reality.

But Cleopatra's mirror image is, of course, one-dimensional. The Roman performance will merely be grotesque caricature rendered with crude dramaturgical techniques and inspired by an even cruder moralism. Such a play might well have been in the popular repertory of the 1580s, something like a Roman *Famous Victories*. The appeal to the Roman populace, Cleopatra insists, will obliterate the dignity of heroic tragedy and the glory of heroic love. Shakespeare's Cleopatra, by implication, thus denies the varletry of censuring London a simplistic moral response to her tragedy: *Antony and Cleopatra* is obviously so much more than Cleopatra's projected Roman play, more than what the Roman populace could appreciate. At the same time, her trepidation – her dramatic vulnerability – points to the lovers' failure to realize their heroic vision

[1] *William Shakespeare: The Complete Works*, ed. Peter Alexander (Glasgow, 1951). This text is cited throughout.

in action. Those mechanic slaves with their rules represent a legitimate measurement which Shakespeare's comprehensive point of view incorporates.

It is very difficult to analyze the efficacy of such dramatic moments which bring the play into the world of the audience and at the same time, paradoxically, reinforce the audience's participation in the imaginative world of the play. This process of what Maynard Mack calls engagement and detachment manipulates not only the individual response of the play-goer but also, in some ritualistic way, the corporate response wherein individuals, with wits as diversely colored as their heads, become an audience.[1] My purpose is not to investigate how this mystery works in the theater; I only want to show that Shakespeare in these latest Jacobean tragedies – and particularly in *Coriolanus* – was manipulating his audience in a new way and that this new way implies a different kind of audience, one which cannot optimistically be expected to make a corporate response.

The famous passage in *Antony and Cleopatra* anticipates precisely the crucial dramatic scene in *Coriolanus*. In both cases the image of public display – Cleopatra exhibited as the prize of Caesar's triumph, Coriolanus standing for election in the market-place – dissolves effortlessly into the image of a demeaning theatrical performance: 'It is a part / That I shall blush in acting' (*Coriolanus*, II, ii, 142–3). More insidiously, the breath of the people, which Coriolanus despises as much as Cleopatra, has the power to determine the value of his performance, his moral worth and his fame.

In *Coriolanus* Shakespeare creates out of the political situation a play within a play. For his performance Coriolanus will be assigned costume, lines, and action. Although the stage directions of the folio give us no instructions, he would also probably require a simple bench or trestle stage assembled for the occasion – such a construction as had proved effective in

the production of *Volpone* in 1605/6. The King's Men owned Jonson's play and therefore the stage property needed for Volpone's performance as mountebank (II, i). Perhaps Jonson's great work reinforced upon Shakespeare's mind the pejorative implications of role-playing, particularly that Italianate role-playing which inspired Shakespeare's original formation of 'mountebank' as a verb (*OED*):

Mother, I am going to the market-place;
Chide me no more. I'll mountebank their loves,
Cog their hearts from them, and come home belov'd
Of all the trades in Rome.　　(III, ii, 131–4)

Coriolanus is literally to approach the people with his platform, in the process emblematizing himself as the most corrupt and dishonest of actors.

Shakespeare thus dramatizes, as the crux of his final tragedy, a theatrical relationship between aristocratic actor and popular audience, the very image which appalled Cleopatra. What completes the image in *Coriolanus* is that the vulgar 'audience' breathing on the hero has another audience breathing on it. The judicious breath of the real audience is bated on both the hero and his witnessing mob. It is not by any means the first time that Shakespeare has identified the act of moral judgment with the theatrical judgment of an audience. In *King John*, for example, at the moral and military stalemate between France and England, the citizens of Angiers, unable to choose between Arthur and John, 'stand securely on their battlements / As in a theatre' (II, i, 374–5). Shakespeare develops the moral enigma of Julius Caesar by characterizing him as an actor performing for that 'stinking breath' which offstage all but overpowers Casca and Caesar himself. In the funeral scene Brutus and Antony, on a constructed pulpit-stage, per-

[1] 'Engagement and Detachment in Shakespeare's Plays', in *Essays on Shakespeare and Elizabethan Drama in Honor of Hardin Craig*, ed. Richard Hosley (Columbia, Mo., 1962), pp. 275–96.

form for the uncertain plaudits of two audiences, one onstage and one in the yard.

What differentiates those earlier plays is that the ambivalences they dramatize do not directly involve any relationship with social class. As Ernest Schanzer observed in connection with *Julius Caesar*, the Renaissance equivalents of John Dover Wilson and Sir Mark Hunter – pro- and anti-Caesarians – might well have been in the audience;[1] but two such men could easily have been sitting, or even standing, side by side. *Coriolanus*, however, intentionally and inevitably strikes a social division within the audience. It is perhaps not a division exact enough to be marked by whether one stands or sits. But the sensibilities and prejudices which *Coriolanus* brings into exacerbating play are unquestionably those largely determined by one's social class, and it seems to me that criticism has, by and large, been too engaged in the partisan business of defending or attacking Coriolanus to recognize and accommodate Shakespeare's obvious dramatic strategy.

The ingredients of this class opposition certainly are not new in *Coriolanus*. The mob has been treated in earlier plays with all of its moral, intellectual, political, and hygienic liabilities. Coriolanus' charges against the people and his arguments for absolute authority are the most common of Shakespearian commonplaces. But *Coriolanus* is nevertheless distinctive, as critical discomfort with the play reveals. The groundling watching *Coriolanus* in 1608 would probably be prepared, as he surely was in the 1590s, to assent to the prejudices against the mob, as in fact the Third Citizen does within the play. But these commonplaces do not appear incidentally as a congenially orthodox support for the English royalty and hierarchy. The social opposition in *Coriolanus* serves as basis for the imagery, theme, and structure; it determines the hero's tragedy. Coriolanus evokes these prejudices not in the spirit of political didacticism but in his visionary loathing.

Explicitly Shakespeare brings aristocratic and heroic appeals into tension with a popular and unheroic world. The noblest Roman of them all does not wish to perform for the breath of those who, because they are not themselves noble, have no understanding of nobility. The people's imagistic association with materialism stigmatizes them as opposed to the Roman ideal of virtue and honor:

> See here these movers that do prize their hours
> At a crack'd drachma! Cushions, leaden spoons,
> Irons of a doit, doublets that hangmen would
> Bury with those that wore them, these base slaves,
> Ere yet the fight be done, pack up. (I, v, 4–8)

In response to this action Coriolanus scathingly refers to 'the common file' as 'our gentlemen', and thematically his sarcasm is apt. The people's identification with money and trade hopelessly vulgarizes them. Volumnia has instilled in her son the aristocratic Roman (and English) attitude toward 'woollen vassals, things created / To buy and sell with groats' (III, ii, 9–10). When these vassals reject Coriolanus, they confirm the aristocratic prejudice against their unsavory breath, as abhorrent to patrician sensibilities as an association with trade:

> You have made good work,
> You and your apron men; you that stood so much
> Upon the voice of occupation and
> The breath of garlic-eaters! (IV, vi, 96–9)

The objection against the mob's breath, so commonly charged in the popular drama, here transcends fastidiousness and represents a desire to protect noble ideals from enc-louding 'opinion'. It is the same desire which provokes Cleopatra's horror of 'thick breaths, / Rank of gross diet'.

Of course one can easily oversimplify the stratification of English society, as historians have notably cautioned us. No doubt the audience was made up of many, both reputable

[1] *The Problem Plays of Shakespeare* (London 1963), p. 33.

and disreputable, who identified with neither patricians nor plebeians – or with both. Nevertheless, the social appeals in *Coriolanus*, both positive and negative, clearly distinguish the aristocracy and the gentry from the vulgar who are 'defiled' by trade, craft, money, and gross diet. Since the play allows no middle ground between the extremes, the mob encompasses more than the poor rabble in 2 *Henry VI*, more than the usual unruly apprentices. From Coriolanus' perspective 'the voice of occupation' incorporates what would be the entire citizen class of London, the City as distinct from Court and Country. After Coriolanus is exiled, the temporary respite – with 'tradesmen singing in their shops' (IV, vi, 8) – suggests nothing so strongly as a Roman holiday for complacent shoemakers; the City world of Simon Eyre emerges, without Dekker's romanticizing, totally at odds with the classical glory of Rome.

Shakespeare juxtaposes two incompatible images of Rome – one idealistic and heroic, the other realistic and antiheroic. Thus the play offers the paradox of a city at once the destined glory of the world and a common bickering village. The glory that was Rome, historically perceived, stands out all the more convincingly in that it struggles against political liabilities endemic to all earthly cities. By Englishing the citizens, Shakespeare ironically gives Rome historical immediacy. At the same time, the patrician ideal of Rome in its startling contrast appeals all the more in its aura of antiquity: it is so decidedly ancient history. The scenic effect of the costuming would likely have encouraged this division between the grand and the common. As John Dover Wilson deduced from the Henry Peacham sketch of *Titus Andronicus*, 'the lower classes [were] played apparently in "modern dress", whereas every effort was obviously made, contrary to the assumptions of our theatrical historians, to attain accuracy in the attire worn by patricians'.[1]

In confronting the aristocratic ideal of Rome with a contemporaneous antagonistic City, *Coriolanus* more than incidentally reflects the social and political turmoil of Jacobean England. E. C. Pettet has argued a topical connection between the uprisings in the play and the Midlands Insurrection of 1607, both fomented in part by scarcity of corn and by hostility toward the gentry.[2] And W. Gordon Zeeveld has demonstrated that Jacobean royalists made allusions to the *tribuni plebis* to impugn the activists struggling for the initiative in James's first Parliament (1604–10).[3] But Shakespeare's experimentation with antagonistic appeals and points of view was perhaps most directly inspired by an instinctive awareness that the audience had been affected by the social and political divisiveness surrounding the playhouse. As Gerald Bentley observes, 'In the years immediately before and after 1608, the London theatre audience was developing the social cleavage which is such a marked characteristic of the Jacobean and Caroline drama and stage.'[4] Bentley is referring, in his important essay, to the year in which the King's Men took over the lease to the Blackfriars after James had evicted the children's company; but the year is also the date most frequently urged for *Coriolanus*. Precise dating, however, is not necessary; for whether it was first performed just before or after 9 August 1608 when the

[1] 'Titus Andronicus on the Stage in 1595', *Shakespeare Survey 1* (Cambridge, 1948), p. 21.

[2] 'Coriolanus and the Midlands Insurrection of 1607', *Shakespeare Survey 3* (Cambridge, 1950), pp. 34–42.

[3] 'Coriolanus and Jacobean Politics', *MLR*, LVII (1962), 321–34.

[4] 'Shakespeare and the Blackfriars Theatre', *Shakespeare Survey 1* (Cambridge, 1948), p. 45: 'The gentry, the court, the professional classes, and the Inns of Court men went to the Blackfriars, the Phoenix, and later to the Salisbury Court; the London masses went to the larger and noisier Red Bull and Fortune and Globe. This new state of affairs was just developing when the King's men had their conferences about the Blackfriars in 1608.'

King's Men arranged for the lease of the private theater, *Coriolanus* grows out of a period when Shakespeare as both playwright and shareholder was having to reckon with new dramatic fashions, new audiences, and even a new playhouse. The play reveals the strain as well as the genius of Shakespeare adjusting to a theatrical environment marked by Jacobean fragmentation, particularly by the growing alienation of that important segment of the London audience typically associated with trade and increasingly characterized as sectarian in spirit. The bonds of national unity which Elizabeth had maintained over religious, economic, and political factions had dissolved; and no area of English life responded to the loss more sensitively than the theater.

One hesitates to urge a predominance of external influences on that creativity which gave us *Antony and Cleopatra* and *Coriolanus*, but out of the bombardment of internal and external stimuli came two distinctly heroic tragedies which for the first time in Shakespeare's career treat aristocratic appeals that are definitively and insistently exclusive. The common people of Rome, Cleopatra knows, cannot respond to heroic love because they are not capable of such passion; they are not heroes.[1] No more are they capable of appreciating Coriolanus' *virtus*; they are not virtuous. Antony and Coriolanus, as Eugene M. Waith has argued, are generically Herculean; they tower heroically above the common rout in their aspirations, actions, and passions.[2] They strive for an excellence to distinguish them from both the bestial and the vulgar:

> Kingdoms are clay; our dungy earth alike
> Feeds beast as man. The nobleness of life
> Is to do thus...   (I, i, 35–7)

Although Antony's 'thus' is assuredly not Coriolanus', both Herculean heroes attempt to achieve a greatness triumphantly beyond the level of clay. They cannot, however, ultimately succeed:

> Here I am Antony;
> Yet cannot hold this visible shape...
>   (IV, xiv, 13–14)

> I melt, and am not
> Of stronger earth than others.
>   (*Coriolanus*, V, iii, 28–9)

But while the ultimate failure asserts the hubris of the protagonists, the heroic attempt is substantial enough to affirm their tragic nobility.

The greatness of Shakespeare's two heroic tragedies (and here I disagree with Professor Waith) lies in the fact that the heroes and the heroics within the imaginative world of the plays have moral relevance to the real world of the audience. Shakespeare does not, that is to say, significantly urge special judgments for Antony and Coriolanus or suggest that in their greatness they rise above morality or create one of their own. Shakespeare is concerned with the moral status of heroes, and he renders Antony and Coriolanus critically from first to last. In fact, the irony frequently crowds both Antony and Coriolanus to the brink of the comic, even the satiric.[3] Shakespeare quite grants that heroes, in an unheroic world, are all but unendurable. The horror of Cleopatra and Coriolanus in contemplating their representation before a vulgar crowd implies that the capacity to be heroic is absurd without the select audience to appreciate heroism.

After I *Henry IV, Julius Caesar, Hamlet,*

---

[1] For the semantic confusion behind 'heroical love', a confusion which encouraged the belief that only the great are subject to this overwhelming passion, see John L. Lowes, 'The Loveres Maladye of Hereos', *MP*, XI (1914), 491–546.

[2] *The Herculean Hero in Marlowe, Chapman, Shakespeare and Dryden* (New York, 1962), passim.

[3] See R. A. Foakes, *Shakespeare: the Dark Comedies to the Last Plays: from Satire to Celebration* (Charlottesville, Va., 1971), pp. 85–93. Foakes discusses the 'distancing' in these plays as Shakespeare's response to the drama of the decade, particularly Marston's and the repertory of the children's companies.

and *Troilus and Cressida* one would expect Shakespeare to bring the idea of the hero under moral scrutiny; heroism, like honor, receives definition and qualification rather early in Shakespeare's career. But only in *Antony and Cleopatra* and *Coriolanus* does Shakespeare treat heroism and honor in restrictively aristocratic manifestations, and this new subject-matter clearly reflects the trend of theatrical fashion. The heroic tragedies to follow – from the plays associated with Beaumont and Fletcher to the Caroline decadence – prove the taste of an increasingly exclusive audience for extravagant treatments of heroic virtue and love. These plays appeal to a concept of honor that becomes more rarified as it receives less definition and qualification. Shakespeare, however, chose to create heroic drama, necessarily exclusive in its moral appeals, for what was still a popular audience, although an increasingly unsettled one. But how was the dramatist to satisfy such an audience, the social fragmentation of which involved moral fragmentation? The same question can be posed in terms of Shakespeare's artistic integrity: how was Shakespeare to write such drama, with its special focus, without losing the all-encompassing vision which was his genius?

In resolving the problem, Shakespeare acknowledges once again that all the world's a stage and proceeds to dramatize the problem. By his very nature Coriolanus is inescapably as divisive a figure for the members of the real audience as for their social and political counterparts on the stage. Daringly, the conflict extends topically from the stage into the audience's immediate frame of reference as spectators of a play, as members of their own social classes, and as citizens of their own earthly city. If the experiment is brilliant, it has the air of a valedictory success; one can understand why Shakespeare wrote no more tragedies. Of the many historical presentiments to be discovered in Shakespeare's work, none is more

profound than the demonstration in *Coriolanus* of the inevitable effect of social divisiveness upon the most public of art forms. Within a few decades following 1608, that effect would involve the closing of the theaters, but not before the loss of national unity had made the drama all but irrelevant.[1]

As Alfred Harbage insists in his *Shakespeare and the Rival Traditions*, Shakespeare remains a dramatist for the popular, not the coterie, theater; but the appeals in these last two tragedies and the audience which those appeals imply suggest distinctions not made in Professor Harbage's general survey.[2] The evidence presented in his study will nevertheless confirm that *Antony and Cleopatra* and *Coriolanus* differ signally from characteristic plays in the popular repertory, plays which appeal beyond antagonistic differences to common social, political, and ethical values. Professor Harbage cites these two works with suspicious infrequency, given their importance; and those few citations overlook the opposing characteristics which make the plays so problematic and provocative. The vision of the absolute aristocratic state no less than that of heroical love rejects – and is rejected by – bourgeois values. The prudent craftsmen and tradesmen are no more inclined to Coriolanus' martial virtue than they are to Antony and Cleopatra's heroic passion. The two plays, in fact, suggest the absurdity of juxtaposing the conflicting points of view much as does *The Knight of the Burning Pestle*, a play of the same period (*c.* 1608). Like the Citizen and his wife who are the jarring and unsympathetic audience for Beaumont's City comedy, the Roman tradesmen will either miss the point or morally disapprove of it. Whereas Beaumont generates comedy, Shakespeare generates tra-

[1] See David M. Bevington, *Tudor Drama and Politics* (Cambridge, Mass., 1968), p. 297.
[2] *Shakespeare and the Rival Traditions* (New York, 1952).

gedy out of the social disharmony within an audience.

Shakespeare, however, uses his unsympathetic audience positively as well as negatively in regarding and evaluating his heroic characters. While Coriolanus' vision is granted its validity, the physical world of the trade and working class offers a system of checks more profound than the hero understands. The moral vision of Shakespeare's two heroic tragedies incorporates the popular, didactic morality of the people: Antony and Cleopatra are certainly overthrown by lust; Coriolanus is indeed a victim of his own pride. But Shakespeare also creates a heroic aspiration beyond that moralism even while aware that the greatness of his tragic Romans must be a limited and qualified one. Cleopatra's theatrical fears, therefore, are symptomatic of a moral comprehensiveness achieved by a playwright manipulating a diverse audience with diverse points of view. And Shakespeare finally, I believe, transcends the diversity.

SHAKESPEARE'S VENUS AND ADONIS SONNETS

C. H. HOBDAY

William Jaggard's anthology *The Passionate Pilgrim*, published in 1599 and attributed on the title-page to Shakespeare, contains versions of Sonnets 138 and 144 (here numbered I and II), three poems taken from *Love's Labour's Lost* (III, V, and XVI), four known to be by other authors (VIII, XI, XIX, and XX) and eleven of uncertain authorship. The most interesting of the last group are the three sonnets on Venus and Adonis numbered IV, VI, and IX, which obviously are connected in some way with Shakespeare's poem. Malone suggested that they, and also XI, which is on the same theme, were 'essays of the author when he first conceived the idea of writing a poem on the subject of Venus and Adonis, and before the scheme of his poem was adjusted'. As XI appears in a different version in Bartholomew Griffin's *Fidessa*, published in 1596, most modern critics reject this view, and regard all four as imitations of *Venus and Adonis* written by Griffin. Dissenters include John Masefield, who considered that IV, VI, and IX 'have the ring of [Shakespeare's] freshest youthful manner',[1] and J. Middleton Murry, who had no doubt that VI at least was written by Shakespeare 'when the thought of a poem on Venus and Adonis was forming in his mind'.[2] The case for Shakespeare's authorship of all three has never been fully considered, and deserves re-examination.

The external evidence is admittedly weak. Jaggard was a completely unscrupulous publisher who attempted to cash in on Shakespeare's popularity by attributing other men's work to him. Not content with including poems by Barnfield, Griffin, Marlowe, and Ralegh in *The Passionate Pilgrim*, he issued a new edition in 1612 which contained poems by Heywood, to the annoyance of both Heywood and Shakespeare. In 1619 he reprinted Munday, Drayton, Wilson and Hathway's *First Part of the Life of Sir John Oldcastle* as Shakespeare's, in the hope that purchasers would mistake it for a play about Falstaff. As evidence for the authorship of the three sonnets Jaggard's word is worthless.

Three small points might be pleaded as external evidence for Shakespeare's authorship. The title-page of the 1612 edition begins: 'THE PASSIONATE PILGRIME. OR *Certaine Amorous Sonnets, betweene* Venus *and* Adonis, *newly corrected and augmented.* By W. Shakespeare.' This seems to attribute the Venus and Adonis sonnets specifically to Shakespeare, but Jaggard may merely have been attempting to exploit the continued popularity of his poem. A manuscript in the Folger Library contains six of the *Passionate Pilgrim* poems (I, IV, VI, VII, XI, and XVIII), all of which except XI are attributed in a different hand to 'W.S.' Although the fact that the writer distinguished between Griffin's poem and the other two Adonis sonnets might be regarded as significant, it is difficult to accept VII ('Fair is my love...') and particularly XVIII ('Whenas thine eye...') as Shakespeare's,

[1] *William Shakespeare* (London, n.d.), p. 244.
[2] *Shakespeare* (London, 1936), p. 88.

and the writer's only authority for his attributions was probably the title-page of *The Passionate Pilgrim*. Slightly stronger evidence, perhaps, is Jaggard's arrangement of the poems. The collection opens with three genuine sonnets, an Adonis sonnet, another genuine sonnet and another Adonis sonnet, and it might be argued that Jaggard concentrated most of his genuine material at the beginning of the book to give intending purchasers the impression that it was entirely by Shakespeare. None of these arguments has any great weight, and any case for the authenticity of the sonnets must rest upon internal evidence.

The case is strongest for Shakespeare's authorship of vi, the only one of the three with any particular merit. It is generally agreed that when writing *Venus and Adonis* Shakespeare derived Adonis' rejection of Venus' advances from Ovid's story of Salmacis and Hermaphroditus, with which he was familiar both in the original and in Golding's translation of the *Metamorphoses*. Sonnet vi is a direct imitation of this story, with Venus substituted for Salmacis and Adonis for Hermaphroditus, and is clearly derived from Golding's version. Here is Golding:

She hides her in a bushy queach, where kneeling on her knee
She always hath her eye on him...
                    He took so great delight
In coolness of the pleasant spring, that straight he stripped quite
His garments from his tender skin. When Salmacis beheld
His naked beauty, such strong pangs so ardently her held
That utterly she was astraught. And even as Phoebus' beams
Against a mirror pure and clear rebound with broken gleams,
Even so her eyes did sparkle fire. Scarce could she
                    tarriance make... (IV, 418–30)

And here is the sonnet:

Scarce had the sun dried up the dewy morn,
And scarce the herd gone to the hedge for shade,
When Cytherea, all in love forlorn,
A longing tarriance for Adonis made
Under an osier growing by a brook,
A brook where Adon used to cool his spleen.
Hot was the day, she hotter that did look
For his approach, that often there had been.
Anon he comes, and throws his mantle by,
And stood stark naked on the brook's green brim.
The sun looked on the world with glorious eye,
Yet not so wistly as this queen on him.
He, spying her, bounced in whereas he stood.
'O Jove,' quoth she, 'why was I not a flood?'

If there were any doubt of the author's debt to Golding, the use of the phrase 'make tarriance' by both would remove it. 'Tarriance' appears only once in the Shakespeare canon, where Julia decides to make her 'longing journey' to Proteus and declares that 'I am impatient of my tarriance' (*Two Gentlemen of Verona*, II, vii, 85–90). The association of 'longing' and 'tarriance' with a woman impatient to see a man who does not return her love seems to support common authorship. It is perhaps also significant that in the sonnet Venus, waiting by a brook, is described as hot with desire for Adonis, whilst in the same scene of *The Two Gentlemen of Verona* a reference to the 'hot fire' of Julia's love is immediately followed by her description of a stream (21–32). An even closer parallel to the sonnet is found in the induction to *The Taming of the Shrew*, where a servant asks Christopher Sly:

Dost thou love pictures? We will fetch thee straight
Adonis painted by a running brook
And Cytherea all in sedges hid.   (ii, 51–3)

Both this passage and the sonnet place Venus and Adonis in the same situation as Salmacis and Hermaphroditus; both refer to Venus as Cytherea; and both use the word 'brook' where Golding speaks of a spring.

The intense heat of the sun (to which Ovid had referred in the Salmacis story only in an incidental simile, but which permeates the whole sonnet) is made palpable in order that the reader may sense the ardour of Venus' desire, whilst the coolness of the brook supplies a physical equivalent to Adonis' chastity. The heat of the day is brilliantly evoked in the opening lines, in which the movement from the general statement of the first line to the realistic detail of the second is typically Shakespearian. The picture of cattle seeking shelter from the heat – one seen with a countryman's eye, like the descriptions of animals and birds in *Venus and Adonis* – is repeated in Sonnet 12, with its reference to 'lofty trees...Which erst from heat did canopy the herd'. The same sultry atmosphere and the same ambiguity between physical and emotional heat as in VI is found in *Venus and Adonis*, lines 175–80:

By this the lovesick queen began to sweat,
For where they lay the shadow had forsook them,
And Titan, tired in the mid-day heat,
With burning eye did hotly overlook them,
Wishing Adonis had his team to guide,
So he were like him and by Venus' side.

In the sonnet the description of the hot day is followed by that of Venus looking 'wistly' on Adonis. On two of the three occasions on which Shakespeare uses 'wistly' in the canonical works the word is accompanied by references to heat – *oven*, *burneth*, *hotly*, *fire* (twice), *glow* and *coal* (*Venus and Adonis*, lines 331–48) and *kindled*, *fires* and *blazed* (*Lucrece*, lines 1,352–5).

The most Shakespearian line in the sonnet, and that which seems to clinch the case for Shakespeare's authorship, is

The sun looked on the world with glorious eye.

Sun, *look*, *world*, *glorious* and *eye*, together with *morn*, which appears in the opening line, all form part of a Shakespearian image-cluster, the other terms of which are *golden*, *rack*, *cloud*, *pale*, *sky*, *kiss*, *heaven*, *earth*, *mist*, *vapour*, *face*, *permit*, *smother*, *stain*, *base*, *steal*, *alchemy*, *ugly* and *splendour*.[1] In view of the obvious connection between this sonnet and *Venus and Adonis*, it is significant that the three examples of this image-cluster in the latter are particularly close to the line quoted:

And Titan, tired in the mid-day heat,
With burning eye did hotly overlook them. (177–8)

And as the bright sun glorifies the sky,
So is her face illumined with her eye. (485–6)

The sun ariseth in his majesty,
Who doth the world so gloriously behold
That cedar tops and hills seem burnished gold.
(856–8)

The three ideas of the sun's glory, its eye, and its looking on the world which are scattered through these passages are brought together in one line of the sonnet. It seems more probable that Shakespeare unconsciously echoed three times a line which he had previously written than that another author concentrated into one line ideas which in Shakespeare's poem occur at intervals of 300 to 400 lines. Thus subject, source, treatment, vocabulary and imagery all concur to support Shakespeare's authorship of VI. As J. C. Maxwell has written of *A Lover's Complaint*, 'none of this would be enough to warrant the attribution of an anonymous poem to Shakespeare, but it would be surprising if they were all, by chance, present in one falsely attributed to him in a volume which also contains a collection of genuine work'.[2]

[1] See *3 Henry VI*, II, i, 21–38 (morning, golden, glorious sun, eyes, racking clouds, pale, sky, kiss, earth, world); *Venus and Adonis*, lines 170–93 (earth, eye, overlook, misty vapours, sky, sun, face, heaven), lines 480–93 (kiss, sun, morn, earth, glorifies, sky, face, eye, clouded, heaven), lines 855–8 (morning, sun, world, gloriously behold, gold); *Lucrece*, lines 773–86 (mists, permit, sun, clouds, golden, morning, vapours, smothered, distain); *Love's Labour's Lost*, I, i, 82–8 (eye, heaven's glorious sun, looks, base, earthly), IV, iii, 22–8 (heaven, kiss, golden sun, morning, eye-beams), 60–9 (heavenly, eye, world, earthly, vapour, sun); *Richard II*, III, iii, 60–81 (earth, sun, clouds, glory, stain, eye, steal); *King John*, III, i, 77–80 (glorious sun, alchemist, splendour, eye, earth, gold); *1 Henry IV*, I, ii, 221–38 (sun, permit, base, clouds, smother, world, ugly mists, vapours, eyes); Sonnet 33 (glorious morning, eye, kissing, golden face, pale, alchemy, permit, basest clouds, ugly rack, world, stealing, sun, splendour, stain, heaven).

[2] *The Poems* (Cambridge, 1966), p. xxxv.

The other two Adonis sonnets, IV ('Sweet Cytherea, sitting by a brook') and IX ('Fair was the morn, when the fair queen of love'), are commonplace pieces of Elizabethan eroticism, and if they had not been included in *The Passionate Pilgrim* it is doubtful whether anyone would have thought of attributing them to Shakespeare. The evidence in favour of his authorship is of two types. First, both appear to be by the same author as VI and to have been written at the same time. None of the three refers to Venus by name; she is 'Cytherea' (IV and VI), 'beauty's queen' (IV), 'fair queen' (IV), 'this queen' (VI), 'the fair queen of love' (IX) and 'silly queen' (IX). 'Cytherea' is not found in *Venus and Adonis* but occurs in *The Taming of the Shrew, Cymbeline* and *The Winter's Tale*, whilst 'queen of love', 'fair queen' and 'queen' are all used of Venus in *Venus and Adonis*. Sonnets IV and VI have several rhymes in common: *brook, green, look, queen, eye, chastity* in IV and *brook, spleen, look, been, by, eye* in VI. Groups of Shakespeare's sonnets written at the same time are similarly linked by common rhymes, as in Sonnets 36–9, where the rhymes *spite, delight* occur in 36 and 37 and *sight, light* in 38, *twain, remain* and *one, alone* in 36 and 39, *give, live* in 37 and 39, and *thee, me* in all four. In both IV and IX there are resemblances of situation to VI; Cytherea and Adonis appear together by a brook in IV and VI, although in IV the brook is unnecessary to the story, and the structure of VI and IX is identical. Each opens with a reference to the beauty of the morning (compare the opening of *Venus and Adonis*), linked by 'when' with a description of the lovelorn Venus waiting for Adonis; VI begins a new quatrain with 'Anon he comes' and IX with 'Anon Adonis comes'; and each concludes in the final couplet with the escape of the embarrassed Adonis. Each begins with verbs in the past tense, shifts to the historic present and then reverts to the past tense. Both use the shortened form 'Adon',

which is also found twice in *Venus and Adonis* (lines 769, 1070). If VI is by Shakespeare, there is therefore a good case for attributing IV and IX to him as well.

The case is strengthened by several parallels between IV and IX and the canonical works. In IV Adonis is described as 'fresh and green'; the same adjectives, with a suggestion of youthful inexperience, are found together in 'How green you are and fresh in this old world!' (*King John*, III, iv, 145) and 'Since first I saw you fresh, which yet are green' (Sonnet 104, line 8), and Adonis speaks of himself as 'green' in *Venus and Adonis*, line 806. The image is continued in IV in a reference to his 'unripe years'. In *Venus and Adonis* Venus calls him 'unripe' (line 128), and he speaks of his 'unripe years' and compares himself to a green plum (lines 524–7). Venus is compared to an angler and Adonis to a young fish in both this stanza of *Venus and Adonis* ('No fisher but the ungrown fry forbears') and in the sonnet ('The tender nibbler would not touch the bait'). Adonis is said to be 'froward' in the sonnet, and the same adjective is applied to him indirectly in *Venus and Adonis*, line 570. There are also a number of links between IV and *The Taming of the Shrew*, apart from the Cytherea–Adonis–brook association; the former's use of 'lovely' in the sense of 'amorous' is paralleled in Shakespeare only in Petruchio's 'a lovely kiss' (III, ii, 125), and the rhyme *toward, froward*, with which IV concludes, occurs three times in the play but nowhere else in Shakespeare. The phrase 'steep-up hill' in IX recurs in 'the steep-up heavenly hill' in Sonnet 7, and there are traces in the former of what seems to be a Shakespearian image-cluster. In IX we find 'love', 'paler for sorow', 'milk-white', 'hounds' and 'wounds'; in *The Two Gentlemen of Verona*, III, i, 227–8, 250, 'whiteness', 'pale for woe', 'milk-white' and 'love'; in *A Midsummer Night's Dream*, II, i, 167, 'milk-white' and 'love's wound'; and in *Timon*,

I, ii, 188–95, 'love', 'milk-white' and grey-hounds'.

Before reaching any conclusion, it is necessary to examine the evidence for the theory that all four of the Adonis sonnets in *The Passionate Pilgrim* are by Griffin. The only links between VI, IX, and XI are the appearance of 'quoth she' in all three and the description of Adonis as a 'youngster' in IX and a 'youngling' in XI. There is evidently some connection, however, between IV and XI, in both of which Venus, sitting beside Adonis, makes advances to him in words and actions, which are cut short by his running away. What is odd is that the version of Griffin's sonnet in *Fidessa* is closer to IV than the *Passionate Pilgrim* text. Sonnet IV has 'beauty's queen', 'refused to take her figured proffer', 'offer', 'ran away' and 'fool'. Lines 9–12 of the *Fidessa* text, which are totally different from the corresponding quatrain in XI, are as follows:

> But he, a wayward boy, *refused her offer*
> And *ran away*, the *beauteous queen* neglecting,
> Showing both *folly* to abuse *her proffer*
> And all his sex of cowardice detecting.

None of these close parallels of phrase are found in XI. There are also some striking differences between XI and the other three sonnets. Sonnet XI, unlike the others, refers to Venus by that name and does not call her Cytherea or a queen. Four of the seven rhymes in XI (and five of those in the *Fidessa* version) are double ones; there are only two double rhymes in IV (including *proffer*, *offer*, which recurs in *Fidessa*) and none in VI or IX. Sonnets IV, VI and IX end with Adonis running away or jumping into the water in the closing couplet, and the poet's only comment on the situation is the final 'ah, fool too froward!' in IV. Adonis skips away in the eleventh line in XI and in the tenth in *Fidessa*, and the final couplet gives the story a personal application:

> Ah, that I had my lady at this bay
> To kiss and clip me till I run away!

These resemblances and differences seem to suggest that Griffin's sonnet, especially in the 1596 version, is a direct imitation of IV rather than the work of the same author. Sir Sidney Lee commented that in *Fidessa* 'Griffin was exceptionally bold in imitating home products, and borrowed much from Daniel and Drayton's recent volumes.'[1] It would hardly have been surprising if he had also borrowed from Shakespeare.

If IV, VI, and IX are Shakespeare's, they may help to solve the main problem of *Venus and Adonis*. The central theme of the poem, as of all four of the Adonis sonnets in *The Passionate Pilgrim*, is the contrast between Venus' passion and Adonis' frigidity, but in Ovid, although Venus takes the initiative, there is no suggestion that Adonis is unwilling to become her lover. His reluctance in Shakespeare's version, as has already been noted, is borrowed from the story of Hermaphroditus, but this fact does not explain how Shakespeare came to make him behave in a way completely contrary to the accepted tradition. The starting-point of the process, I suggest, was Spenser's treatment of the Venus and Adonis story in *The Faerie Queene* (book III, canto i, stanzas 34–8). Spenser is more outspoken than Ovid in his treatment of Adonis' relations with Venus; he twice refers to him as her 'paramoure', and states that she 'ioyd his loue in secret vnespyde'. But he also places the lovers in the same situation as Salmacis and Hermaphroditus:

> And whilest he bath'd, with her two crafty spyes,
> She secretly would search each daintie lim.

This passage probably suggested to Shakespeare that he should expand Spenser's brief narrative into a long poem, in one episode of which Venus would watch Adonis bathing, and as a rough sketch of how the incident might be treated he wrote the sonnet 'Scarce had the

---

[1] *The Cambridge History of English Literature* (Cambridge, 1908), III, 266.

sun...' We cannot strictly say that Adonis is represented as frigid in this sonnet; he does not reject Venus' advances, for she makes none, and his quick dive into the brook might be merely the result of surprise and embarrassment. The reference to his need to 'cool his spleen' is ambiguous, for Shakespeare uses 'spleen' to signify either sexual desire or hot temper. As a subject for a long poem, however, the story was unsatisfactory; the course of true love ran smooth, and the essential element of conflict was lacking. Ovid had solved the problem by inserting Venus' story of Atalanta between the lovers' wooing and Adonis' death. Spenser's depiction of Venus watching Adonis as Salmacis did Hermaphroditus suggested an alternative way of treating the theme; it would be paradoxical and amusing to make Adonis react to Venus' wooing as Hermaphroditus did to Salmacis'. A youth who snubbed a goddess, however ungentlemanly and unattractive, would at least be a more interesting hero than one who passively consented to become her stallion. After writing as an experiment two more sonnets in which Adonis rejects Venus, Shakespeare elaborated on the theme at length in *Venus and Adonis*, but on second thoughts omitted the bathing episode as too obvious an imitation of Ovid and Spenser.

It has sometimes been suggested that he borrowed the frigid Adonis from Marlowe's *Hero and Leander*, which describes how

> Venus in her naked glory strove
> To please the careless and disdainful eyes
> Of proud Adonis that before her lies.
>
> (I, 12–14)

This passage, together with the reference to 'rose-cheeked Adonis' in both poems (*Venus and Adonis*, line 3, *Hero and Leander*, I, 93), clearly suggests that there is some connection between the two, but it is much more likely that Marlowe was indebted to Shakespeare than Shakespeare to Marlowe. If Shakespeare was a member in 1592–3 of Pembroke's Men, who

performed *Edward II*, he must have known Marlowe personally at this time, and either might have seen the other's poem in manuscript. *Venus and Adonis*, a poem of 1,194 lines, was written before 18 April 1593, when it was entered on the Stationers' Company register; Marlowe left *Hero and Leander* unfinished, with only 818 lines written, when he died on 30 May. It seems reasonable to infer that Shakespeare's poem was not only completed but was also begun before Marlowe's. As Marlowe was clearly influenced by the *Henry VI* plays when he wrote *Edward II*, and *The Jew of Malta* may owe something to *Titus Andronicus*, he may well have written *Hero and Leander* in a third attempt to compete with Shakespeare.

After *Venus and Adonis* was printed there would have been no point in Shakespeare's publishing three much inferior sonnets on the same subject, mere shavings from his workshop. They doubtless circulated in manuscript among Southampton's circle and Shakespeare's literary friends, with whom their sophisticated eroticism made them popular. These Ovidian sonnets, and perhaps others of similar character now lost, rather than the more personal sonnets published in 1609, may have been the 'sugared sonnets among his private friends' which, together with *Venus and Adonis* and *Lucrece*, helped to persuade Francis Meres that 'the sweet witty soul of Ovid lives in mellifluous and honey-tongued Shakespeare'. Among those who saw them before 1596 was Griffin, who included an imitation of one of them in *Fidessa*. His theft from Shakespeare aroused unfavourable comment, and he rewrote his sonnet to make his plagiarism less apparent. We can thus arrange and date the poems under discussion in the following logical sequence: (1) the Venus and Adonis episode in *The Faerie Queene* (before 1590); (2) *Passionate Pilgrim*, VI (1592); (3) *Passionate Pilgrim*, IV and IX (1592); (4) *Venus and Adonis* (1592–3); (5) *Hero and Leander* (1593); (6) Griffin's

Fidessa sonnet (1592–6); (7) *Passionate Pilgrim*, XI (1596–9). Finally, copies of Shakespeare's three sonnets, two of the dark lady sonnets and the revised text of Griffin's sonnet fell into Jaggard's hands, and he put them together with three poems from *Love's Labour's Lost* (published in 1598) and other miscellaneous matter to make up *The Passionate Pilgrim*.

ORLANDO: ATHLETE OF VIRTUE

JOHN DOEBLER

That rebellious youth, Orlando, has apparently made *As You Like It* contemporary again. The mod musical-comedy[1] production of the play during the summer of 1969 in the Sylvan Theatre, Washington, D.C., drew crowds of the Colorful Generation. There is enough, especially at the beginning of the play, to explain why. Orlando's first speech is a shout of protest. He tells Adam, the old family servant, about exploitation by the 'older generation' in the person of an eldest brother. Ever since the death of their father Oliver has treated Orlando shamelessly, denying him a relevant education by setting him to mindless tasks. We suddenly know ourselves to be in the Renaissance rather than the twentieth century, however, when Orlando claims as the spring of his rebellion a noble spirit inherited from his father, not the superior moral sense of youth. The combination of blood and manhood – Orlando's beard is just beginning – make his servitude intolerable. His new personality is expressed dramatically in two decisive ways. After violently quarrelling with Oliver, Orlando leaves home. Later, a public declaration of manhood is the wrestling match with the lethal professional, Charles. Both statements are physical as well as verbal. In the quarrel Orlando seizes the throat of an insulting brother, and, of course, the actual contest follows the challenge to Charles. This stage image of the wrestling match is always a memorable part of the current theater experience of the play, but its interest is further

deepened if it is seen in the older context of Renaissance iconography.

Recall that the usurped Duke's daughter, Rosalind, encourages Orlando by invoking the classical prototype of strength: 'Now Hercules be thy speed, young man!' (I, ii, 222).[2] It is well known that Hercules stands for all that is manly and virtuous in innumerable emblems, epigrams, and allusions throughout the literature of Shakespeare's day.[3] Also familiar to students of the Renaissance is the encounter of Hercules with Antaeus, son of Neptune and Earth, one of the most commonly allegorized classical stories about this hero, just as the

---

[1] Peter Seng, *The Vocal Songs in the Plays of Shakespeare* (Cambridge, Mass., 1967), says that the elaborate use of song makes *As You Like It* the first of Shakespeare's 'musical comedies', followed by *Twelfth Night*, *The Winter's Tale*, and *The Tempest* (p. 76).

[2] All quotations from *As You Like It* are from *The Complete Works of Shakespeare*, edited by Hardin Craig (Chicago, 1951).

[3] In Stephen Batman's description of the classical deities as moral allegories in their appearance and attributes, we see the meaning the innumerable representations of Hercules in art could have for the Renaissance: 'Hercules apparayled in a Lions skinne, signyfyth the valiant courage of a woorthy Captyne, also the Prudencie wherewith his mind beinge furnished, he subdued his outrageous affections: the Club, signifieth understanding, throughe which the motions of wicked affections are repressed and vtterly vanquished. *Hercules* was...a Prince of worthye Fame, a mainteiner of Vertue, and a punisher of Vice, such a one as hated those that chose to steal by policye, rather than to win by prowesse.' – *The Golden Booke of the Leaden Goddes* (London, 1577), sig. C4r-v.

theme of Hercules at the Crossroads is the commonplace of the later accretions.[1] The way the Renaissance read the Antaeus story, Hercules (virtue) won victory over the giant Antaeus (vice) by lifting him out of contact with his mother Earth (the base passions).[2] It is easy to see why Hercules and Antaeus were a popular subject of free-standing bronzes, the ideal medium for the expression of power and movement (see Plate VIB).[3] But before Hercules discovered the secret of Antaeus' strength, the giant renewed himself every time he was thrown to the ground, where his mother filled his entire body with vital energy. In other words, the soul must wrench the body away from base desires before eternal victory can be achieved. Shakespeare, of course, is writing a play, not a sermon, and the associations are very lightly handled, kept very subliminal.[4] Indeed, the relationship between 'Antaeus' and the earth is even displaced, for it is Charles who boasts to Orlando: 'Come, where is this young gallant that is so desirous to lie with his mother earth?' (I, ii, 212–13).[5] Finally, just before the

the original source of the interpretation 'of Hercules' victory over Antaeus as the conquest of fleshly lust' (p. 295). For the details of the original classical body of myth, see Robert Graves, *The Greek Myths*, 2 vols. (London, 1955), II, 146–7.

[3] These bronzes were often small, designed to grace the desk of the humanist connoisseur, whether scholar or prince, just as the skull had been introduced as an object of meditation in an earlier century. The theme of the triumph of the soul over the body, however, remained the same. For illustrations and commentary, see John Pope-Hennessy, *Renaissance Bronzes from the Samuel H. Kress Collection* (London, 1965), passim; and his *Italian Renaissance Sculpture* (New York, 1958), Plate 90 (Pollaiuolo) and Figure 142 (Antico). The exquisite rendering by Francesco de Sant' Agata, in the Widener Collection (Plate VI B here) is illustrated on pp. 133–5 of Charles Seymour, Jr, *Masterpieces of Sculpture from the National Gallery of Art* (New York, 1949), commentary, p. 181. This last example is of the Paduan School, first half of the sixteenth century.

[4] Richard Knowles has written an important article on the parallels between *As You Like It* and, among other things, the story of Hercules and Antaeus: 'Myth and Type in *As You Like It*', *ELH*, XXXIII (1966), 1–22.

That not all wrestling matches with allegorical implications are handled in so subliminal a way in the English Renaissance, however, is to be seen from a painted *Allegory* (1571), by Joris Hoefnagel. Two headless nude men struggle before an audience of Elizabethan courtiers in the countryside outside Windsor. According to the commentary published along with the painting in 1926, the wrestlers represent brute force and fraud: *Catalogue of an Exhibition of Late Elizabethan Art* (Burlington Fine Arts Club). A Renaissance Italian sculpture by Vincenzo Danti (1530–76), titled *Honor Triumphant over Falsehood*, shows two nude athletes, illustrated in John Pope-Hennessy, *Italian High Renaissance and Baroque Sculpture*, 3 vols. (London, 1963), Plates, 77. According to his contemporary Vasari, Danti carved this marble sculpture after failing to produce a bronze group of Hercules and Antaeus (Catalogue, p. 78).

[5] As for Shakespeare's familiarity with the classical mythology to be found in Renaissance dictionaries, see DeWitt T. Starnes and Ernest William Talbert, *Classical Myth and Legend in Renaissance Dictionaries* (Chapel Hill, 1955), esp. Chap. v, 'Shakespeare and the Dictionaries', pp. 111–34. On pp. 113–14, Starnes and Talbert offer persuasive arguments to suggest that Shakespeare drew on Thomas Cooper's Latin–English *Thesaurus* (London), which went through five editions,

[1] The allegory of Hercules at the Crossroads was familiar to Renaissance England through several sources described by Hallett Smith, *Elizabethan Poetry* (Cambridge, Mass., 1952), pp. 293–303. Most outstanding is Cicero, *De Officiis*, trans. Nicholas Grimald as *Three Books of Duties to Marcus his Sonne* (London, 1596), bk I, fol. 51v–52r. The above is just one of the many editions in which this famous passage may be found. Nine were printed between 1553 and 1600. Another important source is Richard Lynche's partial translation of Vincenzo Cartari's *Le Imagini de i' Dei* (Venice, 1580), called *The Fountain of Ancient Fiction* (London, 1599), STC 4691, sig. T2r-v. For a listing of pictorial representations of this famous theme in the Renaissance as well as a description of the moral allegory, see Guy de Tervarent, *Attributs et Symbols dans L'Art Profane: 1450–1600* (Geneva, 1958), cols. 209–10.

[2] Thomas Wilson, *The Arte of Rhetorique* (London, 1584), saw all of Hercules' labors in this way: 'What other thyng are the wonderfull labours of Hercules, but that reason should withstand affection, and the spirit for ever should fight against the fleshe' (p. 199). Smith cites the medieval mythographer Fulgentius as

Duke's wrestler is thrown by Orlando, Celia wishes she were Jove: 'If I had a thunderbolt in mine eye, I can tell who should down' (I, ii, 226–7), thus reinforcing the classical context.

As in the case of so many details in his plays, Shakespeare is both carrying over and changing material in one of his sources,[1] the major one, *Rosalynde: Euphues Golden Legacie* (1590), by Thomas Lodge. There the lovers merely exchanged burning looks before the contest; thus, instead of Rosalind's invoking Hercules to assist Orlando, Lodge introduces the classical allusion before anyone accepts the open invitation to fight the awesome wrestler known only as 'the Norman': 'the *Norman* presented himselfe as a chalenger against all commers; but he looked like *Hercules* when he advaunst himselfe against *Acheloüs*: so that the furie of his countenance amased all that durst attempt to incounter with him...'[2] Shakespeare has applied the strength of Hercules to Orlando instead of Charles and deleted the allusion to the labor of Hercules in which he overcomes the river Achelous. It is usually safe to assume that Shakespeare's changes are made for a reason, and the reason in this case is one that may very well have originated in his imagined understanding of the visual effect of this scene in production.

The source is quite specific about the actual wrestling. Entering the lists, Orlando's original, Rosader, is so taken by his first glimpse of Rosalind that the Norman

drave him out of his *memento* with a shake by the shoulder; *Rosader* looking back with an angrie frowne...discovered to all by the furie of his countenance that he was a man of some high thoughts... [Rosader] roughlie clapt to him with so fierce an incounter, that they both fell to the ground, and with the violence of the fall were forced to breathe: in which space the *Norman* called to minde...that this was hee whom *Saladyne* [Oliver] had appoynted him to kil; which conjecture made him stretch everie limb, & trie everie sinew...On the contrarie part, *Rosader* while he breathed was not idle, but still cast his eye uppon *Rosalynd*, who...lent him such an amorous

looke, as might have made the most coward desperate: which glance of *Rosalynd* so fiered the passionate desires of *Rosader*, that turning to the *Norman* hee ran upon him and braved him with a strong encounter; the *Norman* received him as valiantly, that there was a sore combat, hard to judge on whose side fortune would be prodigall. At last *Rosader*...roused himselfe and threw the Norman against the ground, falling upon his chest with so willing a waight, that the *Norman* yeelded nature her due, and *Rosader* the victorie.[3]

We can only guess, however, at how a contemporary production of *As You Like It* might have shown the wrestling match. The dress of Elizabethan wrestlers, for instance, is suggested by one of the standard wood-cuts illustrating the 1577 edition of Holinshed's *Chronicles*.[4] Outer clothes are cast aside in the lower right-hand corner, for the sake of loin cloths and harnesses, while the spectators are dressed in the conventional manner of the late sixteenth century. As for what Shakespeare intended his wrestlers to do on stage, the original First Folio directions provide no more than a 'Wrestle' at the beginning and three lines later a 'Shout' when Charles is thrown. The usurping Duke thereupon commands, 'No more, no more!' and a few lines later says, 'Bear him away', after it is seen that the former champion can no

the last in 1587, for his knowledge of the Hercules–Antaeus myth. The battle is described under the heading of *Antheus* in the first edition, printed in 1565 (*Dictionarium*, sig. B5r).

[1] See the Arden edition of *As You Like It* for a thorough discussion of the larger changes, and Marco Mincoff, 'What Shakespeare Did to Rosalynd', *Shakespeare-Jahrbuch*, 96 (1960), 78–89.

[2] Geoffrey Bullough, *Narrative and Dramatic Sources of Shakespeare*, 6 vols. (London, 1957–66), II (*The Comedies: 1597–1603*), 170.

[3] *Ibid.*, p. 171.

[4] Shakespeare is known to have consulted the unillustrated edition of 1587, but this edition he might have seen as well. The wood-cut, like most of the rest, is used more than once, to accompany the account of a match between Corineus and Gogmagog, a giant, in the time of Brute ('The History of England', p. 15); and again to illustrate the reign of King Ewin, who instructed the youth to keep fit by wrestling ('History of Scotland', p. 23).

longer even speak. Although the source made it clear that the Norman was dead, Shakespeare, no doubt lightening the tone, provides us with no further information about him. The question of what exactly occurred on the stage at the play's first production will probably always remain a mystery, but we do have a record of a theatrically successful handling of this match in a way consistent with the Hercules and Antaeus episode, at a time when the symbolic details of that myth would probably have been entirely forgotten.[1] In 1883 Godfrey Turner reported that he had seen the wrestling match in *As You Like It* done successfully on only two occasions, one of them at Sadler's Wells:

Marston, a Lancashire lad, wrestled superbly and was as agile as a cat...[He] allowed himself to be caught up by Charles so as to lean over the wrestler's shoulder, while his own feet, being lifted clear above the ground were coiled round the giant's firmly planted leg. For a few moments the statuesque position was retained; and then just as Orlando appeared in utmost peril of being thrown, he suddenly regained his footing, reversed the situation, cross-buttocked Charles, and flung him heavily to earth.[2]

This description is consistent with both the little information provided by the first publication of the play in the Folio of 1623 and with the many Renaissance representations of Hercules subduing Antaeus. The Sadler's Wells production has first Orlando and then Charles lifted 'clear above the ground', as in Hercules' legendary defeat of the son of Earth, and then the professional flung to the ground, as implied in the comments made about the defeated Charles, when the Duke orders the speechless wrestler borne away. The only details needed to complete the traditional image of Hercules and Antaeus would be two revivals of Charles after being pinned to the earth by Orlando, before the final lifting of Charles above the ground, his subsequent exhaustion, and the flinging of him to the stage. All of this would call for a very muscular adolescent in Shakespeare's acting company to play the part of Orlando, if

the appearance of Charles is to be convincing as well, but youthful weightlifters were probably as available then as now.

The Herculean pattern in *As You Like It* is completed by Orlando's last 'labor',[3] his defeat of the lioness menacing his unnatural brother in the forest. Hercules and the Nemean Lion, which he strangled with his bare hands, was a very popular subject during the Renaissance, bearing as it did the parallel of the lion which is the Beast of Revelation, a familiar hell mouth second only to the whale and the cauldron as a medieval symbol of the evil forces defeated by Christ in the Harrowing of Hell.[4] Once again Shakespeare has made small

[1] That the associations must have been forgotten or thought totally unimportant as early as 1723 is illustrated by an 'improvement' of the play written by Charles Johnson and staged at Drury Lane in that year. A duel with rapiers is substituted for the wrestling match, presumably in order to fit the dignity and social standing of Orlando. Cited by O. J. Campbell, *The Reader's Encyclopedia of Shakespeare* (New York, 1966), p. 43.

[2] Quoted by Arthur Colby Sprague, *Shakespeare and the Actors* (Cambridge, Mass., 1944), p. 32.

[3] The Labors of Hercules, both the originally codified twelve and later accretions, are still well-known, but the Renaissance artist found them endlessly stimulating. Michaelangelo's pastel drawing of three of them (the Nemean Lion, Antaeus, and the Hydra), at the Royal Library, Windsor, is justly famous. It is illustrated in Mario Salmi *et al.*, *The Complete Works of Michaelangelo*, 2 vols. (London, 1966), II, 464. But they appear in innumerable commonplace and artistically insignificant places as well. See, for instance, *The Psalter* (London, 1594), STC 16318, where a capital letter 'B' shows Hercules battling the Hydra.

[4] Hercules as the type of Christ is elaborated by Knowles, 'Myth and Type in *As You Like It*', pp. 14–18, as part of the pattern of Christian symbolism he sees in the play. He cites a passage in Raleigh's *The History of the World* (London, 1614) where Hercules' descent into the underworld to capture Cerberus is paralleled to Christ's Harrowing of Hell. In *Paradise Regained* (IV, 562–8) Milton saw, as did Spenser in *The Faerie Queene* (II, xi, 34.6–46.9), the parallel of Christ's overthrow of Satan on the third day and Hercules' defeat of Antaeus at the third attempt. Endless examples of these parallels in England and on the continent can be cited. Most famous to the

and significant changes in his source. The emblematic character of the events reported by Oliver is established by the addition of a serpent coiled around the sleeping brother's neck, about to crawl into his mouth, when Orlando approaches and frightens the creature off into the underbrush.[1] This is the brother whose words have been so unjust, about to receive just punishment, but Orlando cannot enjoy his revenge by simply standing by. He must perform the natural offices of a brother, according to the Renaissance Cordelian 'bond'. The Rosader of the source carried a boar spear with which he assailed the hungry lion awaiting the awakening of Orlando's sibling enemy. Shakespeare, however, makes no mention of a weapon in the events reported by Oliver, the boar spear having been appropriated to the costume of Rosalind disguised as Ganymede. Orlando apparently, like Hercules, kills the lion with his bare hands, receiving a wound in the arm, rather than in the breast as described in Lodge's *Rosalynde*.

It is interesting to note that Shakespeare has this second Hercules parallel reported, while showing the first on stage. Clearly, it is more difficult to stage the frightening of a snake and the strangulation of a lion than a wrestling match, but Shakespeare is also a playwright capable of that most famous of all stage directions: *Exit, pursued by a bear*, when he really wants to convey a sense of romantic amazement. We should at least consider the possibility of Shakespeare wanting to place a special emphasis upon the wrestling match, making it a thematic introduction to the role he had outlined for Orlando.

In 'The Athlete of Virtue: The Iconography of Asceticism',[2] Colin Eisler establishes the iconography of the victorious athlete, 'one of the oldest and most powerful symbols of the triumph of virtue in Western culture'.[3] Athletic contests in ancient Greece were supposedly started by Hercules, and thus physical strength and beauty were accepted as signs of divine favor, in turn sustained and earned by the efforts of gymnastic training. Exercise, the practise of order and control, represented constant striving after divine acceptance, a ceaseless struggle for virtuous self-discipline against the temptation of relaxed abandonment to evil and decay, moral and physical.[4] This ideal, endorsed by most Greek philosophy and, of course, still alive in this century, was adopted early by Christian theology. The most important events in the early centuries of the Church were the martyrdoms of Christians in the arena and stadium.[5] Thus the classical image of virtue found a context in the new religion. Peter Damiani, for instance, describes the eleventh-century Monastery of Cluny as a 'spiritual gymnasium'.[6] In earlier centuries an elaborate typology had been worked out. The Greek Father, Saint Chrysostom, 'refers to David frequently as a splendid example of divinely sustained strength, a wrestler who rallies after having received great bodily harm'.[7] Indeed, Bullough, without mentioning the tradition, also hears the Biblical echoes that would have risen to the mind of a Renaissance audience, when, in commenting on the sources of *As You Like It*, he says: 'In Shakespeare and *Gamelyn* the hero is taunted by the wrestler, who in Lodge merely takes him by the shoulder. But the taunting is more dramatic and brings out the David-Goliath element in the encounter'.[8]

Renaissance was Pierre de Ronsard's poem on the Christianized Hercules: *Hercule Chretien*.

[1] Knowles sees another Hercules allusion in this detail: 'This fabulous event is an added reminder of the Hercules whose cradle game...was strangling snakes sent by Hera' (p. 5).

[2] *De Artibus Opuscula XL: Essays in Honor of Irwin Panofsky*, ed. Millard Meiss, 2 vols. (New York, 1961), I, 82–97.   [3] *Ibid.*, p. 82.

[4] *Ibid.*   [5] *Ibid.*, p. 84.

[6] *Ibid.*, p. 85.   [7] *Ibid.*, p. 86.

[8] Bullough, *Narrative and Dramatic Sources*, II, 148.

It is no wonder that the religiously-conscious Renaissance is full of paintings, graphics, and sculptures representing a nude, athletically-built hero – especially Hercules or David – overcoming the forces of evil. The bronze *David* cast by Donatello in mid-fifteenth-century Florence is justly famous (see Plate VIA).[1] Surprisingly, this masterpiece also helps us to draw together the various elements combined by Shakespeare in *As You Like It*. The iconography of the statue has puzzled many art historians by its seeming eclecticism; the combination, for instance, of a nude athlete with a bucolic hat, worn in the fourteenth and fifteenth century for hunting and travel.[2] Eclecticism, however, is what delighted Renaissance man the most: the true relatedness of the seemingly unrelated, revealed to the beholder in a moment of intuitive insight by visual means,[3] a concept controlling a great deal of what we know about late Renaissance imagery.

Donatello's David, just entering manhood,[4] stands with one foot on the severed head of Goliath, foreshadowing Christ, the Second Adam, who as Son of Man will bruise the serpent's head with his heel and defeat the sin that defeated the First Adam.[5] David, stripped for the contest of Faith as the Greek athletes stripped for the gymnasium, is clothed merely in the boots of the warrior and the hat of the rustic. He thus combines many ideals: the nude athlete, Christ, David as the 'Hercules' of the Old Testament, the Christian warrior wearing the Pauline armor of God, the Arcadian Natural Man uncorrupted by exposure to the City of Man, and, ultimately, Virtue itself, triumphant over evil. The bucolic hat, betasseled and beribboned, and suggesting David the Shepherd as a Biblical Arcadian who foreshadows Christ the Good Shepherd, is wreathed in triumphant laurel. Another laurel wreath is at the base of the statue. The generalized Triumph depicted in Goliath's visor is probably an ironic comment by the sculptor.

The successful giants of this world can be defeated by mere boys with hearts divinely inspired.[6] The 'live' wings on Goliath's helmet

[1] For some curious reason, perhaps because Michaelangelo's genius cut off all further comment, David is the subject of only three statues in the Italian Renaissance, those by Donotello, Verrocchio, and Michaelangelo. The differences are a perfect insight into the full range of Renaissance art, from iconography, to literalism, to psychological realism. A baroque concluding statement is made by Bernini's *David* (1623), in the Galleria Borghese, Rome.

[2] H. W. Janson, *The Sculpture of Donatello*, 2 vols. (Princeton, 1957), is the established authority: 'We find ourselves confronted...with the enigmatic qualities of the statue. What message was it meant to convey to the beholder? That it did have a message we can hardly doubt; otherwise why all the puzzling details? But the context into which these features can be fitted continues to elude us' (II, 84). He finally tentatively accounts for these 'puzzling details' by documenting Donatello's contemporary reputation as a homosexual. Are the details then fetishes? Pope-Hennessy, however, *Italian Renaissance Sculpture*, restored the balance even though leaving the subject a mystery: 'An attempt [Janson] to relate the iconography to Donatello's presumed homosexuality is an *ex post facto* interpretation which throws no light on the original intentions of the artist' (p. 285).

[3] Edgar Wind, *Bellini's 'Feast of the Gods'* (Cambridge, Mass., 1948), cites this Renaissance mode of thought: 'Down to...minor details Mantegna's picture demonstrates the union of contraries – that great commonplace of Renaissance thought which pervades Cusanus' *Docta Ignorantia* as it does Politan's *Panepistemon*...' (p. 13).

[4] Both David and Hercules have been equated in the Renaissance mind with the issues confronting the boy turning into a man, like Orlando, whose beard has just begun to grow. Hercules as a very young man is usually associated with the crossroad during adolescence of self-discipline or self-gratification. A topical variant is that of *Massimiliano Sforza at the Crossroads*, illustrated in Andre Chastél, *The Age of Humanism* (London, 1963), Plate VII. Here the subject is clothed and very young indeed, though the allusion is to the nude and muscular Hercules usually represented.

[5] David, like Hercules, was a common type of Christ, but with the added advantage of centuries of Biblical typology. See *The Oxford Dictionary of the Christian Church*, ed. F. L. Cross (London, 1957), pp. 374–5.

[6] The gist of an emblem of David and Goliath, with motto *Quid Immania Corpora Possunt*, cited in

may recall a common Teutonic motif of battle dress, thus suggesting to Italians such as Machiavelli a barbarian invasion of civilization, but the context suggests instead the Philistine as a type of the fallen angel Satan, for wings always identified an angel, just as the stone held in the victor's hand identify him as the Biblical hero of the slingshot.

Orlando, too, is adolescent. He, too, defeats a giant, finds sanctuary in the wilderness, where he leads a bucolic life, and finally comes to represent all that is virtuous in opposition to all that is corrupt. The conflation of the athlete and the Arcadian, both drawn from the Golden Age of classical civilization, is the essential connection relating the seemingly disparate elements of *As You Like It*. Previous scholarship and criticism of this play have put the emphasis one way or another, on the pastoral[1] or on the mythological, just as the art historians have seen no traditional continuity in David's bucolic hat and his nudity. There is, of course, no ultimate conflict between seemingly disparate elements in either the statue or the play, quite the contrary.

Emblemata, ed. Arthur Henkel and Albrecht Schöne (Stuttgart, 1967), col. 1,850.

[1] The excesses of the pastoral school have been succinctly characterized by Harold Jenkins, '*As You Like It*', *Shakespeare Survey 8* (Cambridge, 1955): '*As You Like It* has been too often praised for its idyllic quality alone, as though it were some mere May-morning frolic prolonged into a lotos-eating afternoon' (p. 43). Mincoff points out that in comparison to his source Shakespeare has softened the violence, the cruelty, *and* the pastoralism.

THE UNFOLDING OF
'MEASURE FOR MEASURE'

JAMES BLACK

The 'bed-trick' in *Measure for Measure* has always caused embarrassment of one sort or another. 'This thing of darkness' must be acknowledged, but no critic has managed to assimilate the device fully into his view of the play or quite been able to come to terms with what has seemed to be an 'incompatibility of the intrigues of comedy with the tone of what has gone before'.[1] Schucking was offended by its employment: 'It is astonishing to see with how little self-esteem [Shakespeare credits a woman] here';[2] so was Brander Matthews: 'The artifice itself is unlovely, and it cannot be made acceptable';[3] and so was Quiller-Couch: '[Isabella] is all for saving her own soul...by turning...into a bare procuress.'[4] Apologists claim that in adding this detail to what he carried over from his source and using it to preserve the heroine's chastity Shakespeare thereby made more gentle 'one of the quite horrible situations of the [older] drama'[5] and prevented a forced marriage between Isabella and Angelo.[6] W. W. Lawrence, going outside the play for a justification, asserts that Shakespeare's audiences would have seen nothing wrong with this kind of marriage-device,[7] and G. K. Hunter has adduced an example from real life.[8] But to his impressive marshalling of sources and analogues incorporating bed-tricks Lawrence still adds a slightly uneasy rhetorical flourish: 'Would Shakespeare...have made the ensky'd and sainted Isabella, the gentle forsaken Mariana, and the benevolent Duke use [this] stratagem if he had felt it repugnant

to modesty?'[9] And Hunter's observation on *All's Well* has equal application to *Measure for Measure*: 'the Christian and gnomic overtones of the play...seem to raise issues which cannot easily be resolved by plot-manipulation'.[10] The Arden editor of *Measure for Measure*, though he draws on Hunter's *All's Well* essay, seems to have turned away from these issues: in justifying the bed-trick as strictly within the bounds of legality he disposes of a case, not of the human situation.[11]

Thus the explanations of the bed-trick have mainly been negative ones – Mariana and her accomplices and Shakespeare have done nothing unusual or strictly wrong. Although 'we are meant to approve not only of the Duke's stratagem, but of Mariana's, and even Isabel's,

[1] Philip Edwards, *Shakespeare and the Confines of Art* (London, 1968), p. 118.
[2] L. L. Schucking, *Character Problems in Shakespeare's Plays* (London, 1922), p. 197.
[3] *Shakespeare as a Playwright* (New York, 1913), p. 227.
[4] The New Cambridge Shakespeare *Measure for Measure* (Cambridge, 1922), p. xxx.
[5] R. W. Chambers, 'Measure for Measure', in Anne Ridler (ed.), *Shakespeare Criticism 1935–60* (London, 1963), p. 4.
[6] Ernest Schanzer, *The Problem Plays of Shakespeare* (London, 1963), p. 109.
[7] *Shakespeare's Problem Comedies* (New York, 1960), pp. 38, 83.
[8] The Arden Shakespeare *All's Well that Ends Well* (London, 1959), p. xliv.
[9] *Shakespeare's Problem Comedies*, p. 51.
[10] The Arden *All's Well*, p. xliv.
[11] The Arden Shakespeare *Measure for Measure* (London, 1965), pp. li–lv.

part in it', says Mary Lascelles, the employment of this convention, if it is not justified, can leave us with 'a deep and corroding discontent'. She believes that Shakespeare probably intended, before the end of the play, to offer more justification, but 'considerable items are overlooked and forgotten as he presses on to his consummation. There is, for example, Isabel's behaviour in furthering... Mariana's unpropitious marriage... There is the Duke's behaviour in promoting the affair... These anomalies remain.'[1]

My own approach to *Measure for Measure* is going to be from the point of view that Shakespeare did not simply forget to justify his use of the bed-trick device, nor did he adopt in this play a policy of 'never apologise, never explain'. I believe that he intended the play as it stands (textual corruptions aside) to convey the sense that Mariana in sleeping with Angelo has done something right, and that the play turns upon the positive virtue of her action.

Measure for Measure is set largely in a series of places of confinement or retreat. Claudio is under the strict restraint of prison, as are Barnardine and, to a lesser extent, Pompey. Julietta also is in prison and the late stages of pregnancy, and much of the action takes place in the gaol, where, as A. P. Rossiter has observed, 'the worlds of Mrs. Overdone and Pompey, of Claudio and Julietta, and of Isabella and Angelo all meet'.[2] Escalus and Angelo try Pompey, and Isabella and Angelo face one another, in antechambers to this prison. There also is the St Clare nunnery, on whose threshold we first encounter Isabella. The ethos of this place is conveyed only through the quoting of a single rule, but it is a curious either-or prescription whose terms compel notice:

When you have vow'd, you must not speak with men
But in the presence of the prioress;
Then, if you speak, you must not show your face;
Or if you show your face, you must not speak.
(I, iv, 10–13)

Though Isabella never completes this vow there is no doubt that she has prescribed for herself an ideal kind of nunnery whose rules transcend in strictness those of the actual sisterhood. These rules she wishes for herself, and it appears she would extend them to others as well:

I speak not as desiring more [privileges],
But rather wishing a more strict restraint
Upon the sisters stood, the votarists of St. Clare.
(I, iv, 3–5)

Isabella is not alone in wishing to impose her self-restraints upon others. Angelo would do this as well though his application of the law, of which he is not just a representative but the actual embodiment, for 'Mortality and mercy in Vienna Live in [his] tongue, and heart' (I, i, 44–5). His self-restraint is famous, and of choice, and he soon reveals an awareness that it is something he has imposed upon his nature. He uses the disguise words 'case', 'habit' and 'seeming' for the formality he wears (II, iv, 12–15), appears to affect gravity as energetically as Lucio claims to affect flippancy, and indeed at a moment of intense self-awareness conveys that he might just as easily exchange his austereness for Lucio's kind of demeanour:

Angelo.   Yea, my gravity,
Wherein – let no man hear me – I take pride,
Could I with boot change for an idle plume
Which the air beats for vain   (II, iv, 9–12)

Lucio.   'Tis my familiar sin,
With maids to seem the lapwing, and to jest
Tongue far from heart.   (I, iv, 31–3)

Angelo has adopted gravity as his role, and over the years has carefully built a *persona*, persuading the world – and himself – of 'a kind of character in [his] life' (I, i, 27). His reading of the law has been and is closely tied up with his creation of this character, as is suggested in his reference to 'the state whereon

[1] *Shakespeare's 'Measure for Measure'* (London, 1953). See pp. 121, 137 and 163.
[2] *Angel With Horns* (London, 1961), p. 156.

I studied' (II, iv, 7). The setting through which he moves – we may as well call it the court-room – is dominated by this *persona*, for, as the play never lets us forget, the law exists as it is applied and as it begins to be applied to Vienna it takes on the peculiar stamp of Angelo's repressive character. Thus his courtroom and his very presence stand, like the nunnery of Isabella's ideal, for 'a more strict restraint'.

Within his carapace of legal interpretation Angelo feels protected by the abstract generality of law from having to make difficult personal or human decisions. 'Pretending in [Mariana] discoveries of dishonour', he has been able to make himself 'a marble to her tears, [be] washed with them, but [relent] not' (III, i, 226–30); and thereby has dismissed Mariana to her unique place of confinement, the moated grange. With Isabella he soon adopts a Pilate-like dissociation of himself from the law's supposedly necessary course:

> Your brother is a forfeit of the law...
> It is the law, not I, condemn your brother...
> The law hath not been dead, though it hath slept.
> (II, ii, 71, 80, 91)

This self-preserving technique might be allow-able if adopted only here, in the difficult situation of a sister's pleading for her con-demned brother. But Angelo also uses it in much less pressing circumstances, telling Escalus that no exception may be made for Claudio:

> What's open made to justice
> That justice seizes. (II, i, 21–2)

In considering this case, both with Escalus and Isabella, Angelo heads unerringly for the safe ground of abstract theory. Asked by Escalus to reflect whether he himself might not have erred like Claudio given Claudio's opportunity, he swiftly renders the idea merely academic:

> I not deny
> The jury passing on the prisoner's life
> May in the sworn twelve have a thief, or two,
> Guiltier than him they try. (II, i, 18–21)

And there is a debater's relish in his parrying of Isabella's opening move, which is itself academic:

Isabella.
> I have a brother is condemn'd to die;
> I do beseech you, let it be his fault,
> And not my brother...

Angelo.
> Condemn the fault, and not the actor of it?
> Why, every fault's condemn'd ere it be done
> (II, ii, 34ff.)

These exchanges make clear Angelo's stead-fast refusal to be lured out of the narrowest interpretation of the law, which he will consider only in the letter or theory and not as it personally affects others or himself. His answer to Escalus, ''Tis one thing to be tempted...another thing to fall' (II, i, 17–18) is an academic disposition of an hypothesis, as he has not yet been tempted to his own limits. He is embarrassed and impatient when Isabella insists upon his personal response in Claudio's case:

Angelo.
> I will not [pardon him].

Isabella.
> But can you if you would?

Angelo.
> Look, what I will not, that I cannot do.
> (II, ii, 51–2)

Clearly, in his use of the law he does not *want* room for manoeuvre. The inflexible statute, the irreversible sequence of procedure ('He's sentenc'd, 'tis too late' II, ii, 55), the judge's anonymity (Escalus never addresses him by name while discussing this case, and Isabella calls him Angelo for the first time only when his carnal intentions are clear to her, II, iv, 150) – all of these conventions shield him from the necessity of taking decisions on individual circumstances. In sum, he is as circumscribed and secure in the law as Isabella in her ideal nunnery. And we scarcely need Angelo's admission that he takes pride in his gravity to make us see that these two people, each bounded in his or her chosen nutshell, count themselves kings of infinite space.

But there is no suppressing what is for them the bad dream of sexuality.[1] It breaks through just where Angelo has every expectation of security: a courtroom, a legal debate, the appellant a religious novice. All that passes between them is words, which Angelo always has been able to use to bind with or hide in. While words hold to the meanings their users intend, so long as Angelo can positively label and anathematise 'these filthy vices' in others, and so long as 'be tempted' keeps its proper distance from 'to fall', his legalistic enclosure is secure. Very early in the play, however, it is shown that words are very shaky foundations upon which to build a system of absolute law. The trial of Pompey in II, i degenerates into farce because of the way language lends itself to misuse. The continual malapropisms of Elbow, the prosecuting officer, undermine the dignity of these proceedings from the beginning; and no sooner have the judges Escalus and Angelo attuned their ears to his 'misplacings' than Pompey offers his side of the case in a run of bawdy equivocations, giving hilariously suggestive connotations to the most innocent-seeming words.[2] Escalus eventually begins rather to enjoy the travesty, but Angelo sharply tries to direct the proceedings back on the rails. He impatiently shrugs off Escalus' tolerant bemusement, grills Elbow, and rounds fiercely on Pompey:

Escalus. [*to Angelo*] This comes off well: here's a
    wise officer.
Angelo. Go to. What quality are they of? Elbow is
    your name? Why dost thou not speak,
    Elbow?
Pompey. He cannot, sir: he's out at elbow.
Angelo. What are you, sir?   (II, i, 57–61)

Escalus hereafter tries to keep the quibbling Pompey to strict meanings, but in vain, and Angelo at last loses patience and departs. Escalus eventually lets Pompey off with a warning: in the fog of equivocation he scarcely can do otherwise.

It is difficult to credit Ernest Schanzer's explanation of this scene as having 'been introduced mainly to show the ideal judge at work',[3] for the scene demonstrates the sheer impossibility of judging when neither prosecutor nor defendant can or will stay within the logical bounds of words where law can work. 'As their testimonies unfold through a haze of "misplacings" and irrelevancies', says J. W. Lever, 'time, place and all ethical distinctions lose their contours. "Justice" represented by Elbow, and "Iniquity" by Pompey, seem interchangeable and equally meaningless.'[4] The scene suggests that it is impossible to apply – or to take refuge in – the letter of the law when letters themselves will not yield to organisation or discipline.

In this trial of Pompey the tone also is set for the scene which follows, where in an antechamber to the courtroom Angelo hears Isabella appeal on Claudio's behalf and where despite the terrible gravity of the occasion words soon again begin to veer into equivocation and suggestiveness. Isabella 'speaks, and 'tis such sense That [Angelo's] sense breeds with it' (II, ii, 142–3). He has just come from a courtroom where *double-entendre* reigned, and now, approached by a beautiful girl whose intellect itself stimulates him, and who directs his attention to his own human frailty –

> Go to your bosom,
> Knock there, and ask your heart what it doth know
> That's like my brother's fault –   (II, ii, 137–9)

he finds his legal world of words unbalanced and betraying, his security threatened. Misconstruction follows misconstruction in a run of the kind in which one verbal slip is compounded by another as the speaker continues

---

[1] Claudio 'hath but as offended in a dream', II, ii, 4. And see *Hamlet*, II, ii, 260–2.
[2] See J. W. Lever's Arden Edition notes on II, i, 88–112.
[3] *The Problem Plays of Shakespeare*, p. 116.
[4] The Arden *Measure for Measure*, pp. lxvi–lxvii.

unaware or even as he tries to correct the impression – as when Samuel Johnson, having unwittingly caused mirth by the solemn pronouncement that a woman had 'a bottom of good sense', tried to retrieve the situation by adding that he meant she was 'fundamentally sound'.[1] 'O perilous mouths,...Hooking both right and wrong to th'appetite' (II, iv, 171–6), Isabella will cry in dismay when she fully understands Angelo's drift. Meantime, ignorant of any sensual coloration in her words, or of his alertness thereto, she says 'Heaven keep your honour safe' and 'save your honour' ('From thee', responds Angelo under his breath, II, ii, 162), and tells him 'I am come to know your pleasure'. The terms of her offer to bribe Angelo with prayers (II, ii, 150–6) are curiously suggestive,[2] and her strenuous avowal of willingness to die is charged with a 'sensuality of martyrdom':

> Were I under the terms of death,
> Th' impression of keen whips I'd wear as rubies,
> And strip myself to death as to a bed
> That longing have been sick for, ere I'd yield
> My body up to shame. (II, iv, 100–4)

Words are associated with the law and with rank: condemnation and reprieve live in Angelo's tongue, and Isabella says 'That in the captain's but a choleric word / Which in the soldier is flat blasphemy' (II, ii, 131–2). The play began with the Duke's test to see 'If power change purpose, what our seemers be', and now as Angelo goes further into temptation both power *and* words change purpose. In this moral whirligig, which exemplifies Lear's 'change places, and, handy-dandy, which is the justice, which is the thief?' (*King Lear*, IV, vi, 157–8), Angelo changes from judge to ravisher, Pompey from bawd to hangman – 'a feather will turn the scale', says the Provost (IV, ii, 28). Angelo may well ask, 'The tempter, or the tempted, who sins most?' (II, ii, 164), and Abhorson expatiate upon how 'every true man's apparel fits your thief' (IV, ii, 41–5).

Indeed, a key to the non-absoluteness of words in moral contexts is provided by the executioner's portmanteau name. He is by his trade 'abhorrent', and as a 'whoreson' seems a lively embodiment of what as the law's instrument he punishes. His name also incorporates and perhaps gives ambivalence to the word which Isabella uses more than any other to express her hatred of vice: 'There is a vice that most I do abhor' (II, ii, 29); 'such abhorr'd pollution' (II, iv, 182); 'That I should do what I abhor to name' (III, i, 101).

It is little wonder that in a world of such shifting possibilities the prison has no lack of inmates, or that Isabella and Angelo should seek refuge in the nunnery and the self-constructed enclosure of reputation and legal absoluteness. Despite these precautions, however, Isabella finds herself eventually in the confine of a terrible dilemma which delimits movement as effectively as any actual chain. When she and Claudio come together for the first time, in III, i, they are like the claustrophobe of Angelo's fancy (II, iv, 19–26), struggling in ever-growing panic against the press of dreadful alternatives.

The philosophy which will free all from their confinements is never far to seek in the play. It is stated at the outset:

> If our virtues
> Did not go forth of us, 'twere all alike
> As if we had them not. Spirits are not finely touch'd
> But to fine issues. (I, i, 33–6)

There is repeated insistence that not only must the professors of virtue 'issue' their talents, but also they must stand-in for others and do so in such a way as wholly to be the person sub-

[1] *Boswell's 'Life of Johnson'*, ed. Sydney Roberts (London, 1960), II, 384.
[2] Connoisseurs of the so-called Freudian slip might note how the words 'sickles' and 'tested' may be combined, especially as they associate in this speech with 'stones' and 'up...and enter'. F. R. Leavis coined the phrase 'sensuality of martyrdom' ('The Greatness of *Measure for Measure*', *Scrutiny*, X (1942), 234).

stituted for. 'In our remove, be thou at full ourself', says the Duke (I, i, 43) when commissioning Angelo to 'supply [his] absence' (I, i, 18). Two scenes later he tells Friar Thomas that he has delivered to Angelo 'My absolute power and place' (I, iii, 13). The meaning is not restricted to that of office-bearing: Angelo soon is invited by Escalus to put himself in Claudio's shoes and to ask himself whether, if he had been given the opportunity, he 'had not sometime in [his] life / Erred in this point...' (II, i, 8–16). The invitation is swiftly turned aside, but returns later when Isabella says to Angelo:

> Go to your bosom,
> Knock there, and ask your heart what it doth
>   know
> That's like my brother's fault... (II, ii, 137–9)

This is intensified to

> If [Claudio] had been as you, and you as he,
> You would have slipp'd like him, but he like you
> Would not have been so stern; (II, ii, 64–6)

and then more passionately and prophetically to

> I would to heaven I had your potency,
> And you were Isabel! Should it then be thus!
> No; I would tell what 'twere to be a judge,
> And what a prisoner. (II, ii, 67–70)

By these graded steps, as it were, the dialogue comes to the greatest of all examples of substitution for others:

> Why, all the souls that were, were forfeit once,
> And He that might the vantage best have took
> Found out the remedy... (II, ii, 73–5)

It is all splendid talk of the necessity of loving and feeling for one's neighbour as oneself. But fired as it may be by desperation and danger, it is still – it seems we may say *only* – talk. To Isabella's evangelistic fervour Angelo returns 'Why do you put these sayings upon me?' (II, ii, 134). Shortly after citing Christ's supreme example of substituting Himself for others – finding 'the remedy' – Isabella can say 'We cannot weigh our brother with ourself' (II, ii, 127); and realising she

cannot dictate the terms of her martyrdom will stand on 'More than our brother is our chastity' (II, iv, 184). She is being challenged to go beyond words when Angelo asks 'What would you do?' (II, iv, 98). As they do in the Gospels, words must find enactment, else

> Heaven in my mouth,
> As if I only did but chew his name.
>
> (II, iv, 4–5)

As Angelo has put the letter of the old law into effect, so Mariana sets the letter of forgiveness and love in act. This she does through the bed-trick. In its simplest terms this is a liberating action for her: it initiates her release from the moated grange, where for five years she has hidden herself away, grieving not only for a dead brother but also for Angelo's broken promise (III, i, 225–9), and feeding her melancholy with songs which 'please her woe'. In sleeping with Angelo she acts as a substitute, literally giving her body in place of someone else's. She is more than a convenient body, however, for in Angelo's apprehension she *is* Isabella. Hers is the first act of wholehearted substitution: although Angelo was enjoined to be 'at full' the Duke he has not exercised power as the Duke would do, nor can Isabella substitute for her brother in the manner which Angelo has proposed. Putting herself so fully in another's place, Mariana makes good the moral dicta that till now have been not much more than splendid pronouncements, and makes of the bed-trick – to quote Isabella talking theory – 'no sin at all, but charity' (II, iv, 66).

If Shakespeare needed the bed-trick to resolve his plot, he has made a virtue of necessity. We also should note that this action of Mariana's takes place in the most confined of settings. Angelo

> hath a garden circummured with brick,
> Whose western side is with a vineyard back'd;
> And to that vineyard is a planched gate,
> That makes his opening with this bigger key.
> The other doth command a little door
> Which from the vineyard to the garden leads;

There have I made my promise
Upon the heavy middle of the night
To call upon him.   (IV, i, 28–36)

This setting – the bed within the garden-house (v, i, 211) within the walled and locked garden within the gated and locked vineyard – would seem to pattern out the labyrinth of dilemma into which Isabella, Claudio and Angelo have wound. It answers also, keys and all, to the confines and wards of Claudio's prison; while the very arrangements for Angelo's deception – the 'repair in the dark' which will have 'all shadow and silence in it' (III, i, 245) – also suggest restrictions which go beyond even the nunnery's.

If you speak, you must not show your face;
Or if you show your face, you must not speak.

It is as if Mariana, encountering darkness like a bride, has reached into all those confines where the others are enthralled: from this bedroom of darkness and silence events turn back toward light and freedom. The 'repair' in the dark is a remedy as well as an assignation.

Tensions wound up by fearful debate in the first half of the play find partial release through activity in the second half. Isabella has to go over the assignation route twice with Angelo and then acquaint Mariana with the whole matter (IV, i, 36–59). Maidenhead-for-maidenhead inspires head-for-head as a substitute for Claudio – and Barnardine – is found in Ragozine. The purpose is once again to deceive, and save, Angelo and thus buy time for Claudio. But Isabella is told by the Duke that her brother has been executed. She must make her own repair 'in the dark' – that is, be tested on her forgiveness of Angelo's trespass while still ignorant of Claudio's preservation.

The public setting of the final scene is heavily stressed (IV, iii, 95–6; IV, iv, 4–5, 9; IV, v, 9; IV, vi, 15). From the pent-up atmosphere of court, prison, and grange the action is removed to the open and public space by the city gates, where under the Duke's stage-management (cf. IV, vi, 1–8) each character in turn is made to play out actions of self-enfranchisement. Mariana is first: after Isabella has, on the Duke's prior instructions, accused Angelo and then been 'arrested' for slander, Mariana enters heavily veiled. The Duke's command both echoes and overrides the nunnery's rule:

First, let her show her face, and after, speak.
                                        (v, i, 170)

Mariana fulfils this command both literally and symbolically, showing her face and declaring herself in public for the first time in five years. The Duke also 'shows his face' when, after leaving and returning in his Friar's habit, he is unhooded by Lucio. These two dramatic enactments of 'coming out' lead of course to the unmasking of Angelo.

But an even more dramatic issuing-forth has yet to be undertaken by Isabella. Still with every reason to hate Angelo, believing her brother to be dead, and with Angelo's own ordainment of his penalty and the Duke's legalistic explication of the case fresh in her ears – 'An Angelo for Claudio; death for death' – Isabella is begged by Mariana to take Angelo's part. The play suddenly compresses into two brief speeches the opposites that have warred throughout:

Mariana.   Sweet Isabel, take my part;
        Lend me your knees, and all my life to come
        I'll lend you all my life to do you service.
Duke.
        Against all sense you do importune her.
        Should she kneel down in mercy of this fact,
        Her brother's ghost his paved bed would
            break,
        And take her hence in horror.   (v, i, 428–34)

The Duke invokes the 'sense' of the law, the 'fact' of an unjustly dead brother and natural as well as legal revenge, family honour (which counted much with Isabella before, II, iv, 178 and III, i, 71), and even the superstition of a certain kind of morbid religiosity. Mariana appeals as Isabella formerly pleaded with

Angelo, in the terms of redemptive substitution and self-sacrifice: 'take my part' and 'all my life to come I'll lend you all my life' – offering her own life in place of what Isabella may in justice demand, Angelo's death. Mariana, 'craving no other nor no better man' than Angelo and offering herself thus, is spiritually at one with Juliet, who earlier in prison answered the Duke's question so affirmatively: 'Love you the man that wrong'd you? Yes, as I love the woman that wrong'd him' (II, iii, 24–5). It is now Isabella's turn to join their company; and she who talked so much about mercy is again being asked to *do* something, indeed something physical. For the whole scope of Mariana's plea should be noticed: she asks only a silent gesture:

> Sweet Isabel, do yet but kneel by me;
> Hold up your hands, say nothing; I'll speak all.
> (v, i, 435–6)

This to Isabella, whom we remember to have been not only morally but also physically unyielding:

> Had [Claudio] twenty heads to tender down
> On twenty bloody blocks, he'd yield them up
> Before his sister should her body stoop
> To such abhorr'd pollution,

she has said (II, iv, 179–82), and to Claudio's face,

> Die, perish! Might but my bending down
> Reprieve thee from thy fate, it should proceed.
> I'll pray a thousand prayers for thy death;
> No word to save thee.   (III, i, 143–6)

Therefore it is an act of self-conquest (and a great stage gesture) when Isabella falls on her knees.

She does more than kneel, however. Mariana asked only for a silent appeal – 'Say nothing; I'll speak all' – but Isabella goes the second mile to speak on Angelo's behalf:

> Look, if it please you, on this man condemn'd
> As if my brother lived.   (v, i, 442–3)

The legalism of her plea for Angelo has been strongly denounced: Ernest Schanzer, for example, says 'One's spirit recoils at hearing this girl, who had not a word to say in excuse of her brother but rather admitted the justice of his doom, now plead, with all the finesse of a seasoned attorney, on the most purely legalistic grounds for her would-be ravisher and the judicial murderer of her brother'.[1] But such a response overlooks at least three factors. First, so far as Isabella knows she is addresssing in the Duke a judge who up to now has invoked the strict letter of the law, and so she must plead the letter if Angelo is to have any chance. Second, it is in itself a striking reversal that the letter is being cited, not to kill as in Claudio's situation, but to save. And third, it ought to be recognized that the real force of this plea lies not so much in its terms as in the fact that Isabella is interceding for Angelo at all. The stubborn Barnardine is rightly admired for his determined refusal to co-operate with his executioners: he is 'absolute for life'.[2] But the formerly stubborn Isabella has now surpassed Barnardine in that she is absolute for someone else's life, and that life her enemy's. Perhaps Barnardine and Isabella together illustrate the Duke's distinction between a grace that 'stands' and a virtue that 'goes' (III, ii, 257); this is the distinction between the 'old' and 'new' Isabellas as well.

So Isabella's own enfranchisement from the exactness of 'measure still for measure' is being enacted when she pleads for Angelo. The reciprocal virtue of her action is expressed in Romeo's joyful realisation that in loving Juliet, his 'enemy': 'My intercession likewise steads my foe' (*Romeo and Juliet*, II, iii, 54). Kneeling in public with Mariana, Isabella has 'shown her face', and she has spoken as well. Thus she has come fully out of the nunnery, where

> If you speak, you must not show your face;
> Or if you show your face, you must not speak.

[1] *The Problem Plays of Shakespeare*, p. 101.
[2] J. W. Lever has anticipated my use of this phrase: Arden *Measure for Measure*, p. lxxxviii.

She sees the narrowness and irreversible nature of justice. Having formerly cried out for 'Justice! Justice! Justice!' (v, i, 26), she now can say 'My brother had but justice.' The 'but' contains a whole statute of limitations.

Just as Isabella shows her face so too has Angelo's been shown, and what he knows about himself painfully revealed to the world. No-one who feels that Angelo is treated too leniently has fully taken into account the city-gate setting and the public humiliation there endured (to Shakespeare's contemporaries it was a recognised factor in punishment). The exposure of so essentially withdrawn a man and the breaking through of his *persona* is in itself a punishment which if it does not exactly fit the crime certainly fits the offender. To Angelo execution would be preferable, entailing as it does the concealment of prison and the oblivion of death: it is the public session he wants curtailed:

> No longer session hold upon my shame.
> But let my trial be mine own confession.
> Immediate sentence, then, and sequent death
> Is all the grace I beg. (v, i, 369–72)

The soul-searching Angelo underwent before sinning, his remorse and fear when his villainy has, as he thinks, succeeded (IV, v, 18–32), and the penitence he expresses when caught (v, i, 472–5) – all these cannot be left out of the reckoning; and as his public humiliation is prolonged the audience may sum up, with the Duke, 'Your evil quits you well.'

The theme of releasing is formally enacted once more when Claudio is brought on 'muffled'; then revealed and pardoned. This unwrapping, Mariana's unveiling, and the Duke's being unhooded, together with the more metaphorical uncovering of Angelo, have all been foreshadowed in a word of the Duke's – 'unfold'. He uses this word at his very first appearance to mean 'explicate' or 'reveal'; and in greeting this day of revelation for so many of his subjects suggests releasing with 'Look, th'

unfolding star calls up the shepherd' (IV, ii, 202). With these implications of the truth making free, the word comprehends both the range of the play's events and the Duke's part in them.

But although the Duke 'like power divine, Hath looked upon [Angelo's] passes', it does not follow that he should be seen as God.[1] It is not so much divine power as resourcefulness and good luck which enable him to counter Angelo's attempted double-cross (IV, ii, 113f.). In becoming the Friar he undergoes, like others, his own process of self-removal: though he does this voluntarily, some sort of drastic action obviously has been dictated by Vienna's condition. The Duke has been a secretive man – 'I love the people', he says, 'But do not like to stage me to their eyes' (I, i, 67ff.) – and only Escalus seems to know him well. Retiredness encourages rumour, and even Friar Thomas seems to think that his ruler's disguise may have a nefarious motive (I, iii, 1–6). It is therefore salutary that the Duke–Friar must perforce listen to Lucio's slanders, as well as see his prison. At the play's end he indicates that he is not God (or even a Friar) by making himself one partner in the marriage-pairings which have the earthy membership of Lucio and his paramour. The emphasis, in this final scene, upon action and gesture makes it fairly clear that although Isabella is silent after the Duke's proposal she may not necessarily be equivocal in accepting. 'Give me your hand and say you will be mine' is followed directly and conclusively by 'He [Claudio] is my brother too' (v, i, 490–1), a firm indication that the Duke has received the sign he asked for. In the marriage-pairings he is associated with men and women: wedlock qualifies the 'too much

---

[1] Lever (*ibid.*, pp. lvii–lviii) discusses the theory of the play as allegory of the Divine Atonement with the Duke symbolising the Incarnate Lord, outlined in studies by G. Wilson Knight, Roy W. Battenhouse and Nevill Coghill.

liberty' which formerly turned to restraint (I, ii, 117–20), and is the best assurance that none of them will any longer 'forswear the full stream of the world and...live in a nook, merely monastic' (*As You Like It*, III, ii, 440–1).

Measure for Measure, as I see it, is about human beings who in an uncertain world are shut up against themselves and from one another. They find release and fulfilment in 'going forth' through self-abnegation and forgiveness. The play illustrates that a fugitive and cloistered virtue is of equal uselessness with a buried talent, and that noble ideals are supposed to be put into action. In making Mariana's trick an important part of the ethical fabric of *Measure for Measure* Shakespeare has wedded a traditional comic device to a serious moral intention. They are not at all strange bedfellows.

© JAMES BLACK 1973

I   Rosso Fiorentino, *The Descent from the Cross* (Pinacoteca, Volterra)

II El Greco, *The Burial of the Count of Orgaz* (chiesa de Santo Tomé, Toledo)

III Bronzino, *Venus, Cupid and Time* (National Gallery)

IV Tintoretto, *The Last Supper* (chiesa di San Giorgio Maggiore, Venice)

Painting on the West Face of the Wall which divides the Nave from the Chancel of the Chapel of the Trinity at STRATFORD upon AVON in WARWICKSHIRE

V   Wall-painting of the Last Judgement (the chapel of the Trinity, Stratford-upon-Avon)

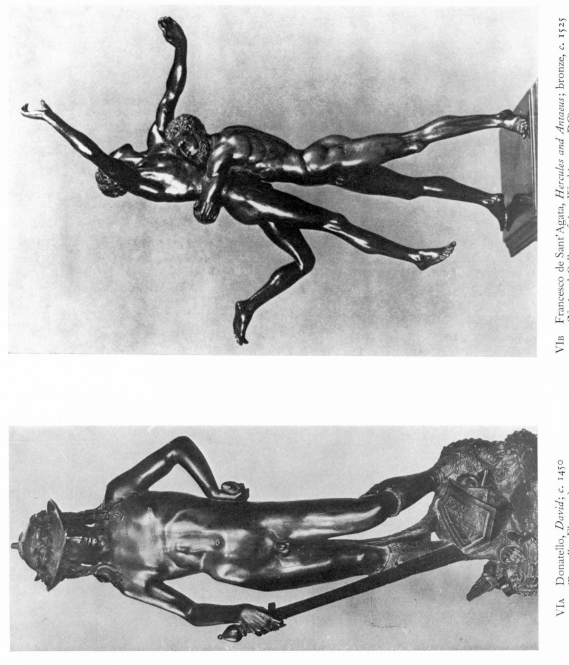

VIA Donatello, *David*; c. 1450
(Bargello, Florence)

VIB Francesco de Sant'Agata, *Hercules and Antaeus*; bronze, c. 1525
(National Gallery of Art, Washington, DC)

VII *Antony and Cleopatra*, Royal Shakespeare Theatre, 1972. Directed by Trevor Nunn, designed by Christopher Morley, with music by Guy Woolfenden. Richard Johnson as Antony and Janet Suzman as Cleopatra.

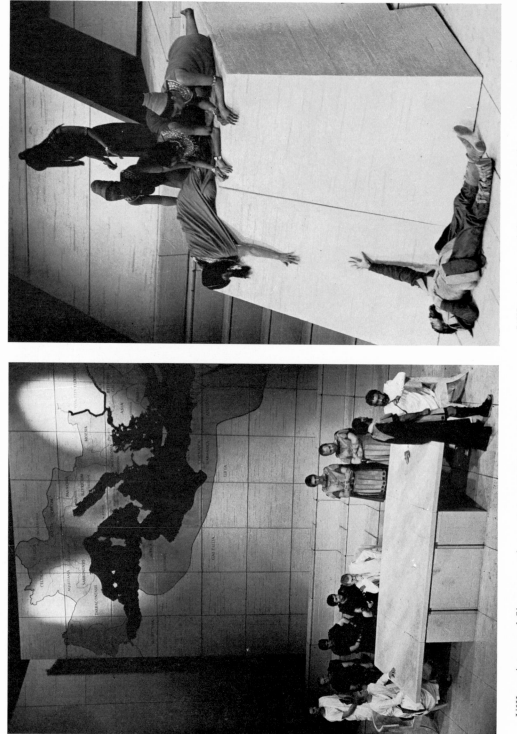

VIIIa *Antony and Cleopatra*, with round the table (l. to r.), Corin
Redgrave as Octavius, Raymond Westwell as Lepidus,
Patrick Stewart (standing) as Enobarbus, and Antony

VIIIb *Antony and Cleopatra*, with (l. to r.) Antony, Cleopatra,
Wendy Bailey as a Waiting Woman, Mavis Taylor Blake
(standing) as Iras, Rosemary McHale as Charmian and
Edwina Ford as a Waiting Woman

SHAKESPEARE AND THE EYE

CECIL S. EMDEN

Interpretations

Shakespeare's frequent interpretations of the expressions in the eyes of his characters may be said to provide a valuable type of evidence about their dispositions and conduct. We can, moreover, often notice that the dramatic quality of a play is enhanced as a result of the availability of such information. One or two descriptions of incidents in which analysis is a feature are quoted here, at the outset, as furnishing a useful prelude to what follows.

Philip the Bastard finds need at a critical juncture to try and infuse a sense of self-confidence in King John; but has little hope of being persuasive. He tries to bolster up the King's courage when he is faint-hearted, being faced with a menacing situation. The Bastard exhorts him to change his timorous appearance to that of stoutness of heart: 'Let not the world see fear and sad distrust / Govern the motion of a kingly eye!' (v, i, 46–7). Some years later the weak-spirited and shifty Duke of York argues in favour of the competence of Richard II to act as monarch. Though using assured language, he proves unconvincing when he addresses his companions, urging them to support the King against Bolingbroke's implicit threats to usurp the throne: 'Yet looks he [Richard II] like a king. Behold his eye, / As bright as is the eagle's, lightens forth / Controlling majesty' (III, iii, 68–70). The Duke hopes to sustain the King's cause by asserting that he has a look of energy. His description is spirited in form, but too far from the truth to carry conviction. In both these instances a vain attempt is made to control the course of history by interpreting the expression of a king's eyes in a favourable light.

In an episode in *Much Ado* the reputation of Hero is questioned, though she is a young woman of impeccable record. The Friar defends her by pointing out that, upon her being charged with misconduct, 'in her eye there appear'd a fire, / To burn the errors that these princes hold / Against her maiden truth' (IV, i, 164–6). He claims, in fact, to have noticed a convincing glow of protest in her eyes when she is publicly denounced; and his interpretation proves to be correct.

A remark by Cassio about Desdemona, in *Othello*, offers an enlightening analysis of her facial expression: 'An inviting eye, and yet methinks right modest' (II, iii, 24–5). No sinister implication seems to be insinuated here. He is only making an attempt at a reasonable explanation of what may well have been a complex countenance.

Sometimes several pairs of eyes have expressions that are interpreted collectively. In I *Henry IV* a radical change of mood, as shown in the faces of the crowd, is vividly depicted. After Richard II's eventual failure to retain either the people's admiration or respect, it is said that groups of his subjects, when confronted by him 'rather drowsed and hung their eyelids down, / Slept in his face, and render'd such aspect / As cloudy men use to their adversaries, / Being with his presence glutted, gorged and full' (III, ii, 81–4). This picturesque sketch of the resolutely listless and unresponsive citizens is remarkable for its lively appreciation of the way in which the opinion of the masses can change quickly and completely.

Characters, both early and late in the order of the plays, imply that they can determine what is going on in the minds of others by looking closely into their eyes. Richard II tells John of Gaunt: 'Uncle, even in the glasses of thine eyes / I see thy grievèd heart' (I, iii, 208–9). Leonato, when Borachio's vileness is being exposed, in *Much Ado*, says: 'let me see his eyes, / That, when I note another man like him, / I may avoid him' (V, i, 245–7). And Othello, when suspecting that his wife has been unchaste, demands of her: 'Let me see your eyes. / Look in my face' (IV, ii, 25).

How far the expression of the eye can be affected by the parts of the face adjacent to it can be interesting matter for speculation. In one or two passages in the plays, references to the brows include the eye itself. The most explicit of these passages is in Goneril's violent denunciation of her husband, the gentle Duke of Albany, in *King Lear*: 'Milk-livered man!... / Who hast not in thy brows an eye discerning / Thine honour from thy suffering' (IV, ii, 50–3). In *Measure for Measure* also we find: 'There is written in your brow, provost, honesty and constancy' (IV, ii, 146–7). The inclusion of his eyes is surely implied here; and this is so even though 'the brow' is capable of being interpreted in a general sense as reflecting character.

We have occasional evidence of Shakespeare's acceptance of the fact that the expressiveness of the eyes can depend on the movement of the brows, or parts of the cheeks, or the framework round the eye, especially, but not exclusively, the eyelids. The importance of this framework is apt to be overlooked; but

those, like artists, who study such matters know how significant it can be.

A convincing example is to be found in Lady Capulet's remarks to Juliet concerning the attractive qualities of Count Paris: 'Read o'er the volume of young Paris' face / And find delight writ there with beauty's pen. / ... And what obscured in this fair volume lies / Find written in the margent of his eyes' (I, iii, 82–7). Clearly the word 'margent' is suggested by the earlier mentions of a volume; and, equally clearly, the volume she had in mind was a scholarly type of Elizabethan book with its explanatory notes in the margin. This metaphorical illustration is particularly apt in intensifying Lady Capulet's argument.

A few words in *The Tempest* provide further support for Shakespeare's recognition of the framework of the eye as an indication of its expression. Sebastian comes to realise that Antonio wants him to join in a plan to murder the King of Naples. He, therefore, speaks insinuatingly to Antonio hoping to induce him to declare himself: 'The setting of thine eye and cheek proclaim / A matter from thee;...' (II, i, 220–1). Commentators have interpreted 'setting' as 'fixed look'; but a more likely meaning is 'outline'. This accords with an early sense of the word. Moreover, such an interpretation makes the mention of 'cheek' more understandable.[1]

Kinds of expression

Most of the descriptions of the expressions in eyes that are part of people's everyday appearance seem to fall into two main classes, those that are distinctly pleasant and those that are distinctly unpleasant. Shakespeare does not seem to have found that more than a few in either of these classes provided him with scope for the enlivenment of imagery. His language in this sphere is in fact apt to be literal and even

[1] See also *The Merchant of Venice*, I, i, 52; *Pericles*, I, iv, 51.

commonplace. This is hardly surprising because static situations are less likely to stimulate high-wrought descriptions than those where there is abundant activity. Notable among the pleasant qualities mentioned are kindliness, cheerfulness, valour, and amiability – a group that may well reflect the author's personal preferences. Among the unpleasant qualities that are prominent are rapaciousness, lust, pitilessness, and a truculence that extends at times into a propensity to criminal violence. It is sufficient to quote one or two examples of the phraseology used in each of the two classes.

Orlando asks Rosalind to 'let your fair [benignant] eyes and gentle wishes' (I, ii, 167) attend him at his wrestling match. The nurse in *Romeo and Juliet* remarks to Juliet: 'An eagle, madam, / Hath not...so fair [handsome] an eye / As Paris hath' (III, v, 220–2).[1] One of the revilers of Richard III describes his eyes *tout court* and without qualification as 'murderous' (IV, i, 56) and another as 'deadly' (I, iii, 225). Perhaps they thought that brevity was best suited to malediction.[2] A few people in the plays are remarkable for a constitutional liability to disclose anger in their eyes. An example is Imogen's comment on 'the hourly shot / Of angry eyes [of Cymbeline]' (I, i, 89–90).

Cleopatra's observations about Octavia's normal expression may seem at first sight to be exceptional in standing half-way between the two extremes of commendation and disparagement. But it is clear that she means to be palpably scornful when she characterises Octavia's eyes as 'modest' (IV, xv, 27), and, on another occasion, as 'sober' (V, ii, 54).

In contrast with habitual expressions in eyes, those that are transient, especially if generated by tense, strongly-felt situations, naturally have an invigorating influence on the descriptions of so sensitive a playwright as Shakespeare. When he is involved with this category, the visible reaction noticeable in the eye of a character, as a result of emotional disturbance, stirs his imagination strongly. Scenes comprehending such sentiments as eagerness, indignation, excitement, fear, and sense of guilt provide typical examples.

The time-serving Duke of York, already mentioned, having changed his allegiance, is fulsome in his account of the favourable welcome provided by Londoners on the arrival of the usurping Bolingbroke. The onlookers of the procession are pictured as eager and excited; and the Duke wants to emphasise the impressiveness of the occasion: 'You would have thought the very windows spake / So many greedy looks of young and old / Through casements darted their desiring eyes / Upon his visage...' (V, ii, 12–15). And there are, of course, several passages characterised by a warlike spirit to be found in *Henry V*, such as the King's address to his troops before Harfleur: 'For there is none of you so mean and base / That hath not noble lustre in your eyes' (III, i, 29–30). 2 *Henry IV* includes a particularly stirring sketch of the outward tokens of personal valour. Just as the abortive tourney is about to begin, the appearance of the two contestants is portrayed: 'Their eyes of fire sparkling through sights of steel / And the loud trumpet blowing them together' (IV, i, 120–1). The atmosphere of this impassioned scene is conveyed in a masterly manner, partly due to the incisive language used.

Excitement of various kinds can make the eyes flash or glisten; and, as a result of mental turmoil, they may glare, or even revolve. In *Macbeth* the Thane of Ross rushes on to the stage eager to impart the news of a mighty victory: 'What a haste [urgency] looks through his eyes!' (I, ii, 47). Or the eyes may glow with indignation, as when Cicero, in *Julius Caesar*, 'Looks with such ferret and such fiery eyes / As we have seen him in the Capitol, / Being

[1] See also *Antony and Cleopatra*, I, i, 2.
[2] See also *Richard III*, IV, ii, 67.

cross'd in conference with some senators' (I, ii, 186–8).[1] Othello, overcome by jealousy, is contemplating the murder of his wife. She tries to divert him from what seems to her to be some delusion forming in his mind, certainly ominous, possibly horrific. She cannot resist hinting at her suspicions: 'And yet I fear you, for you are fatal then / When your eyes roll so...' (v, ii, 40–1).

An effect of sudden fear is to make people stare and blanch at the same time. Cassius tells Casca, on the frantic night before the Ides of March: 'You look pale, and gaze, / And put on fear, and cast yourself in wonder' (I, iii, 59–60).[2] Helpless, hopeless sense of fear is often contagious. Its effect can spread at a rapid pace where people meet easily by reason of their living in close proximity in towns and cities. At a critical stage in *King John* Hubert tries to convey to the King the sense of shock, apprehension and distress visible among the citizens in the streets at the talk of Arthur's death: 'And he that speaks doth gripe the hearer's wrist, / Whilst he that hears makes fearful action, / With wrinkled brows, with nods, with rolling eyes' (IV, ii, 190–2). This can claim to be the most accomplished of Shakespeare's portrayals of street scenes. The vividness of his imagination is expressed in notably laconic and effective language.

Oppressive sense of guilt has much in common with fear. Hubert himself, the suspected murderer of Arthur, is pictured as being depraved and panic-stricken at the same time: 'The image of a wicked heinous fault [misdeed] / Lives in his eye; that close aspect of his / Does show the mood of a much troubled breast' (IV, ii, 71–3). He has the appearance of a haunted wretch.[3]

Sometimes the expressions in people's eyes have, in contrast to those just discussed, an active rather than a passive quality. They may be classed as provocative. For instance, a distasteful or obnoxious look in the eyes of one person can arouse strong feelings of, say, resentment, dismay, or aggravation in another. Few situations are more distressing than one in which someone unexpectedly finds an old friend behaving in a standoffish manner without apparent cause. Brutus is particularly inwardlooking when he is about to engage in a conspiracy to assassinate Julius Caesar. His near friend, Cassius, finds him unamiable and aloof, to say the least; and he complains: 'I have not from your eyes that gentleness / And show of love as I was wont to have'[4] (I, ii, 33–4). But Cassius has his censorious as well as his sensitive side, and regards Julius Caesar as unduly formidable, with an eye that could 'awe the world' (I, ii, 123). Several distinguished Romans have critical views about the expressions in the eyes of their friends.

Eyes sometimes have the appearance of defiance. Henry IV watches the Earl of Worcester closely when he is addressing some offensive remarks to him, and observes on his face a churlish, glowering look. He dismisses him from his presence, 'for I do see / Danger and disobedience in thine eye' (*1 Henry IV*, I, iii, 15–16). In the event, Worcester finds cause to regret his temerity.

Extreme passionateness coming close to mental derangement can produce, among other unpleasant facial expressions, a look of outrageous and gratuitous disdain. Early in *The Winter's Tale*, for instance, Polixenes tells Camillo about the astonishing discourtesy with which he is being treated by his host, Leontes, who is suddenly overmastered by a frenzied jealousy of him. He reports that 'even now I met him / With customary compliment, when he, / Wafting his eyes to th' contrary [i.e.

[1] See also *Julius Caesar*, II, i, 242.
[2] See also *Macbeth*, V, iii, 11–12; *King John*, IV, ii, 106–7; *1 Henry IV*, I, iii, 142–3.
[3] See also *Richard III*, I, iv, 166.
[4] Cf. *Julius Caesar*, I, ii, 194, 202–3.

aside and away], and falling [i.e. protruding] / A lip of much contempt, speeds from me...' (I, ii, 370–3). The combined action of eyes and mouth betoken violent animosity. Both aversion and rancour are conspicuous. This graphic picture exemplifies Shakespeare's supreme capacity for contriving a dramatic effect. It is, in fact, just what is required to excite the curiosity of the audience and whet their appetite for the sensational situations that are soon to follow.

A most powerful aid to duplicity is by means of counterfeit expression in the eyes. Many people, for instance, can assume a genial, even affectionate look when their real feelings are running in an entirely contrary direction. It is natural that this device is frequently employed in the plays so as to heighten tension. There are several examples in *Macbeth* where characters try to practise this kind of deception. Early in the play Lady Macbeth advises her husband how best to assure those around them that there are no sinister plots in preparation: 'Your face, my thane, is as a book where men / May read strange matters. To beguile the time / Look like the time, bear welcome in your eye, / Your hand, your tongue; look like the innocent flower, / But be the serpent under't' (I, v, 59–62). Later on, the roles are reversed; and it is Lady Macbeth who requires the same kind of injunction. Her husband tells her to pretend to Banquo, whom he is plotting to have murdered, that he is regarded by them as a valuable friend: 'Present him eminence [i.e. treat him with specially honoured attention] both with eye and tongue' (III, iii, 31). They do not have to dissemble for long: within hours Banquo is dead.

In *Julius Caesar*, Brutus, of all people, acts in the same double-faced manner as the Macbeths. He charges his fellow-conspirators: 'Good gentlemen, look fresh, and merrily; / Let not our looks put on [reveal] our pur-poses' (II, i, 224–5). The need for such imposture is also brief, but for different reasons, when King Lear is deceived by the guile of his daughter Regan who for a short time pretends that she is still loyal to him though he has been insulted by Goneril, her sister. He tells Regan that Goneril's eyes 'are fierce, but thine / Do comfort and not burn' (II, iv, 171–2). The unfortunate man is soon disillusioned.

Now and then we can learn about counterfeit expressions in people's eyes indirectly, by implication. The conversation of a character having a capacity for peculiar violence of emotion, or at least for the pretence of it, can enable us to visualise his looks without our being supplied with definite information on the subject. Perhaps the best example is Richard of Gloucester (soon to be Richard III) on the occasion of his wooing Lady Anne. His success in this project depends, of course, largely on skill in faking his looks, and the versatility he displays in pressing his suit. At first he adopts a pathetic strain, with eyebrows doubtless raised appealingly. Almost immediately his eyes dilate with admiration. When she accuses him of crimes which had caused her suffering, his tactics take an adventurous turn, and, with his eyes riveted on hers, he challenges her to kill him so as to satisfy her need for revenge. By degrees he undermines her resistance; and we can imagine his eyes appearing radiant with incipient triumph. The hypnotic powers which his eyes could exercise in circumstances which might seem to be unpropitious are proof that Shakespeare regarded him as a master of duplicity; and yet, oddly enough, nothing explicit is said here about his looks and the way they are varied.

Eccentric metaphors

By a strange fancy of the men of letters of Elizabethan times the eye is occasionally made to represent both the mind and intellectual qualities and activities such as judgement, opinion, attention, discernment, and even conscience. Metaphorical usages like these were doubtless regarded by the stylists as tokens of literary elegance. Today, however, they tend to be obscure, and even tiresome. But they have a particular interest, as we shall notice later on, when discussing the enlargement of the influence of the mind as opposed to that of the eye, in matters of love.

Benvolio, when advising Romeo to look out for a more forthcoming inamorata than Rosaline, makes a suggestion: 'Go thither [to a party], and with unattainted eye [unprejudiced mind] / Compare her face with some that I shall show' (I, ii, 85–6).[1] This extract is comparable with some words of Mark Antony, justifying himself to Octavius Caesar by alleging that he cannot 'with graceful eyes [i.e. mild, assenting mind]' make wars to his own disadvantage[2] (*Antony and Cleopatra*, II, ii, 64).

The distinctions between mind, judgement, and opinion in the present connection are sometimes slight, but doubtless made for reasons considered to be adequate. Brutus, addressing his fellow-conspirators about the degree in which they were actuated by the public interest in entering into a plot to assassinate Julius Caesar, says that a proper understanding of their 'purpose' in 'the common eyes' (II, i, 178–9), meaning the judgement of the populus, would ensure the maintenance of their good reputations. Besides several similar instances in the plays, there is the celebrated sonnet which begins: 'When, in disgrace with fortune and men's eyes [opinion] ...' (Sonnet XXIX).[3] Discernment, akin to judgement, is discussed between Albany and his wife Goneril, in *King Lear*. There is a contention between them relating to evidence affecting a proposed line of conduct. He says to her: 'How far your eyes [discernment] may pierce I cannot tell...' (I, iv, 346).[4]

The straining of metaphors when 'eye' is made to represent 'conscience' seems fantastic by present-day standards. Henry V declares: 'If little faults, proceeding on distemper, / Shall not be winked at, how shall we stretch our eye [conscience] / When capital crimes, chew'd, swallow'd and digested / Appear before us?' (II, ii, 54–7). A more dramatic instance of this kind of diction occurs when Macbeth soliloquises during the process of planning crime: 'The eye wink at the hand' (I, iv, 52). This may be interpreted, as the context indicates: 'May my conscience overlook the deed!'

Nowadays some of these metaphors might be described not merely as strained, but grotesque. Henry V, for instance, uses phrases which would seem outlandish to us today when he is intent on inducing his troops to look grim and ghoulish in the face of the enemy. He thus exhorts them: 'But when the blast of war blows in our ears, / ... Then lend the eye a terrible aspect; / Let it pry through the portage of the head / Like the brass cannon; ...' (III, i, 5–11). This type of language was, we may suppose, sufficiently lurid to satisfy the most sensation-loving of the groundlings.[5]

Shakespeare's frequent eccentricity of the kinds noticed in the preceding paragraphs must often have seemed strange even in his own times. It may be attributed to a streak of whimsicality. But we may also regard it as an indication of the large extent to which the eye was in the forefront of his fancy as a suitable metaphorical illustration.

[1] See also *Romeo and Juliet*, I, ii, 49–50.
[2] For 'eyes' as 'attention', see *Hamlet*, I, ii, 256–7; *1 Henry IV*, I, ii, 205–6.
[3] See also *Richard III*, III, vii, 111–12; IV, iv, 177.
[4] See also *Much Ado*, V, i, 219–21.
[5] See also *Cymbeline*, V, v, 394–5; *Othello*, II, i, 38; *1 Henry IV*, III, ii, 70.

Eyes and mind in matters of love

For a time the chief rival to the eyes as the most influential factor in early love was the heart which had a traditional connotation of emotion. But the heart was soon challenged by the mind. Its use came to imply a combination of emotional and mental activity, or even mental activity alone.

Biron (Berowne), in *Love's Labour's Lost*, was an early exponent of the practical importance of the part played by the eyes in the first stages of love. He remarks, in regard to women's eyes: 'They are the ground, the books, the academes / From whence doth spring the true Promethean fire' (IV, iii, 299–300). And he proceeds to develop his theme, pointing out that love, when established, 'adds a precious seeing to the eye', and does not merely stimulate activity unseen 'immurèd in the brain'. Comparable points of view, but charged with deeper feeling, are expressed by the hero in *Romeo and Juliet* which was first produced in the following year (1595). He describes love as 'a fire sparkling in lovers' eyes' (I, i, 189). A little later on, but still early in the play, the status of the mind comes up for discussion. Romeo's confessor and adviser is surprised at his sudden change of allegiance from Rosaline to Juliet, and, with a friendly touch of irony, half-chides him: 'Young men's love then lies / Not truly in their hearts, but in their eyes' (II, iii, 67–8). He doubtless meant to imply: 'If you had used your mind rather more and your eyes rather less in regard to Rosaline, you might have saved yourself some disquiet.'[1]

Near the beginning of *A Midsummer Night's Dream*, which was first produced in the same year as *Romeo and Juliet*, Helena has personal grounds for insisting on the principle that 'Love looks not with the eyes, but with the mind' (I, i, 234), for she is piqued at Demetrius' sudden and unexpected admiration of Hermia's beauty and his scorn for her own physical attractions. Her jealousy of Hermia, in fact, may well have disposed her to prefer mental rather than ocular means of appraisal. After a while Lysander, having been bewitched into deserting Hermia and falling in love with Helena, tells the latter, by way of explanation of his changed behaviour, that 'reason says you are the worthier maid' (II, ii, 116) and that 'Reason becomes the marshal to my will, / And leads me to your eyes, where I o'erlook [peruse] / Love's stories written in love's richest book' (120–2). He plainly asserts that his action is controlled by his mind; and he explains rather than qualifies this statement by adding that he is entranced by Helena's eyes. His advances, however, prove futile, for magic continues to spread confusion. Eventually the tangle is unravelled, and Demetrius finds that after all he is in love with Helena, not, as he makes clear, because of the influence of either his mind or his eyes alone, but of both of them acting in conjunction – 'all the faith, the virtue of my heart, / The object and the pleasure of mine eye, / Is only Helena' (IV, i, 166–8).

The amount to be learnt from these extracts regarding Shakespeare's views on the question of eyes *versus* mind may be somewhat limited. The volatile flights of fancy and mysterious magical happenings tend to lessen the significance of some of the remarks made by the lovers. We must be satisfied with concluding that, in recounting the progress of their blandishments, his inclination was towards the view that eyes and mind must work together in beneficent collaboration. In later years, however, this attitude is clarified. For instance, Olivia, at the time of her dalliance with Cesario (Viola), in *Twelfth Night*, at first feels 'his' perfections 'With an invisible and subtle stealth, / To creep in at mine eyes' (I, v, 280–2). But, almost at once, she appreciates the weight of the arguments for reasoned judgement: 'I do…fear to find / Mine eye too great a flatterer

[1] See also *Hamlet*, IV, iii, 4–5.

for my mind' (292–3). Thus we have grounds for supposing that the influence of the mind is gaining increased recognition.

We should not neglect the possibility of a connection between this development and Shakespeare's proneness to the use of the kind of metaphor mentioned above, where the eye is made to represent not only the mind but such intellectual functions as judgement and discernment. Some of his eccentric metaphors may seem a little strange to us, but they may well have subconsciously affected his views about the relative scopes of eye and mind in matters of love, and thus conduced to tilt the balance in favour of the mind.

We must, however, recognize that, at the advent of mutual tenderness, the eye has for Shakespeare a particular and momentous significance. Portia, when just about to admit to Bassanio that she has fallen in love with him before he is competent to declare his love for her, tells him half-playfully: 'Beshrew your eyes! / They have overlooked me [charmed me by witchcraft] and divided me; / One half of me is yours, the other half yours, – / Mine own I would say: but if mine then yours, / And so all yours' (III, ii, 14–18). Romeo, in a more impassioned mood, cannot restrain himself from protesting to Juliet that he is so captivated by her eyes that he would risk death rather than cut short his visit to her. She tells him that, if her kinsmen find him in the Capulet garden, they will murder him, to which he replies: 'Alack, there is more peril in thine eye / Than twenty of their swords!' (II, ii, 71–2). This might seem to be something of a *façon de parler*; but it is more likely to exemplify the degree of exaltation to which Shakespeare's suitors can attain when under the first fascination of a lady's eye. At that stage his more ardent male characters indulge in fantastic notions about their thraldom. Angelo, in *Measure for Measure*, admittedly not a typical lover, but certainly a strenuous admirer, goes so far, when contem-

plating the charms of Isabella, as to 'feast upon her eyes' (II, ii, 179).

The first occasions when tender feelings are experienced simultaneously by both lovers can be particularly affecting. Prospero, soon after Ferdinand and Miranda meet, reflects, in a complacent aside: 'At the first sight / They have changed eyes' (I, ii, 440–1). They have in fact reciprocated those distinctive, intimate glances that imply a mutual falling in love. This picture must have pleased its author, for he used it in his preceding play, *The Winter's Tale*: 'Your precious self had not then crossed the eyes / Of my young playfellow' (I, ii, 79–80).

Figurativeness is freely used in describing these early stages, with the object of intensifying the emotions. An estimable example of this type of portrayal, one of the most delightful scenes in all the plays, is that where Florizel and Perdita woo in the moonlight, as recounted by Perdita's presumed father, the old shepherd. He speaks with an unexpected sense of poetical feeling when confiding in Polixenes at the sheep-shearing feast: 'He [Florizel] says he loves my daughter. / I think so too; for never gazed the moon / Upon the water as he'll stand and read, / As'twere, my daughter's eyes; and to be plain, / I think there is not half a kiss to choose / Who loves another best' (IV, iv, 171–6). This glimpse of Florizel discerning in Perdita's eyes the depth of her love for him must surely be unrivalled as an illustration of Shakespeare's close understanding of the vital part played by the eyes in bringing young hearts together. It is a passage to be cherished.

Any study of Shakespeare's treatment of the eye in relation to drama should pay some attention to the development of his interest in the subject and of his proficiency in dealing with it. There is only room here to add a few brief supplementary remarks. The first play in which he paid any considerable attention to the subject is *Love's Labour's Lost*. His diction there is experimental; and, naturally enough, his discussions about the qualities of the feminine eye are inclined to be ornate and even precious, perhaps consciously so. The play has been suitably described as 'a comedy of affectations'. Nevertheless the subject clearly intrigued him. Dr John Dover Wilson has commented on the extreme frequency of the mention of eyes in this play; and he observes: 'It is eyes, eyes all the way...' He believes that there is a planned significance in this conspicuous recurrence. In the later plays Shakespeare's diction usually resumes its unpretentious tones. As he comes to appreciate more fully the important part played by the eye in the interpretation of human character and in the intensification of dramatic effects, his manner gains in impressiveness and actuality. It must soon have become apparent to him that admirable opportunities for disclosing the efficacy of the eye would be found in the plays in which he planned a good many sensational incidents. This supposition is borne out by the considerable number and the liveliness of references to the eye in three of the most notable tragedies, *Romeo and Juliet*, *Julius Caesar*, and *Macbeth*. The English history group of plays, including as it does many tragic happenings, also provides plenty of examples. It is remarkable how frequently the eye is an object of particular interest where murder and sudden death are involved. It seems strange that this observation does not apply to *Hamlet*. This is a puzzle which can be added to those with which this play abounds.

If we wished to point to the play which includes the largest amount of expressive phraseology regarding the topics we have been considering, the choice might well be *Julius Caesar*, though it would probably be agreed that this play does not head the list for imagery that is both vivid and picturesque. It was written in mid-career; and, in the years that followed, the high standard of the descriptions in which the eye features is well maintained. This may be taken as indicating that Shakespeare recognised that attention to this aspect of characterisation could contribute substantially to lively and lifelike presentations of his plays.

© CECIL S. EMDEN 1973

NO ROME OF SAFETY:
THE ROYAL SHAKESPEARE SEASON 1972
REVIEWED

PETER THOMSON

The 1972 season, despite Trevor Nunn's understandable public hedging, was intended to be a very special one for the Royal Shakespeare Company. It saw Shakespeare's four Roman plays 'performed in a group for the first time anywhere', Rank Strand Electric's new computer system for stage lighting 'used for the first time', what the programme called 'radical alterations' to the auditorium designed to bring it closer to 'the "one-room" relationship between actor and audience' that will be a feature of the company's Barbican theatre, and the installation of complex hydraulically-operated staging to permit sudden transformations of the whole stage picture.

Of at least equal theatrical significance (though, by contrast, quite unsung) was the confirmation of a change in casting policy. The three-year contracts that were a feature of Peter Hall's organisation have been replaced by single-season contracts. If this does not represent a total surrender, it is certainly a retreat; and its artistic implications are unmistakable. The British actor, we are to assume, comes ready-trained to this as to any other repertory theatre, there to be *deployed* by the British director. There is no time for serious discovery in such a system, no possibility of evolving a style of acting that will distinguish this company from every other. (Against Yeats's search in London for a professional actress to play Deirdre, Synge 'would rather go on trying out people for ten years than bring in this ready-made style of acting that is so likely to destroy

the sort of distinction everyone recognises in our company'.) So what is to be distinct about the Royal Shakespeare Company? On the evidence of 1972 not the acting – unless through the locally superb performance; and such individual excellence you might see also at the Bolton Octagon, the Chester Gateway, or the Swansea Grand – but the staging. A false emphasis, surely. It's harder, of course, to train actors than to costume them, and the rewards are often less immediately apparent. But the life of the theatre is in the actor, not the edifice, nor the lighting, nor the costumes and stage properties. The announced total cost of the alterations during the winter of 1971/2 is 'approximately £90,000', and right enough by me that the Royal Shakespeare Company should have that kind of money. What, I wonder, is the actor's share? There were too many subsidiary actors, in 1972, who seemed quite simply inadequate, ill-at-ease with Shakespeare's language and evidently unable to sustain a conviction of their own importance. Did they feel less crucial to the season than the new stage? That way lies artistic bankruptcy and the first hydraulically-operated Bingo Hall in England. It is in its acting that the Royal Shakespeare Company should aim to excel. The current emphasis on conspicuous expenditure exposes those weaknesses of the acting company that it may at worst be intended to disguise. It is an obstruction that could be overcome by a single artistic decision. There is enough money in Stratford not only to employ

139

but also genuinely to care for a uniquely-talented group of actors. Meanwhile the revival of *The Comedy of Errors* ten years after its first production provoked unfavourable comparisons with the original performance. What the actors achieved was not precision itself but the shadow of precision. They lacked exuberance because they lacked the skill that earns it. Synge's metaphor will serve to define my response to the performance as a whole. Here was a ready-made cast in a production once made splendidly to measure. I do not intend to make any special comment on the 1972 *Comedy of Errors*. 'The present newly-cast revival', said the programme, 'is the production's fourth at Stratford.' The reasons for pumping it back into the repertoire after seven years were, I suspect, more cogent off-stage than on it, and I find it hard to see how the actors stood to benefit. Not many prizes are given for dancing in dead men's shoes. As it was, the production highlighted the inflexibility of the company's middle actors. Hazlitt would have regretted their lack of the *gusto* essential to comedy, and in the Roman plays a general lack of urgency. It is a long time since the fifty-lines-and-under speaking parts were played so badly at Stratford, and that, however you look at it, is serious.

The Royal Shakespeare Company offers itself (not willingly) as a model of 'director's theatre', and in 1972 it was conspicuously so. Why should Trevor Nunn, by all accounts a modest and kindly man, have set himself the task of directing all four of the Roman plays? It was bound to stretch him beyond likely endurance. Another question. Why, by selecting a group-title for the season, did he invite comparison with the Wars of the Roses season of 1964? I can see why he has gone out of his way to resist the comparison in his public statements, but still, why did he invite it? He must have felt either challenged or trapped into laying his reputation on the line. 'What a

director needs to know', Stephen Joseph was liable to say, 'is how and when the cast likes tea.' And that may be the kind of overstatement needed to re-adjust the balance between actor and director. John Russell Brown has come firmly to the view that 'the actor must be much more freed from directorial control if he is to discover this particular kind of richness that lies hidden within Shakespeare's text, and the audience's focus of attention needs to be almost wholly upon him'.[1] I don't suppose that Trevor Nunn would quarrel with this; but his productions do. To some extent, he is victim as well as beneficiary of present theatrical assumptions; but, as artistic director of the Royal Shakespeare Company, he must have agreed, tacitly at least, to whatever conditions at Stratford he has not created. Some indication of the restlessness of British actors in a director's theatre has been given in 1972 by the formation of The Actors' Company. Ian McKellen, one of its founder-members, has very politely made the point that in the National Theatre and in the Royal Shakespeare Company 'the actors are one of the last things to happen in the process of putting on a production'.[2] It is sufficient for my case that McKellen should *think* this true. Directors would strenuously deny it, I'm sure. Nunn's own method, however, seems partly to corroborate McKellen's view. He begins, I think, with a unifying idea of the play, which is then reinforced by Christopher Morley's design. The test of every detail is its relationship with the basic idea, which thus becomes a simple equivalent to Stanislavsky's 'through-line of action'. It is in the working of the idea towards theatrical effectiveness that the actors become involved, 'one of the last

[1] The quotation is from Professor Brown's 'Originality in Shakespeare Production', *Theatre Notebook*, xxvi, 3 (1972), but similar views are put forward by the same writer in 'Free Shakespeare' in *Shakespeare Survey 24* (Cambridge, 1971).

[2] In an interview with Gordon Gow reported in *Plays and Players*, 19, no. 12 (September 1972), 36–7.

things to happen in the process of putting on a production'. I am not suggesting that Nunn has pre-determined what his actors will do – his rehearsals are freer than were Peter Hall's, for example – but he has decided what will be *meant* by what they do. Inevitably he must select from what is 'offered up' at rehearsal those ideas that tend to corroborate his prior view. In *Shakespeare Survey 24*, John Russell Brown argued that this forceful pursuit of a unifying idea is an over-severe limitation on the presentation of Shakespeare's variety. The 1972 season might have provided Professor Brown with an ideal text. It has certainly carried me towards a fuller acceptance of his arguments, particularly where they look to the liberation of the actor from the demand for definitive performance.

I need to pause there. I find myself on the edge of accusing Trevor Nunn of dictatorial excesses, and I don't mean to. It is one of the curses of 'director's theatre' that it blurs the distinction between personal attack and the exploration of ideas. Nunn admits to his productions nothing that he could not para-phrase. It is my own view that his theatricality is an overlay on a disparately unadorned interpretation of the text. There is something almost frugal about his published views of the Roman plays. Nowhere does he argue that they bore any special relationship in Shakespeare's mind. What they share for him is, quite simply, Rome – and the politics of Rome as Shake-speare pictured them at four different historical crises. He thinks of the growth from small tribe to City-state (*Coriolanus*), to Republic (*Julius Caesar*), to Empire (*Antony and Cleopatra*), and to a decadence that is the prelude to Gothic conquest (*Titus Andronicus*). He would concede the possibility of revealing literary develop-ment by performing the plays in the reverse order, but his own greater interest is in political structures and contrasts. His case for grouping the plays is the moderate one that

'it's interesting for an audience to be able to see Shakespeare return on four separate occasions in his writing lifetime, to a society which clearly fascinated him'.[1] In the event, there was too much insistence on continuity in the visual presentation, and an alertness to political analogy that drew too much of the plays' weight with it and became this season's parti-cular interpretative distortion. But Nunn, how-ever the scholars may squirm, is not careless of Shakespeare's text. His attempts to realise his responses theatrically are more wayward than the responses themselves. They seem sometimes imposed rather than inherent, an expensive gift-wrapping on an unpretentious gift.

This was particularly the problem of *Coriolanus* with which the season opened. To understand what Nunn was doing here, we need to take a closer look at the winter's reconstruction work in the Royal Shakespeare Theatre. The alterations to the auditorium involved, most importantly, the thrusting out of the stage some eighteen feet from the proscenium arch. It is on this forestage, forty feet wide, that the majority of the action in all the plays takes place. You can't, of course, put a tennis-court in a hen-roost and expect the bounce to be entirely even. The audience at Stratford is still placed for easy viewing through the arch, and the dominant scenic impression when the stage is bare is of corridor-like depth rather than thrust. Furthermore, the sightlines this season were sometimes dreadful. It was exciting to sit in the front row for *Julius Caesar* and have that magical red carpet hurtle down the stage at me, but whenever the stage was raised its leading edge was an obstructive and dominant part of the scenic image. On my first visit to *Coriolanus* I sat ten seats in on Row G of the stalls, and noted down during act I, 'Sightlines bad from here.' My point is only that things have not altogether improved.

[1] In an interview with Margaret Tierney reported in *Plays and Players*, 19, no. 12, pp. 23–7.

The circle, I'm sure, is a gainer by the new arrangement, and to a lesser extent the gallery. The stalls are worse off than they were before. There is no acoustic drawback if we except a spot downstage centre from which curious resonances are set up. My major reservation is about the claims made for the new one-room actor/audience relationship. The 1972 season failed for two obvious reasons to put this really to the test. It failed, firstly, because the battery of lights separated the stage from the auditorium quite as decisively as the proscenium arch would have done, and secondly, because the really spectacular changes were not in the auditorium but on the stage itself. Until the late advent of *Titus Andronicus*, it was the elaborate hydraulic mechanism that commanded our attention, not the forestage-slab, and the most adventurous of the lifts were upstage of the proscenium. I very much doubt whether there is any chance of a one-room situation in the Stratford theatre, but the final judgement must await a different approach to designing on the new stage. Christopher Morley, who planned the alterations, was Nunn's senior designer throughout the season. The basic setting, described in the programme as 'flexible "stone" textured', had massive wing-blocks angled in upstage as they have often been in Morley's previous work at Stratford, and a slanted ceiling suspended over the forestage. These, as well as the stage floor, were made up of off-white paving blocks, oddly sticky in appearance like the chunks of nougat you can still find in some confectioneries. Brightly lit, as it was for most of *Coriolanus* and *Julius Caesar*, it became over-dominant after an hour or so. The canopies and coloured lighting of *Antony and Cleopatra* burnished it wonderfully. It wasn't until this third play that the movable stage showed its real worth. The sudden creation of Pompey's ship, complete with mast and slung sail, was fascinating to watch, the transformation from Egypt (full stage with cushions and canopies) to Rome (forestage only, with a wall map of the Empire filling the proscenium arch) scarcely less so; but the crowning trick of the acrobatic stage came with the creation of Cleopatra's Monument. The whole stage floor heaved, swung, and bent to make it. The heavings of *Coriolanus* seemed, by comparison, purposeless, a ceaseless turmoil, 'as if this earth in fast thick pants were breathing', or as if a designer's whim demanded a change of level for each change of scene. Despite its dazzling newness, this hydraulic stage can strangely echo the excesses of nineteenth-century productions: once again each shift of location can command a whole different stage picture. In designing Tree's *Julius Caesar*, Alma-Tadema needed to know what Hann and Harker could paint (scene-painting, I suppose, is a dwindling craft) and the stage-hands manipulate. Beyond that, he was limited only by the mechanism of the stage and his own imagination. In designing Nunn's *Julius Caesar*, Morley needed to know only what his lifts could be made to do. If we can accept a preponderance of straight lines and Roman right-angles (how many of Shakespeare's plays are as right-angled as these?), they are, in fact, very versatile. And they have the priceless advantage of transforming the stage picture so quickly that the flow of the action is not interrupted. In 1972, the contrary values of the unit set were on display in *The Comedy of Errors*, and in *Antony and Cleopatra* there were happy signs of a marriage between the two styles. What a pity, though, that III, i survived only until the public previews. No twentieth-century theatre has ever been better equipped to show Ventidius in triumph with Pacorus dead.

Coriolanus opened with a massed entry, a downstage march and a brief mime of Romulus and Remus suckled by the She-Wolf. At the dispersal of the silent scene, a patrician trampled on the ill-clad body of a starving plebeian. Smeared with Lancastrian grime, and costumed in grey rags, the Plebeians were placed in a kind of dirty shanty-town. Menenius stood like a bar of soap among blackheads. Indeed, the cleanliness of the patricians was a constant correlative of Coriolanus's fastidiousness. As Menenius, Mark Dignam treated the plebeians like unruly grandchildren. He quelled them without raising his voice: and he handled the verse with equal composure. It was one of the season's pleasures to hear Dignam and Raymond Westwell, another senior actor, demonstrating how Shakespeare's verse can relax the voice of the actor who speaks it with pleasure. For too many of the company, Ian Hogg included, the throat tends to tighten around the pentameter. Hogg spoke Coriolanus badly wherever the need was for a sustaining of verbal rhythms. It was a severe defect, that blinded many critics to his fine pointing of those moments of emotional hiatus that accompany Coriolanus's fumbling compromises. I remember particularly the bitter play on 'mildly' (III, ii), and the throwing down of his sword before:

> Pray be content.
> Mother, I am going to the market-place.
> (III, ii, 130–1)

Hogg said this as 'Pray be content (pause) mother. (Long pause, and then in gathering crescendo) I am going to the market-place!' Back, that is, to the verminous, grey slum of the plebeians, which offends him utterly. It was, in many ways, a strange piece of casting. Hogg has a flashing, piratical smile and a bearing expressive of compressed energy, but he is not patrician. I was reminded of Eric Bentley's comment on Robert Ryan's playing of the role: 'if Coriolanus is not an aristocrat he is just a disgruntled gladiator'.[1] There was something, in Hogg's performance, of the temperamental sporting star, a George Best sulkily crossing Manchester to help the welcoming City defeat a shaken United. He was,

in other words, charismatic, but not as Shakespeare's Coriolanus is charismatic, who will be to Rome 'as is the osprey to the fish, who takes it / By sovereignty of nature'.

The production's major visual shock came with the entrance of the Volsces. Echoing the play's opening, they swept downstage after a massed entry, to be stopped short by a suddenly lit fire. They were costumed and made up as Aztecs or Indians, primitive tribesmen. After the rout of Corioles, the remnant would gather round a camp-fire (I, x), and the revitalised army carried totem poles in place of standards (IV, vii). As Tullus Aufidius, Patrick Stewart wore a mandarin moustache and a superb black pony-tail, and spoke with an unemotional oriental lilt. His 'I was moved withal' in answer to Coriolanus's 'would you have heard / A mother less? Or granted less, Aufidius?' (V, iii, 192–3), was made threateningly ambiguous by the tonal inscrutability; but local felicities are insufficient justification for so deviant a reading. There was something altogether haywire about the Volsces. No others spoke like Stewart. Their soldiers, senators and lords were prone to enigmatic stillness, but the servingmen of IV, v were traditional stage cockneys. The decision to set Roman and Volscian civilisation so sensationally apart had not been thought through. There is, anyway, flimsy evidence for it. There is nothing alien about Roman morality to the Volscian soldiers who quarrel with Menenius and conspire against Coriolanus. It was, I suspect, an example of that imposed theatricality to which I have referred. Stewart moved about the stage with a feline grace that led readily into the bisexuality of his greeting to Coriolanus:

> But that I see thee here,
> Thou noble thing, more dances my rapt heart
> Than when I first my wedded mistress saw
> Bestride my threshold. (IV, v, 115–18)

[1] Bentley's review is reprinted in *What is Theatre?* (New York, 1968), pp. 134–8.

But the polarity for which the production strove is not present in the text. It seemed like role-playing unanchored to the play itself, and certainly of no use in defining the political conflicts on which the Roman scenes were made to pivot.

The Roman opposition of plebeians and patricians was both more effective and more consistent. The finest moments of political confrontation were attended always by the admirably-played tribunes. By letting their voices simply say the words, and by seeming always to be confiding in each other, Raymond Westwell and Gerald James found secret corners all over the stage. They were content not to create so much as to indicate revolutionary processes, like Marxist opportunists exploiting social confrontations without themselves resorting to terrorism:

> Let's to the Capitol,
> And carry with us ears and eyes for th' time,
> But hearts for the event.   (II, i, 258–60)

It was the younger and more spirited patricians whom they most offended, and who became Coriolanus' strongest supporters. (I don't know whether Nunn intended this. In *Julius Caesar* the younger senators supported Brutus more eagerly than their elders.) Coriolanus was never any political match for these tribunes. He reconciled himself to his quest for the popular vote as he later reconciled himself to his defection to the Volsces, by making a game of it. Even so, it seemed perverse to have him delivering the appeal for the plebeians' voices in a downstage spotlight. The interestingly characterised First Citizen (man-with-a-grievance) laid heavy ironical stress on his reply to Sicinius' question, 'How now, my masters, have you chose this man?' 'He has our *voices*, sir.' The conduct of the crowd in this scene made good sense of Sicinius' closing words to Brutus:

> To th' Capitol, come.
> We will be there before the stream o' th' people;
> And this shall seem, as partly 'tis, their own,
> Which we have goaded onward.   (II, iii, 257–60)

It was only in physical action that this Coriolanus excelled; and here he was not well served by the production. The battle at Corioles had a bit of everything – smoke, strobe, realism, stylisation, ballet, mime, wrestling, sword-fights. A fight-arranger's cadenza, composed by shuffling clichés on a raked stage. The skirmish in the Capitol was unsatisfactory too. Having tossed burning cloths at the patricians, the plebeians fled. Why? I thought they were winning. Perhaps they thought we wouldn't notice if it happened fast enough. Hogg himself was physically exultant in these scenes; but act I was unbelievably messy. The pale playing of Virgilia and Valeria, and even Margaret Tyzack's much stronger Volumnia, was swallowed up in the general confusion. My note at this stage was, 'They aren't telling the story.' The first interval followed act I (the second followed IV, ii). After it everything improved, but it was an abiding defect of the production that it seemed more concerned to interpret than to render the fable.

The production of *Julius Caesar* was coherent and too slow-footed. It opened with deafening drum-beats, the unrolling of a wide red carpet, a massed entry, and a mime of Brutus crowning Caesar with laurel. There followed a raised-arm salute and the shout of 'Caesar!' The programme informed us, above references to Mussolini, Napoleon, Hitler, Mobutu, and Sheikh Karume, that 'Caesar has been a model for other military dictators seeking to impose the legend of themselves on history', and Mark Dignam certainly looked the part. His war injuries have given his lip a permanent curl, which can express a worldly tolerance as it did in Menenius, but which can also be cold and cruel as it was here. There was nothing attractive about this Caesar, except perhaps to the National Front. He was pathetic only insofar as he was brittle, a man without dignified access to his private self. Particularly in contrast to John Wood's precise, ascetic Brutus he seemed unthinking, even unintelligent. It was implied by the production's emotional balance that Rome was well rid of Caesar, that Brutus' fastidious liberalism held no prospect of good government, particularly since Patrick Stewart's Cassius was slow-witted to the point of stupidity, that Antony might have done much, but that the steely and utterly loveless Octavius would do more. At the end of the play there was a pointed ambiguity. Octavius' invitation to Antony to '*part* the glories of this *happy* day' was followed by his immediate brisk exit *right*. Alone on stage, Antony shook his head slightly, and slowly walked off *left*. It was a clear advantage of performing the plays as a group to be able to end thus, without a conclusion.

Caesar's Rome was a police state, with black-armoured soldiers to enforce the law. The tribunes fell suddenly silent when two of these blackshirts made the long cross from upstage left to downstage right. It was a nicely-judged interpolation. These same soldiers would later provide a bodyguard to protect Caesar from the well-intentioned Soothsayer and Artemidorus; but it was a strange production feature that they stood by during the assassination. Brutus made some slight gesture to the pair standing stage left, but what of those stage right? It seemed an unintended implication that the conspirators had allies in the ranks of the army. The first heavy stress of John Wood's Brutus fell on his answer to Cassius' querying whether he would want Caesar crowned:

I would not, Cassius; yet I love him well.

(I, ii, 82)

Wood aimed to express the nervous tension of a man only too well aware of the contradictions in his own loyalties. At times there was the hint of a stammer. Perhaps the precision of Brutus's delivery had been cultivated to overcome it, the effort of will of a highly-strung intellectual. In the quarrel-scene his self-possession was profoundly threatened, and the deliberateness, so insulting to Cassius, no more than the forced restraint of a lost temper. The mindlessness of Caesar's strong-arm police was bound to pain this sensitive man. From the opening dialogue with Cassius and on through the play, Wood showed clearly what is both Brutus' greatness and his weakness, that he can understand politics only by analogy with the conduct of his own life. He was not only self-possessed, but self-absorbed. Cassius, whatever his illusions, had no effect on him. I thought the reading of Cassius too partial. 'Seldom he smiles', says Caesar, but Patrick Stewart grinned incessantly. In the storm and in the quarrel he was operatic, never patrician, never of adequate stature. There was no sense that Brutus loved him. John Wood's greater concern with his own thought-processes seemed the condition even of his tolerance of the 'slight' Cassius. Casca was more interesting. Gerald James gave him a dry, donnish pedantry: 'I saw Mark Antony offer him a crown; yet 'twas not a crown neither, 'twas one of these coronets....' The other conspirators fell within the area of this company's weakness. The assassination will often be better done. Perhaps it had lost fire outside the rehearsal room. Brutus' deliberate slitting of Caesar's throat should have been horrifying, but it wasn't. Even Cassius' convulsive stabbing of the corpse until forcibly restrained by Brutus lacked true conviction.

It is one of the curiosities of the play that Brutus and Caesar say scarcely anything to each other. Nevertheless, the pivot of the first part of this performance, which took its single interval after IV, i, was the juxtaposition of the two main scenes in act II. Brutus thought through his soliloquy. Caesar fretted when he was alone. Both men had black servants (an immediate image of slavery), but Brutus was tender where Caesar was peremptory. Portia was treated with respect, the physically demonstrative Calphurnia with embarrassment. When the conspirators had gone, and he was alone again, Brutus began to shiver; a nice detail, matched in the subsequent scene by having the confident Antony flop carelessly into Caesar's thronelike chair. The scenes were both thoughtfully directed, but there were some puzzling design features. Brutus' 'orchard' contained a single dead tree, and Caesar's courtyard was dominated by a massive statue of himself, roped as if in storage or in transit. This clumsy piece, spotlit, would later become Caesar's Ghost and an attendant spirit at the Battle of Philippi. I thought it ridiculously obtrusive.

The entrance of Antony's servant after the assassination was marked as a dividing point in the play by the bringing up of the lights. Both before and after his funeral oration, Richard Johnson's Antony was often morose; but he spoke the great speech with authority despite the awkward downstage placing of the pulpit. I was surprised to find the crowd as grey and almost as dirty as in Coriolanus. They had an impossible job trying to react to Brutus and Antony with their backs to the audience and confined to a thin ribbon of stage between the pulpit and the corpse, particularly since they were too few to do what was required of them. The designer had been too influential here, as he had in the placing of the interval. There is no case for making IV, i a postscript to the funeral and the slaughter of Cinna the Poet, but it had been decided to give Brutus and Cassius a real tent for their quarrel, and that needed an interval's setting. The tent was not only unnecessary, but out of keeping, and the transformation from outside to inside was much less impressive than the fine one at the monument in *Antony and Cleopatra*. Brutus dominated the quarrel, his tension hovering constantly around breaking-point until the unnamed *poet* (a drunken soldier in a comic wig)

gave him a harmless pretext for the release of anger. The sobs that escaped him on 'Portia is dead' were part of the same release. The dual account of her death was retained, but there was some suggestion (not a firm one) in Brutus' handling of his papers that he had read the information only just before he announced it. It was merely to humour an overwrought man that Titinius, Messala, and Cassius agreed to march to Philippi.

As in *Coriolanus*, the play dwindled in its battle scenes. The decision had been made to costume the two armies exactly similarly, which made a point about Civil War but didn't do much for the plot. It was, perhaps, as a contrast to Octavius' formality that Antony sat by Brutus' corpse to speak his elegy. The opposition was physically vivid. A swarthy, black-bearded, black-haired Antony in uneasy alliance with a blond, pink-skinned, clean-shaven Octavius. We were intended to look for a sequel.

In *Antony and Cleopatra* the stage looked fine, and the actors dominated the director – to his credit. After the discipline of white light and half-light in the previous two plays, the billowing canopy and coloured light of the opening mime promised the visual richness which followed. The black-clad Roman soldiers were conspicuously severe amid the display of Antony's dotage. They were more at ease in the colder light of the Roman scenes. It was a contrast that found an echo in Richard Johnson's portrayal of Antony. 'He was disposed to mirth; but on the sudden / A Roman thought hath struck him' (I, ii, 79–80). Every aspect of the production enforced this opposition (in an insistence on the unifying idea, there is always a threat of theatrical tautology), but I was intrigued by Johnson's use of physical posture to imply mental schism. In Rome he stood straight, and spoke decisively, as in the assertive quelling of Octavius at 'I am not married, Caesar' (II, ii, 127). In Egypt he was slightly stooped, self-consciously ageing, the vacillating Antony divided against himself. His inability to choose between a land or sea battle was entirely convincing, its ground thoroughly prepared. I had not expected such compassionate acting from Johnson, who has always lacked the great actor's vivid life-of-the-eyes. It was a characterisation centred on melancholy, melodically spoken, and with a concern for detail that did not blur the general outline. (A contrast, in this last, with Wood's Brutus?) If it failed at all, it was in the establishment of a full relationship with Cleopatra. But that was, perhaps, more a result of the view of the play pressed home by Janet Suzman as Cleopatra. It was the view that Cleopatra's worthiness is nowhere in evidence before act v. Miss Suzman was gloriously dressed, witty, graceful and sexually alert – Enobarbus was quite in earnest when he swore that 'Age cannot wither her, nor custom stale / Her infinite variety' (II, ii, 239–40) – but she was also frivolous and evidently superficial. She played best the scenes which she could control. Her delivery of the rebuff to Charmian, which brought to a halt the teasing references to her liaison with Caesar, was impeccably timed; a pause, a half-smile, and then the confession which she made erotic, 'My salad days, / When I was green in judgment...' (I, v, 73–4). This mastery of the comic line was characteristic. It was the same concern for the beautifully perfected that informed her dying. Miss Suzman had some difficulty in reconciling this aspect of the character with the phrenetic beating of the messenger and the panic-stricken flight to the Monument, but it would misrepresent my response if I were to quibble further with the performance of the two principals. I missed Ashcroft and Redgrave. I hope, some day, people will be as sorry to have missed Johnson and Suzman. And let them add a word for Patrick Stewart's quiet-spoken Enobarbus, improbably avuncular and good-humoured in mutton-chop whiskers, but widening the play's image of friendship with every conversation he held. There was nothing wrong with the idea of having him die with the weakest of whimpers, lying still and supine on a dimly-lit raked stage throughout his final speeches; but, in practice, it was theatrically untidy. Had we come already to depend on the scenery to complete the stage picture, so that the bare stage was visually frustrating? There is, as I have already suggested, a disturbing possibility that the mobile staging will prove to have contributed to this retreat into the past. William Poel is juddering in his grave.

A major problem in staging *Antony and Cleopatra* is to maintain momentum. Until the first interval, at the end of act II, there was no slackening. The story was clearly told, despite Shakespeare's unusually clumsy introduction of the Pompey episodes. The loutish scene on Pompey's galley was carried with gusto. Corin Redgrave's stiffness as Octavius was not all acted, but his distaste was palpable. He did his job, which was to make Octavius entirely unsympathetic, a killjoy and a lubricious puritan. Such men enter Egypt in the hope of finding blue films to confiscate. The second act of this production (from III, ii to IV, iii) was more daring, and, if it failed, failed bravely. They attempted to present the dwindling energies of Egypt without surrendering the audience's attention. This was the slow movement, played predominantly in a minor key. The last act began softly. There was no exaggerated triumph after Antony's temporary victory, and the entry of Cleopatra and her court to the accompaniment of tinkling bells was a witty theatrical reminder of the effete alternative to war. The sudden rush of Cleopatra's panic-stricken flight to the Monument was finely staged. The canopy had collapsed and the cushions were strewn about. It was an image of departed glory. It was here that Antony stabbed himself. There followed the magnificent transformation to the Monument. This was so genuinely a fortress, so visibly impregnable, that its capture by the Roman soldiers achieved the status of a major event. It was in its aftermath that Cleopatra could prepare herself for a deliberate and stately death.

I saw *Titus Andronicus* before it had had time to settle, and before the establishment of its final detail. There may, then, be apparent inaccuracies in my review that are not wholly so. I wonder, for example, whether it ever came to be more brightly lit. I found myself generally peering at the stage, on which an apron of half-light (the play was performed almost exclusively downstage of the proscenium) was backed by impenetrable upstage darkness. Apart from the side-lit green of the hunt-scenes, and despite the gaudy nights of Saturninus, the resultant mood was one almost of parsimony after the splendours of *Antony and Cleopatra*. Even the raked stage was still, its whiteness smothered in a dark carpet, and only isolated set-pieces and the provision of Titus' house with an unspectacular *above* made the locations scenically distinct from each other. In its reliance elsewhere on descriptive properties, this was the season's most Elizabethan production.

It opened unconvincingly, with the bringing on of a life-size statue of the late Emperor, half-clad on a couch, eating grapes. The image of decadence was thus over-enforced from the start, and John Wood's degenerate Saturninus revealed as a chip off an old and possibly syphilitic block. This did not seem to me the Rome Titus greets on his return:

> Kind Rome, that hast thus lovingly reserv'd
> The cordial of mine age to glad my heart!
> Lavinia live; outlive thy father's days,
> And fame's eternal date, for virtue's praise!
>
> (I, i, 165–8)

And Titus cannot be lightly dismissed as 'out of

touch' or 'misled'. His reasons for declining candidature for the Empire are authoritative:

> Give me a staff of honour for mine age,
> But not a sceptre to control the world:
> Upright he held it, lords, that held it last.
>
> (I, i, 198–200)

The play describes, not the continuance of an established decadence, but the overthrow of virtue until its promised restoration through Lucius Andronicus. Trevor Nunn had persuaded himself that it gives a picture of Rome in decline and imminent fall; but that is writing on a different scale. What has *The Spanish Tragedy* to say about monarchical Spain?

The bias of the opening scene obscured Titus' fatal error in supporting Saturninus, a choice which ruins Rome with its Gothic consequences and calls out the patriotic treachery of Lucius. In the comparison of Lucius to Coriolanus (IV, iv, 67), there was a clear chance to link the season's last play to its first. Nunn gave both roles to Ian Hogg, but the resemblance went little further. Hogg played Lucius without a hint of flamboyance. An inserted soliloquy at the end of III, i had him holding the crucifix that he wore round his neck, and there were further explicit references to his Christianity in the oath to Aaron (v, i), and in the taking of bread and wine after the final slaughter. The oafish sadism of Chiron and Demetrius was the strongest possible contrast to this good man. In v, i Lucius was more isolated than the captured Aaron among the Goths, who found in Aaron's table of horrors a cause for admiring laughter. The lack of action for the Goths at and after the fatal banquet is a damaging lacuna in the play, and these plausibly brutish barbarians made a stronger impression than could be comfortably fobbed off at the play's skimped end. Not so Calvin Lockhart's disappointing Aaron. The physical presence was there, but without vocal backing, so that he wasted more Shakespearian opportunities than most of the company got within reach of.

The play had the season's strongest cast; and though I thought Margaret Tyzack too cool for the lusts of Tamora and Janet Suzman unresolved about Lavinia, each of them had fine moments. But the impression that remains most vividly with me is of the contrast between Colin Blakely's weighty playing of Titus and John Wood's perilously frivolous treatment of Saturninus.

What should I say of this performance of John Wood's? It was clever and indulgent, inventive and destructive, memorable and possibly quite unforgivable. I thought at various times of Caligula, Cloten, Kenneth Williams, Louis XI, and the terrified mad king of Ghelderode's *Escurial*. There is warrant in the text for the selfish, indecisive voluptuary that Wood presented, but at some point in rehearsal, invention seems to have superseded perception. The marriage to Tamora became the pretext for an inserted skipping entrance in a fancy cloak. The hunting horns found out his hangover, and he slapped his cheeks ringingly to rouse himself. By now he had earned several laughs, and sacrificed any right to judge Titus' sons. In the inserted transvestite revelry before IV, ii, he lay stretched on a couch, too ill to open his eyes, until he toppled off and staggered comically out to vomit. In IV, iv, undressed and with his wig awry, he tossed Titus' arrows over his shoulder at the cyclorama, then flopped onto his throne to be patched towards dignity by a crowd of courtiers. News of Lucius' treachery evoked a tantrum, and he belaboured Aemilius' breastplate with the silken sleeve of his purple smock. Perhaps I am being over-solemn. This shrunken-shanked, fragile man, too effete to stay upright on the cover of *The Yellow Book*, was a potent image of degeneracy, and even if the gags were familiar, Wood's angularity and tartness gave them an aura of the unexpected.

But the problems came with the last scene, when the clowning is for Titus to do, and when Saturninus must avenge a murder by killing in his turn. Blakely here had the disturbing power of the grotesque, but Wood remained confined to the burlesque. He committed suicide (why? out of fright?) by biting something from, I think, his ring, and falling in a ludicrous spasm from the couch on which he stood. Is this not all bound to undermine the last scene's tenuous hold on us?

Colin Blakely, you might have thought, had been at different rehearsals. He had substance and severity from the start. He was sturdy, weather-beaten, and grandly ageing, a man more suited to the containment of passion than to its expression. The events of the play forced him consistently out of character. His anger, like his pride, is physical rather than verbal. He can kill Alarbus and even Mutius without shouting; but then, there are usually people near enough to hear what he quietly says. This is no longer so after the first tumultuous scene, when Saturninus has led Tamora off:

Titus, when wert thou wont to walk alone...
(I, i, 339)

Blakely said this in bemused awareness of an astonishing reversal. For him, the events of the play were literally unspeakable. The attempts to comfort Lavinia, in particular to feed her, were painful to watch. Eventually he would kill her by a sudden jerking break of the neck, without further disfigurement.

There was never any chance that this Titus would flourish in the Rome of this Saturninus. The melancholy little scene in which Marcus kills the fly was the aftermath of Titus' terrible laugh in III, i. 'Why dost thou laugh? It fits not with this hour', asks Marcus, and Blakely gave in slow reply, 'Why, I have not another tear to shed'. At that point, or near it, his physical repose was lost, and he developed the fitful bouncing motion that culminated in his bizarre dance at the banquet, a pattern of movement almost as declaratory as Serjeant Musgrave's. I did not see Olivier's Titus, but I feel privileged to have seen Blakely's. It stands solidly behind my disappointment over a modest Aaron, the uneasiness about so demon-strative a Saturninus, and the interest of seeing how strongly Lucius could be made to play.

I ought, perhaps, to add that the production was more notable for its restraint than for any indulgence in physical excess. The tale is nastier than was its telling.

© PETER THOMSON 1973

THE YEAR'S CONTRIBUTIONS TO
SHAKESPEARIAN STUDY

1. CRITICAL STUDIES

reviewed by NORMAN SANDERS

When so much of the criticism of Shakespeare during the present century has, after the manner of Bradley and Knight, tended to move naturally into the wider issues of the plays, it is refreshing to come across a book which concerns itself with one specific technical aspect of them, which turns out to have real critical implications. Such is E. Jones's *Scenic Form in Shakespeare*[1] which focuses our attention on the scene as *the* basic dramatic unit in the plays. The early chapters offer a virtuoso display of perception on such topics as the nature of the theater audience, the creation of the 'audience mind', the basically simple design of the big set scenes, the variety of patterns in information-giving scenes, the methods of increasing and retarding tempo, and the nature of dramatic time. At every point Jones's schematizations are illustrated by brilliant close analyses of particular scenes (outstanding examples are the discussions of *Titus*, III, i, and *Caesar*, I, ii), extended discussion of the pacing of scenes in complete plays, and the whole question of the time-scheme in *Othello*. He detects in the Histories and Tragedies a two-part structure with each section being characterized by its own theatrical unity of time. In the second part of the book he views *Othello*, *Lear*, *Macbeth*, and *Antony and Cleopatra* in the light of his defined types of scenic form; and it is in these essays that his technical analyses become a genuinely illuminating critical approach which reinforces the interpretations of some plays derived from the work of other critics (e.g.

Macbeth), while with others (e.g. *Antony and Cleopatra*) difficulties that perplexed other men are explained away by a new way of looking.

Time in a more philosophical sense is the subject of F. Turner's recent book.[2] His starting-point is the concept of 'time as dynamic, as process and becoming' and his concern is 'with the arsenal of thoughts, feelings, and attitudes with which Shakespeare attacks the central problems of man's temporal nature and his relationship with his environment of time'. He traces with some subtlety in the plays and poems Shakespeare's handling of historical, sequential time, the dynamic and personal experience of time, time as the realm opposed to the eternal, as the agent of growth and decay, as cycle and rhythm, as occasion, as revealer and unfolder of the hidden, as cause and effect, as harmonious and disharmonious rhythm. At no point in these discussions does Turner labor his idea, and there is real insight into the ways these various themes are emphasized and into the theatrical forms they assume, with perhaps the most completely satisfying account being that of the Sonnets.

W. Clemen's *Shakespeare's Dramatic Art*[3] is also an exercise in technical analysis. Half of the volume comprises previously-published papers on Shakespeare's use of various

[1] The Clarendon Press, Oxford, 1971.
[2] *Shakespeare and the Nature of Time. Moral and Philosophical Themes in Some Plays and Poems of William Shakespeare* (Oxford University Press, 1971).
[3] Methuen, 1972.

dramatic devices; but Chapter 1 is a new preliminary sketch on Shakespeare's art of preparation, by which Clemen means such things as the announcement of new characters, the gradual working towards catastrophe or climax extending over several acts, the employment of omens, dreams and portents, the use of irony, the concealed hints, prophetic imagery, and characters' premonitions. He rejects any approach to his subject by means of classification and claims that only by recognizing and demonstrating the interdependence and co-operation of individual methods of preparation can we grasp the topic's complexity. After some good introductory remarks on the nature of drama and the demands it makes on the playwright, Clemen offers specimen analyses of eight plays, all of which are characterized by the kind of responsiveness to language and theatrical effect and the unpretentious subtlety that we have come to expect from him. One hopes that this essay is really a report on work in progress.

The self-reflecting aspect of the plays is much in vogue at the moment, and two recent books are devoted to it. T. Weiss uses the plays up to *Twelfth Night* to trace those elements which indicate that the poet was continually obsessed with his own art.[1] The chapters on the early Comedies are somewhat overwritten and contain a mixture of the obvious and the perceptive. However, Weiss can be very acute on how the poetry works, and he makes a good case (at the cost of some narrowing of the plays' overall effects) for a Shakespeare at first caught up with the glittering sound of words and self-absorbed, but in whose hands words increasingly 'found radiance and power through the absorption in and of the world'. J. L. Calderwood[2] also takes the plays to be about themselves. After a somewhat self-regarding introduction on the subject of metadrama, he rides his theory rather hard through five of the early plays so that *Titus*

presents us with the rape of language and the mutilation of the poet's tongue when his spirit is obliged to submit to the requirements of a theater barbarized by popular sensationalism and classical authority; *Love's Labour's Lost* shows us the impossibility of reconciling poetry with dramatic form; *Romeo and Juliet* reveals an erotic lyricism sealed off from a plague-ridden milieu; *Richard II* records the divorce of the poet–dramatist from his surrounding world order; and in *A Midsummer Night's Dream* we witness the marriage of all the elements of Shakespeare's art into a complete harmony. Perhaps it should be noted that once one has dragged through the first chapter, the essays on the plays all contain useful observations, with the discussion of *A Midsummer Night's Dream* as a meditation on dramatic art being quite distinguished.

It has been generally agreed for 400 years that Shakespeare's Comedies are 'relevant' and I suppose it was inevitable that their special relevance for the relevant generation would be demonstrated. The opening chapter of H. M. Richmond's new book warns us about the originality of his approach and tells us about the really up-to-date features of the playwright's erotic ideas.[3] Actually this transpires to be a snappy version of the old nineteenth-century view of how sweet the Swan of Avon must have been in real life because his plays contain such nice thoughts and feelings. Richmond believes that 'Shakespeare consistently seems to advocate a basic change in his audience's conventional idealism of sexual love, a sceptical modification sufficiently extraordinary and universal to bear as directly on our modern behaviour as anything in Freud or Fromm' and contends that the only mature lovers are those

[1] *The Breath of Clowns and Kings* (Atheneum, New York, 1971).
[2] *Shakesperean Metadrama* (University of Minnesota Press, 1971).
[3] *Shakespeare's Sexual Comedy: A Mirror for Lovers* (Bobbs-Merrill, New York, 1971).

who evolve a detached yet participating role in sexual relationships and manage to maintain their sturdy independence as human beings. Thus, the witty skeptics like Biron, Katharina, and Petruchio come in for a good deal of praise at the expense of fatally idealistic lovers like Romeo and Othello in a series of essays which are always lively, often perceptive, remorselessly practical, and based on the conviction that names like Mario Savio and Cody's Bookshop resound with the universal allusiveness of Voltaire and the Bastille.

R. A. Foakes[1] concentrates on the form the comic spirit assumed in the Dark Comedies and the Last Plays. During his final phase Foakes believes that 'Shakespeare learned how to liberate himself from a commitment to character presented with psychological and linguistic consistency' so as to achieve special effects, noticeably those of distancing the audience to prevent empathy. Foakes's ultimate aim in this exceptionally well-planned book is to examine the dramatic structures and tonality of the Romances so as to challenge the critical orthodoxy's stress on ideas, themes, patterns, and symbols. After a strangely weak discussion of *All's Well That Ends Well*, which largely ignores the issue of dramatic structure and focuses on the roles of Lavatch and Parolles, Foakes considers rewardingly the genres of satirical comedy and tragedy and the problems they present, and provides absolutely first-rate accounts of *Measure for Measure* and the plays of Marston and Tourneur in these kinds. In the section on the Last Plays Shakespeare is seen combining 'techniques learned in earlier plays to create a dramatic world in which human intentions, the will, the act of choice, play a very subdued role, and actions by characters are referable to a psychological condition or compulsion, or to chance, or the influence of an uncertain heaven'. While the discussion of *The Tempest* is conventional, those of *The Winter's Tale* and particularly of *Cymbeline* are unusually

good in demonstrating Shakespeare's construction of play structures that are like the action of our own lives. Some of the railing comic characters, like Thersites and Jaques, are viewed by C. R. Reaske[2] not very convincingly as being the possessors of the kind of wisdom and self-knowledge which the tragic heroes attain only at the end of their lives.

Love's Labour's Lost receives most of the attention afforded the early comedies this year with a good general essay by T. M. Greene,[3] which has a new interpretation of the Masque of the Nine Worthies and lays heavy stress on the suggestion of a possible ideal that a society can achieve. J. J. Anderson,[4] on the other hand, takes the play to have an unemphatic Morality basis directing the audience's attention towards human responsibility rather than spiritual perfection. Two articles concentrate on special aspects of the same play, with J. H. Kodama[5] working from a theatrical production to give an interesting reading of the problematical final lines, and B. Thorne[6] comparing the use of parallel characters with that of Lyly's *Endymion*, but claiming that Shakespeare rebuts Lyly's other-worldly philosophy. The good work done in recent years in establishing *A Midsummer Night's Dream* as one of the profoundest of the Comedies is continued by A. D. Weiner[7] in an excellent paper which

[1] *Shakespeare. The Dark Comedies to the Last Plays: From Satire to Celebration* (Routledge and Kegan Paul, 1971).

[2] 'Shakespeare's Railers and Tragic Heroes', *Michigan Academician*, II (1969), 99–103.

[3] '*Love's Labour's Lost:* The Grace of Society', *Shakespeare Quarterly*, XXII (1971), 315–28.

[4] 'The Morality of *Love's Labour's Lost*', *Shakespeare Survey 24* (Cambridge University Press, 1971), pp. 55–62.

[5] 'Armado's "You That Way; We This Way"', *Shakespeare Studies* (Japan), VIII (1969–70), 1–17.

[6] '*Love's Labour's Lost:* The Lyly Gilded', *Humanities Association Bulletin*, XXI (1970), 32–7.

[7] '"Multiforme Uniforme": *A Midsummer Night's Dream*', *English Literary History*, XXXVIII (1971), 329–49.

discusses the play in terms of the images that the poet implants in our imagination and the emotional reactions they elicit, and the extent to which it may be viewed as Shakespeare's 'Defence of Poesie'. More limitedly, J. A. S. McPeek[1] skillfully traces Shakespeare's refinement and reconstruction of fragments of the Psyche myth from *The Golden Ass*, and M. C. Jochums[2] delineates the role of the fairy world in controlling the human characters while providing an external motivation for the progress of the action.

Two articles take up different themes in *The Merchant of Venice*. S. Barnet,[3] in a good essay, contrasts Bassanio's prodigality and intuitive responses in harmony with time with Shylock's usurious calculation which risks nothing while selling time; and N. Carson[4] argues that the main theme concerns Elizabethan ideas about desert and merit which reflect contemporary debate about election and free grace. L. Howard[5] also looks back to the learning of the age, suggesting that Portia's mercy plea agrees with and diverges from the system of rhetoric found in Fenner's *Arte of Logic and Rhetoricke*.

Among the middle Comedies, *Twelfth Night* for once does not take the major share of attention, although there is a fine new consideration of the whole play by W. von Koppenfels.[6] Both A. R. Cirillo[7] and D. J. Palmer[8] make illuminating use of the way the experience of Arden in *As You Like It* reflects the audience's experience of the play itself. The former in a well-argued piece shows how Shakespeare uses the forest world to poise the ideal against the real; while Palmer stresses how the balancing of character against character requires from us the 'provisional assent of "if"'. More conventionally A. Downer[9] traces the effects on character of the court-to-forest movement; and A. Wolk[10] brings the scheme of triple temptation found in *Rosalynd* closer to the moral center of the play in a discussion of the

roles of Jaques and Jaques de Boys. Somewhat unusually, the work done this year on *Much Ado About Nothing* is stylistic. W. W. Morgan[11] considers how Shakespeare employed and transcended his conventions in the use of prose and verse in the play; T. J. Stafford[12] takes it to be a satirical 'artistically unified statement on the language customs of the courtly versifier'; and R. Berry[13] eschews imagery for vocabulary study to establish how the idea of 'knowing' is both verbally and conceptually central to the play.

Our attention to the word is also demanded by F. M. Pearce[14] in *All's Well That Ends Well*, where she sees our response to the bed-trick being prepared for by verbal analogues long before the event takes place; and the trick's perpetrator herself is interestingly compared

[1] 'The Psyche Myth and *A Midsummer Night's Dream*', *Shakespeare Quarterly*, XXIII (1972), 69–80.

[2] 'Artificial Motivation in *A Midsummer Night's Dream*', *Illinois State University Journal*, XXXII (1970), 16–21.

[3] 'Prodigality and Time in *The Merchant of Venice*', *Publications of the Modern Language Association of America*, LXXXVII (1972), 26–30.

[4] 'Hazarding and Cozening in *The Merchant of Venice*', *English Language Notes*, IX (1972), 168–77.

[5] 'Portia's Reasoning in the Trial Scene of Shakespeare's *The Merchant of Venice*', *Neuphilologische Mitteilungen*, LXXIII (1972), 103–9.

[6] 'Twelfth Night', *Das Englische Drama*, I (1970), 134–56.

[7] '*As You Like It*: Pastoralism Gone Awry', *English Literary History*, XXXVIII (1971), 19–39.

[8] '*As You Like It* and the Idea of Play', *Critical Quarterly*, XIII (1971), 234–46.

[9] 'The Game of Love and Marriage', *The Hues of English: NCTE 1969 Distinguished Lectures*, pp. 33–57.

[10] 'The Extra Jaques in *As You Like It*', *Shakespeare Quarterly*, XXIII (1972), 101–5.

[11] 'Verse and Prose in *Much Ado About Nothing*: An Analytic Note', *English*, XX (1971), 89–92.

[12] '*Much Ado About Nothing* and its Satiric Intent', *Arlington Quarterly*, II (1970), 164–74.

[13] '*Much Ado About Nothing*: Structure and Texture', *English Studies*, LII (1971), 211–23.

[14] 'Analogical Probability and the Clown in *All's Well That Ends Well*', *Shakespeare Jahrbuch*, CVIII (1972), 129–44.

with and contrasted to Viola by W. H. Magee.[1] Ranging more widely over the same play, A. Leggatt[2] uses characterization, verse and prose modes, and the mixed responses called for to argue that Shakespeare is deliberately testing the Romance values against a known reality. Two critics attempt to account for the mixed texture of *Measure for Measure*: M. Rosenberg,[3] in a provocative essay, dubs the play a themeless fantastic trick, but traces in the sub-textual indications how the sexual relationship between the Duke and Isabella is made plain throughout the play; and B. Beckerman[4] is inclined to see the dramatic shift in act III as being the result of deliberate artistic choice which tells us much about what the play is really about. The double nature of the Duke of dark corners is illuminated by C. L. Gent's[5] consideration of the character in the light of book IV of *Il Cortegiano*; and S. Reid[6] has no doubt that the play persuades us in social terms that only limited sexual satisfaction is attainable. *Troilus and Cressida* is provided with a good introductory essay by D. Mehl,[7] who is particularly interesting on the levels of speech in the play, one aspect of which – the use of neologisms for satirical ends – is the subject of fascinating and learned discussion by M. Sacharoff and T. McAlindon.[8] The satirical intention of the play as an attack on contemporary conventions of courtly love is the subject of a scholarly article by C. Asp;[9] but Sacharoff[10] in another article, claims that the unsound judgments of Thersites drastically weakens the case for the play's being a satire at all.

The effect of the pressures of public life felt at the royal, personal level are explored by P. Edwards[11] in his British Academy Lecture. He suggests that Shakespeare proposed two antithetical ways in which a person and his public office are related: either a unity of being in which the private and the public roles are co-extensive and inseparable (e.g. in *Richard II* and *Lear*), or a division in which the royal robe is simply an external beneath which the individual can remain adaptable and flexible. In a book-length study of the same topic, J. C. Bromley[12] is convinced that 'at bottom all Shakespeare's kings...were destroyed by the fact and burdens of royalty' with only Lear transcending at last the world of history and politics. The book is written in a lively, provocative manner and is at certain points profound (e.g. the analysis of the character of Henry IV). The author concentrates always on the qualities of leadership, political decisions that lead to success or failure, and the inevitable personal cost of political success. However, the very concentration on individual kings, together with his rejection of the idea that Shakespear espoused a political orthodoxy, often leads Bromley to some strange final judgments, the most noticeable of which is the completely

[1] 'Helena, a Female Hamlet', *English Miscellany*, XXII (1971), 31–46.
[2] '*All's Well That Ends Well*: The Testing of Romance', *Modern Language Quarterly*, XXXII (1971), 21–41.
[3] 'Shakespeare's Fantastic Trick: *Measure for Measure*', *Sewanee Review*, LXXX (1972), 51–72.
[4] 'A Shakespearian Experiment: Dramaturgy of *Measure for Measure*', *Elizabethan Theatre II*, ed. D. Galloway (Macmillan, 1970), pp. 108–33.
[5] '*Measure for Measure* and the Fourth Book of Castiglione's *Il Cortegiano*', *Modern Language Review*, LXVII (1972), 252–6.
[6] 'A Psychoanalytic Reading of *Troilus and Cressida* and *Measure for Measure*', *Psychoanalytic Review*, LVII (1970), 263–82.
[7] '*Troilus and Cressida*', *Das Englische Drama*, I, (1970), 184–203.
[8] *Publications of the Modern Language Association of America*, LXXXVII (1972), 90–9.
[9] 'Th' Expense of Spirit in a Waste of Shame', *Shakespeare Quarterly*, XXII (1971), 345–57.
[10] 'Thersites as Crucial Figure in Shakespeare's *Troilus and Cressida*', *Humanities Association Bulletin*, XXI (1970), 3–9.
[11] 'Person and Office in Shakespeare's Plays', *Proceedings of The British Academy*, LVI (1970), 93–109.
[12] *The Shakespearean Kings* (Colorado Associated University Press, 1971).

one-sided view of Henry V whose Agincourt victory is considered by Bromley to be 'really a defeat, both moral and spiritual'. Altogether this is a book well worth reading by those who know their Shakespeare well; but it is likely to lead the uninformed sadly astray at times.

R. B. Pierce's book *Shakespeare's History Plays*[1] more conventionally extends the discussion of the analogy of the family and the State, by exploring such subjects as the dichotomy or unity of the monarch's private and public lives, impersonal *versus* familial elements, the use of the Prodigal Son tradition, the idea of the inheritance of noble character, the static and dynamic use of the State–family correspondence, and Shakespeare's development of the concept of family. Pierce pursues these topics in terms of those relationships that had a particular interest for Renaissance commentators: husband–wife, father–son, master–servant. The role of the mother also receives some interesting comment, as do the dramatic functions served by the marriages of Henry VI, Edward IV, and Richard III; but owing to the excessive emphasis on the Prodigal Son motif in the analysis of the Henry IV–Hal relationship, the Prince emerges as a far less complex figure than he actually is. While this book has some individually fine things in it and isolates well one aspect of the plays, and so is useful, it does not alter our view of the History Plays in any significant way.

Although H. B. White's *Copp'd Hill Towards Heaven*[2] does not deal with the History Plays, it does argue that Shakespeare was a Platonic political philosopher and so may be considered at this point in the review. White pairs *Timon* with *A Midsummer Night's Dream*, taking the former play to depict the decline of the *polis* and the latter to be about the founding of a new city. A rather different scheme is detected in the Final Plays, with *Cymbeline* suggesting that human and national regeneration lies in the hands of forceful exiles of spiritual power, Pericles being seen as a ruler Platonically educated through a series of miracles so that he resembles his historical namesake, and Prospero emerging as Shakespeare's philosopher–king who knows how men should live. The book offers an interesting and strange view of familiar plays, although it leaves out much that is important in them.

Among the History Plays, the second tetralogy receives as usual the bulk of criticism. A. L. French[3] uses the events of the Woodstock murder to explicate the themes of title, name, and honor in *Richard II*; and the ambiguities surrounding the play's two main characters are explored by S. Homan[4] and Helmut and Jean Bonheim,[5] with the former detailing the various parts of the play which elicit a divided response in the audience, and the latter associating Bolingbroke with fertility imagery and Richard with that of sterility to argue that the play presents a political versions of the universal pattern of Nature. The Garden scene in the same play is taken by W. Schrader[6] and G. Seehase[7] to be Shakespeare's method of incorporating a consciousness of the common people and their opinions. In a very good article, J. Hoyle[8] demonstrates a continuity between the play and *Henry IV* by pointing to the developing use of emblematic images, particularly those of sun/ice and moon/Fortune.

[1] Ohio State University Press, 1972.
[2] Mouton, 1970.
[3] '*Richard II* and the Woodstock Murder', *Shakespeare Quarterly*, XXII (1971), 337–44.
[4] '*Richard II*: The Aesthetics of Judgment', *Studies in the Literary Imagination*, V (1972), 65–72.
[5] 'The Two Kings in Shakespeare's *Richard II*', *Deutsche Shakespeare-Gesellschaft West Jahrbuch* (1971), pp. 169–79.
[6] 'Shakespeare – Sprecher des Volkes und Repräsentant des Humanismus', *Shakespeare Jahrbuch*, CVIII (1972), 7–23.
[7] 'Shakespeares Publikumsnähe in *König Richard II*', *Shakespeare Jahrbuch*, CVIII (1972), 53–63.
[8] 'Some Emblems in Shakespeare's Henry IV Plays', *English Literary History*, XXXVIII (1971), 512–27.

Two critics take up central issues in the two parts of *Henry IV*. M. O. Thomas[1] examines the various means employed by Shakespeare in his treatment of Holinshed in Part 1 to ensure an increasingly favourable reaction to Hal by the audience, and F. Manley[2] subtly links the pattern of personal and political betrayals in Part 2 to justify Hal's actions in the final scene. The whole Falstaff problem is raised again by H. Schumann,[3] and H. J. Genzel[4] discusses Goethe's fragmentary continuation of the Fat Knight's story. In a good general discussion of *Henry V*, U. Suerbaum[5] comes to grips with the central critical problem of whether the play is the culmination and epic statement of Shakespeare's historical thought or is a failure to dramatize a questionable political doctrine – a topic on which neither H. R. Coursen,[6] who sees the king as a portrait of the nearly perfect total politician, nor D. Cook,[7] in her analysis of the structural symmetry of the play, has any reservations.

The earlier historical trilogy is the subject of several full-length studies. David Riggs[8] devotes a book to querying the adequacy of the homiletic approach which tends to make some choric characters the thematic spokesmen while ignoring the concerns and values of whole classes of characters who are far more dramatically central. He notes that passages of overt moralizing so beloved of the dialectic critics are 'often flat, dull, and perfunctory; they cannot compete imaginatively with the celebration of human capabilities that establishes our main angle of vision on the events being presented'. He finds a more fruitful approach to these plays *via* the dramatist's treatment of the heroic ideal:

these plays keep saying that the received ideals of heroic greatness may be admirable in themselves, but they invariably decay, engender destructive violence and deadly rivalries, and, in the process make chaos out of history. They lead to anarchy because the notions of 'honor' that regulate the heroic life can never be securely realised within any stable, historical form of national life.

The stages of Shakespeare's treatment of this ideal are seen to be (a) the reshaping of heroic values he found in Tamburlaine in the person of Talbot; (b) the revaluation of the heroic conception of character; (c) the reappraisal of the heroic tradition itself. The strengths of the book lie in its reassertion of the plays' dramatic qualities, the constant awareness of the rhetorical modes and their functions, and the perception of the importance of the juxtaposition of characters. A book well worth reading, although one does have reservations about the neatness of the pattern Riggs constructs. C. M. Kay[9] provides us with the most thorough study of the verbal and theatrical imagery of the plays to date, and W. Billings[10] offers a well-written and acute essay on the way in which the structure supports the heroical irony the plays contain.

Two interesting articles by French scholars focus our attention on the theological content of *Richard III*. F. Fauré,[11] with a good deal of subtlety, uses the evidence of the language of

[1] 'The Elevation of Hal in *1 Henry IV*', *Studies in the Literary Imagination*, V (1972), 73–90.

[2] 'The Unity of Betrayal in *2 Henry IV*', *ibid.*, pp. 91–110.

[3] 'Zum Falstaff-Problem in *Heinrich IV*', *Shakespeare Jahrbuch*, CVIII (1972), 106–10.

[4] 'Falstaff in der Sicht Goethes', *ibid.*, pp. 97–105.

[5] '*Henry V*', *Das Englische Drama*, I (1970), 96–113.

[6] 'Henry V and the Nature of Kingship', *Discourse*, XIII (1970), 279–305.

[7] 'Henry V: Maturing of Man and Majesty', *Studies in the Literary Imagination*, V (1972), 111–28.

[8] *Shakespeare's Heroical Histories: 'Henry VI' and its Literary Tradition* (Harvard University Press, 1971).

[9] 'Traps, Slaughter, and Chaos: A Study of Shakespeare's *Henry VI* Plays', *Studies in the Literary Imagination*, V (1972), 1–26.

[10] 'Ironic Lapses: Plotting in *Henry VI*', *ibid.*, pp. 27–50.

[11] 'Langage Réligieux et Langage Pétrarquiste dans *Richard III* de Shakespeare', *Etudes Anglaises*, XXIII (1970), 23–37.

the early scenes to argue that Shakespeare conceived the play as a serious attempt at Christian dramaturgy; and P. Sahel,[1] while admitting the strong presence of a providential scheme, nevertheless believes that the emphasis is primarily on the relationship between ethics and politics. However, W. E. Sheriff[2] views it as quite a different sort of play and claims that it has a distinct comic content in that the deceiver is at last himself deceived and the conclusion leaves us with the comedy of England's return to normality. The art by which Shakespeare makes credible his most grotesque piece of comedy in the same play – the wooing of Lady Anne – is ably examined by D. S. Smith.[3] *King John* receives a little attention from P. D. Ortego[4] who analyzes the play as a revelation of historical truth; and from R. Weimann,[5] who shows how Shakespeare blends Renaissance humanism and elements of the folk theater to produce a Faulconbridge who is the only legitimate representative of social responsibility.

Julius Caesar is furnished with a good general introduction by W. Riehle,[6] which covers most aspects of the play and stresses heavily the theme of political reality; and the built-in ambiguity in the portrayal of the main characters is isolated in different ways by W. F. McNeir,[7] and by R. J. Kaufmann and C. J. Ronan,[8] who also stress the various intersections of psychic and political control being dramatized. It is the same topic of the public–personal conflict that receives attention in studies of *Coriolanus*. D. C. Hale[9] uses the two-part structure of Shakespearian tragedy to argue that each of the two elements in the conflict is the focus of one half of the play; and P. G. Zolbred[10] makes an illuminating comparison (marred only by inaccurate French quotations) between the protagonist and Alceste of *Le Misanthrope*. Two particular speeches get some close analysis: D. Hale[11] argues again for the central importance of the

Fable of the Belly, and A. H. Bell[12] gives a persuasive reading of Volumnia's instructions to her son in III, ii, suggesting a new punctuation of them. In a book devoted to *Antony and Cleopatra*, P. J. Traci[13] approaches the play through analysis of the characters as people and symbols, the cosmic and geographical spread, the comedy and the bawdy and their effect on audience response, the kinds and range of love explored, and the mortal, immortal, magical, comic, degrading, and irrational faces of human affection. The final chapter is the most original part of the volume, which puts the (to me) new idea that the structure of the play follows the pattern of coition: the comedy and celebration of the first half being the love-play of the protagonists that leads to their sexual union, followed by the death of Antony, the

[1] 'Les Voies des Hommes dans *Richard III*', *ibid.*, pp. 91–103.
[2] 'The Grotesque Comedy of *Richard III*', *Studies in the Literary Imagination*, V (1972), 51–64.
[3] 'The Credibility of the Wooing of Anne in *Richard III*', *Papers on Language and Literature*, VII (1971), 199–202.
[4] 'Shakespeare and the Doctrine of Monarchy in *King John*', *College Language Association Journal*, XIII (1970), 392–401.
[5] 'Vice-Tradition und Renaissance-Gestalt in *King John*. Zu Aufbau und Funktion des Bastards', *Shakespeare Jahrbuch*, CVIII (1972), 24–34.
[6] '*Julius Caesar*', *Das Englische Drama*, I (1970), 114–33.
[7] 'Shakespeare's *Julius Caesar*: A Tragedy Without a Hero', *Akademie der Wissenschaften und der Literatur Jahrgang 1971*, II, 37–52.
[8] 'Shakespeare's *Julius Caesar*: An Apollonian and Comparative Reading', *Comparative Drama*, IV (1970), 18–51.
[9] '*Coriolanus*: The Death of a Political Metaphor', *Shakespeare Quarterly*, XXII (1971), 197–202.
[10] 'Coriolanus and Alceste: A Study in Misanthropy', *ibid.*, XXIII (1972), 51–62.
[11] 'Intestine Sedition: The Fable of the Belly', *Comparative Literature Studies*, V (1970), 377–88.
[12] '*Coriolanus*, III.ii.72–80: "Cryptic" and "Corrupt"', *English Language Notes*, IX (1971), 18–20.
[13] *The Love Play of 'Anthony and Cleopatra': A Critical Study of Shakespeare's Play* (Mouton, 1970).

birth of Cleopatra's 'baby', the death of Cleopatra, and the rebirth of the Emperor Antony recreated by her love. Their union is cosmic even as it is connected with 'that very act of love by which the artist "shackles accidents, and bolts up change" in the work of art that is his created child'. However, the demonstration is not nearly so totally undeniable as Traci claims. Four articles concentrate on different themes in the play: H. Erskine-Hill[1] uses *The Faerie Queene* to good effect to discuss the dramatization of intemperance in Antony and temperance in Octavius; P. Rackin[2] suggests that the sexual ambiguity of a boy actor's Cleopatra embodies the clash between the theory of poetry as imitation of Nature and that which postulates the poetic creation of a Golden world to which the truth-criteria for extra-poetic experience do not apply; and M. Fujita[3] considers the concept of royalty found in the play by connecting it with civic pageantry in contemporary England. Among the essays on special aspects, R. Hapgood[4] tackles the very difficult task of defining the sonic tone of the whole; B. Miyauchi[5] gives a confused commentary on act v; and the distinguished Australian poet, A. D. Hope[6] contrasts Shakespeare's genuine poetic tragedy with Dryden's 'pathetic comedy'.

In one of the best books to appear on the Tragedies for some time, R. A. Brower[7] explores the probable analogies between the Shakespearian heroic and that of Graeco-Roman literature. He is less concerned with heroic ideas and images than with the poetic idioms that Elizabethan translators and dramatists created in their attempts to domesticate the language and attitudes they found in the heroic poetry of the Ancients. After a perceptive discussion of the heroic and diabolic idioms in *Othello*, Brower provides us with a wider context for the hero than any single play can give in a most learned study of the Elizabethans' absorption of Homer, Vergil, Seneca, and Ovid,

and the way Shakespeare's heroic draws so many strands from classical concepts. Although *Titus* is seen as giving evidence of an ability to dramatize violence and disorder and create representatives of directed heroic action, civilized life, order and peace, it is in his discovery of North's Plutarch that Brower believes Shakespeare found a version of the ancient heroic in a language so familiar that he could in turn transform it as a writer of tragic drama. There are individual essays on *Caesar*, *Troilus and Cressida*, *Hamlet*, *Antony and Cleopatra*, *Coriolanus* and *Lear*, all of which are packed with brilliant insights into the nature of the tragic heroes and their special predicaments in the worlds they inhabit. This is a book which no-one seriously interested in Shakespeare's works can afford not to read.

In another book, K. F. Thompson[8] looks at a different literary tradition and concentrates on Shakespeare's methods of incorporating into his plays the conventions of courtly romance, the story and plot of the revenge play, the tradition of the didactic nature of

[1] 'Antony and Octavius: The Theme of Temperance in Shakespeare's *Antony and Cleopatra*', *Renaissance and Modern Studies*, XIV (1970), 26–47.

[2] 'Shakespeare's Boy Cleopatra, the Decorum of Nature, and the Golden World of Poetry', *Publications of the Modern Language Association of America*, LXXXVII (1972), 201–12.

[3] 'The Concept of the Royal in Shakespeare', *Shakespeare Studies* (Japan), VII (1970), 1–32.

[4] 'Hearing Shakespeare: Sound and Meaning in *Antony and Cleopatra*' *Shakespeare Survey 24* (Cambridge University Press, 1971), pp. 1–12.

[5] 'Preliminary Remarks on *Antony and Cleopatra*, Act v', *Kagoshima Studies in English Language and Literature*, I (1970), 1–13.

[6] 'All for Love, or Comedy as Tragedy', *The Cave and the Spring: Essays on Poetry* (Adelaide, 1965), pp. 144–65.

[7] *Hero and Saint: Shakespeare and the Graeco-Roman Heroic Tradition* (The Clarendon Press, Oxford, 1972).

[8] *Modesty and Cunning. Shakespeare's Use of Literary Tradition* (University of Michigan Press, 1971).

drama, and the doctrine of natural correspondences. He divides the canon into a Shakespearian apprenticeship when conventions were elaborated and embellished, a Globe period when conventions were used in an increasingly compressed and abbreviated way, and a final phase when they were employed in an expansive and leisurely fashion. The book contains much good comment and throws a great deal of light on many problems of interpretation, but the overall impression is that while Thompson's approach can be rewarding as a critical tool for the early comedies and the Romances, it has very little to offer so far as the Tragedies are concerned. An article by N. Takei[1] contains a good deal of intelligent comment on the Tragedies while arguing that tragedy is the result of the invasion of the heroes' dreams into their real lives; and B. Miyauchi[2] makes a case for the value of structural study of the same plays.

Two different views of *Titus* are argued by J. Shadoian,[3] who claims it is a perfectly adequate play if judged on essentially theatrical, immediate, and visceral terms; and by W. B. Toole[4] who admits an artful structural design, but sees failure in the unresolved conflict between the atmosphere of mounting horror and the demand for increasing sympathy for the main character. Shakespeare's other tragic failure, *Timon*, is explicated in terms of the alchemical metaphor by D. M. Bergerson.[5]

There are two full-length studies of *Hamlet* by N. Alexander[6] and H. Fisch.[7] Alexander's is an intelligent, closely-argued work which elaborates his view of the play as a movement from a single act of poisoning through the inner play's double poisoning and on to a duel in which four characters die of poison. The various stages in this pattern are discussed with much use made of iconographical learning: the Ghost's relation to the recreation of the past, the seven soliloquies as pointers to the states of Hamlet's consciousness, the central symbolism

of the play-within-the-play, brilliant tough-minded analyses of the Graveyard scene and of Hamlet's relationship with Ophelia, and the ramifications of the duel. The book is truly a product of our age in its assertion that death is the absolute that defines life: 'The play offers its audience some hope that it is possible to play these rôles with a triumphant human dignity that can outface even the skull in the graveyard. The play offers its audience the certainty that "the rest is silence".' How modern! – but also how Jacobean! Fisch has a rather different view as he explores whether there is room for introducing into the canon of the play's criticism the notion of the Covenant. He is fully aware that he is seeing the play in terms of his own beliefs, but is prepared to follow the Hebraic component's presence in the fable, characters, patterns of images, and soliloquies, as the hero (like Moses) receives a revelation from the world of eternity, sets it down in his tablets, and descends from his rampart-mountain to dedicate himself to a path which necessitates the rejection of all previous loyalties. The covenant thus made, he moves to an inevitable tragic doom but harnesses his instinctual fury to become the divine instrument of salvation and a moral purge to his society. One has reservations about Fisch's reading of the piece, which is little

[1] 'Dreams as Metaphorical Visions – A Study of Shakespeare's Major Tragedies', *Shakespeare Studies* (Japan), VIII (1969–70), 18–47.
[2] 'The Structure of Shakespearean Tragedy', *Kagoshima Studies in English Language and Literature*, II (1971), 99–147.
[3] '*Titus Andronicus*', *Discourse*, XIII (1970), 152–75.
[4] 'The Collision of Action and Character Patterns in *Titus Andronicus*: A Failure in Dramatic Strategy', *Renaissance Papers 1971* (1972), pp. 25–39.
[5] 'Alchemy and Timon of Athens', *College Language Association Journal*, XIII (1970), 364–73.
[6] *Poison, Play, and Duel: A Study in Hamlet* (Routledge and Kegan Paul, 1971).
[7] *Hamlet and the Word: The Covenant Pattern in Shakespeare* (Frederick Ungar, 1971).

different in the long run from the usual Christianizings of it, but there can be no doubt about the perception, learning, and intelligence displayed in his book. E. Prosser has revised her *Hamlet and Revenge*[1] by adding summaries of the historical assumptions of her first three chapters and an appendix on the relevance of political approaches to the play; and D. Mehl[2] has a fine general account which stresses the complex reality of Hamlet's world and the nature of the play's tranquillity at the end. There is an intelligent essay on the way in which Hamlet approaches and refines his role as revenger so as to become truly heroic in the first volume of a new periodical devoted to Renaissance studies;[3] three of the roles the Prince performs are defined by B. T. Stewart;[4] and C. Davidson[5] emphasizes the nature of evil in the play and its purgation through Time's workings rather than the hero's. Various special topics are dealt with to some advantage: R. W. Battenhouse[6] smells Christian heresy in the Ghost's sufferings; Hamlet is seen to arrive at the idea of the Mouse-trap by different means in attractive pieces by P. S. Gourlay[7] and A. Hayter;[8] Polonius' devious stratagems are examined by L. N. Jeffrey;[9] and the whole play's influence on three later writers is discussed by R. M. Seiler,[10] who draws together the Prince and Prufrock; by C. Vandersee,[11] who sees parallels between Hamlet and Henry Adams; and by J. D. Golder,[12] who describes Ducis' neo-classical French version of 1769.

C. Davidson's *The Primrose Way*[13] attempts to see what Shakespeare meant in certain areas of *Macbeth* by examining the background of the period during which it was written by means of the books and pamphlets published between the death of Elizabeth and the date of the play's composition. The author works his way through most of the ideas (ambition, loyalty, murder, guilt, regicide, disloyalty, etc.) and tests the forms they assume in

the play against a very wide reading of the period's utterances on these topics. It is most useful to have this historical commentary on the play this well done. Two other articles try to illuminate the play by outside reference: S. Iwasaki[14] uses Jacobean beliefs about conscience to probe Macbeth's psychology; and J. Satin[15] draws some parallels between the hero's mental state and features of Dante's *Inferno*. There are also two good notes on the image connections in Macbeth's soliloquy after his wife's death by F. Pyle,[16] and on the elements of obscurity in Shakespeare's use of the Thane of Cawdor by D. Murdock.[17]

Apart from R. Lengler's[18] general essay on *King Lear* which is strong on the relationships

---

[1] Stanford University Press, 1971.
[2] 'Hamlet', *Das Englische Drama*, I (1970), 157–83.
[3] M. Rose, 'Hamlet and the Shape of Revenge', *English Literary Renaissance*, I (1971), 132–43.
[4] 'The Three Faces of Hamlet', *Essays in Memory of C. Burleson*, ed. T. G. Burton (East Tennessee State University Press, 1970).
[5] 'The Triumph of Time', *Dalhousie Review*, L (1970), 170–81.
[6] 'Apocatastasis of *Hamlet's* Ghost', *American Notes and Queries*, IX (1970), 57–8.
[7] 'Guilty Creatures Sitting at a Play: A Note on *Hamlet*, Act II, Scene 2', *Renaissance Quarterly*, XXIV (1971), 221–5.
[8] '"The Murder of Gonzago"', *Ariel*, III (1972), 29–33.
[9] 'Polonius: A Study in Ironic Characterization', *The CEA Critic*, XXXIII (1971), 3–7.
[10] 'Prufrock and Hamlet', *English*, XXI (1972), 41–3.
[11] 'The Hamlet in Henry Adams', *Shakespeare Survey 24* (Cambridge University Press, 1971), pp. 87–104.
[12] 'Hamlet in France 200 Years Ago', *ibid.*, pp. 79–86.
[13] Westburg and Associates, Iowa, 1970.
[14] 'Macbeth as a Case of Conscience', *Studies in English Literature* (Tokyo), LXVII (1970), 13–28.
[15] '*Macbeth* and the *Inferno* of Dante', *Forum*, IX (1971), 19–23.
[16] 'The Way to Dusty Death', *Notes and Queries*, XIX (1972), 129–31.
[17] 'The Thane of Cawdor and *Macbeth*', *Studia Neophilologica*, XLIII (1971), 221–6.
[18] 'King Lear', *Das Englische Drama*, I (1970), 204–22.

between the main characters and the allegorical elements in the hero, most of the work done on the play this year deals with particular matters. A new essay by G. Wilson Knight[1] is always an event and no-one can afford to miss the spectacle of a now easily-recognized mind moving easily from the fact of Gloucester's imaginary leap from the Dover cliff to visions of mortality. P. Milward[2] argues that Shakespeare gives a fresh exposition of Christianity in the play by placing it in an unwonted context of paganism; J. H. Jones[3] views Lear's realization of his delusion of self-sufficiency in the light of Matthew 5: 33–7 and *King Leir*; A. J. Tough[4] makes a vague comparison between the world of the play and that encountered in *Wuthering Heights* which does not hold up in its details; and H. Seller[5] claims that in both this play and *Othello* dramatic irony creates a situation in which we see the characters preparing for a final resolution in which the irony itself is discovered by them.

It would appear that, after *Hamlet*, *Othello* is the play that forces upon critics a critical approach via character analysis, and it is certainly a rewarding one in this year's work. For example, R. Berry[6] has a good essay emphasizing the theme of disbelief and attempted conviction in the various relationships the play deals with and Shakespeare's conveying of the fact of the ultimate inscrutability of the human soul. J. P. Sisk[7] concentrates on the precariousness of the control of self, events, and environment; and D. R. Godfrey[8] proves just how absent this quality is in the different kinds of jealousy represented by the central characters. Advocating 'pluralistic criticism', S. E. Hyman[9] uses Iago for his demonstration of how much richer the texture of the work appears to be when the various limited and partial methods of approaching the character – Vice-figure, Satanic presence, Judas-figure, latent homosexual, stage Machiavel, artist-manipulator – are held simultaneously

in the mind so that they may provide a more satisfying mutually corrective interplay than any single critical vocabulary can give us. The work on Desdemona is rather thin, with J. Overmyer[10] managing to say little or nothing about the character in her modern view, and U. Püschel[11] claiming that she is a feminist ahead of her time in her desire for an equal partnership in marriage. M. D. Faber[12] sees a Morality pattern sub-structure to Desdemona's summoning in v, ii; and T. Siphagil[13] maintains that Othello's demand to see her eyes in the Bedroom scene would have been recognized by a Biblically-aware Jacobean audience as a search for evidence of adultery. There are some interesting points made in P. Cronin's[14] analysis of the peculiar expressiveness of Othello's speeches as revelations of his character, as there

[1] 'Gloucester's Leap', *Essays in Criticism*, XXII (1972), 279–82.

[2] 'The Religious Dimension of *King Lear*', *Shakespeare Studies* (Japan), VIII (1969–70), 48–74.

[3] '*Leir* and *Lear*: Matthew 5: 33–7, the Turning Point and the Rescue Theme', *Comparative Drama*, IV (1970), 125–31.

[4] '*Wuthering Heights* and *King Lear*', *English*, XXI (1972), 1–5.

[5] 'Some Effects of Dramatic Irony in *King Lear* and *Othello*', *California English Journal*, VI (1970), 38–41.

[6] 'Pattern in *Othello*', *Shakespeare Quarterly*, XXIII (1972), 3–20.

[7] 'The Cybernetics of Othello', *New Orleans Review*, II (1970), 74–7.

[8] 'Shakespeare and the Green-Eyed Monster', *Neophilologus*, LVI (1972), 207–20.

[9] *Iago: Some Approches to the Illusion of his Motivation* (Atheneum, New York, 1970); see also *Shenandoah*, XXI (1970), 18–42.

[10] 'Shakespeare's Desdemona: A Twentieth-Century View', *University Review*, XXXVII (1971), 304–5.

[11] 'Zur Aufführung des *Othello* durch das Staatstheater Dresden', *Shakespeare Jahrbuch*, CVIII (1972), 111–21.

[12] 'The Summoning of Desdemona: *Othello*, v, ii, 1–82', *American Notes and Queries*, IX (1970), 35–7.

[13] '*Othello*, IV, 2, 29–36: A Note', *English Language Notes*, IX (1971), 99–100.

[14] 'Language and Character in *Othello* – Part 2', *London Review* (Winter 1970), 3–14.

are in J. W. Draper's[1] connecting the reversal of love idea and the setting of politics and war. The University of California Press has re-issued Marvin Rosenberg's now-classic study[2] of the acting history of the major roles.

Shakespeare's earlier love-tragedy is the subject of a perceptive essay by I. Leimberg,[3] who compares the structure of Romeo and Juliet's love-affair and the events surrounding it with the rhythms she detects in the sonnet cycles. Striking a more modern note, R. Berman[4] claims the play for the Existentialists in its contrasting of a permanent cosmic world with the temporality of the human world of the lovers. There is a very good paper on the first meeting of the lovers by K. McLuskie,[5] who sees the masque as both the brief image of one moment of harmony in which the lovers can come together and also the central point of reference for the whole play. The Friar and the Nurse are somewhat oddly paired by A. Schlösser[6] as the voices of the ordinary people of Verona.

A good example of how other nations' literatures can help in elucidating some of the problems of the Romances is furnished by N. Rabkin[7] in his analysis of the analogies between the late novels of Thomas Mann and Pericles and The Tempest. The first of these two plays is also the subject of an elegantly scholarly paper by J. P. Brockbank,[8] who provides a most satisfying commentary on the resurrection theme. The second play is the subject of a good general introduction by H. Oppel;[9] and one aspect of the play's miraculous construction is discussed by W. F. McNeir,[10] who stresses the way space and time are condensed so that there is a remarkable integration of spectacle and theme. Using the figure of Prospero as his focus, R. Uphaus[11] indicates the same play's advocation of reform rather than retribution, with the Epilogue being used to express the hope that the audience have learned the lesson it preaches. Two critics use different approaches

in an attempt to demonstrate the coherence of The Winter's Tale, with W. Blissett[12] employing imagery and plot to affirm that the play's two halves are mirror-images of each other with the centre at the bear's mouth; and Michael Taylor[13] making an intelligent and knotty exploration of the ideas of knowledge and innocence and the way they lead to a Blakean celebration of the marriage of the flesh and the spirit in both generations. The problems posed by Leontes' characterization also receive some attention from L. S. Champion[14] in his demonstration of how the part demands an empathetic participation by the spectator similar to that needed in the Dark Comedies; and from

[1] 'The Contrast of Plot and Setting in Othello', Rivista di Letteratura Moderna e Comparata, XXIII (1970), 165–7.
[2] The Masks of Othello (University of California Press, Reprint Series, 1971).
[3] 'Romeo and Juliet', Das Englische Drama, I, (1970), 60–78.
[4] 'The Two Orders of Romeo and Juliet', Moderna Språk, LXIV (1970), 244–52.
[5] 'Shakespeare's "Earth-Treading Stars": The Image of the Masque in Romeo and Juliet', Shakespeare Survey 24 (Cambridge University Press, 1971), pp. 63–70.
[6] 'Komplex Wirklichkeit und Dialektik in Romeo und Julia', Shakespeare Jahrbuch, CVIII (1972), 35–52.
[7] 'The Holy Sinner and the Confidence Man', Four Essays on Romance, ed. H. Baker (Harvard University Press, 1971), pp. 33–53.
[8] 'Pericles and the Dream of Immortality', Shakespeare Survey 24 (Cambridge University Press, 1971), pp. 105–16.
[9] 'The Tempest', Das Englische Drama, I (1970), 223–44.
[10] 'The Tempest: Space-Time and Spectacle-Theme', Arlington Quarterly, II (1970), 29–58.
[11] 'Virtue in Vengeance: Prospero's Rarer Action', Bucknell Review, XVIII (1970), 34–51.
[12] 'The Wide Gap of Time: The Winter's Tale', English Literary Renaissance, I (1971), 52–70.
[13] 'Shakespeare's The Winter's Tale: Speaking in the Freedom of Knowledge', Critical Quarterly, XIV (1972), 49–56.
[14] 'The Perspective of Comedy: Shakespeare's The Winter's Tale', College English, XXXII (1971), 428–47.

J. P. Thorne[1] in an original close reading of the two forms of syntax used in the depiction of the character's jealous utterances. J. F. Holland[2] makes good use of *Pandosto* to display a consistent pattern in the handling of Autolycus, the Oracle, and the happy ending.

The attempts to order the apparent chaos which is *Cymbeline* continue. H. M. Richmond,[3] stressing the critically-overworked observation that the play's events coincide with Christ's birth, argues that the complex structure is ordered by the theme of the elusiveness of the full truth and the inadequacy of legalistic verdicts; while M. M. Schwertz[4] finds that Imogen, as the ideal of personal, familial, and national integrity, is at the heart of Shakespeare's multi-level relationships. The legendary, mythological, and historical models used to convey the actions and motives of Imogen and Iachimo are closely scrutinized by R. J. Schoek;[5] and J. Rudolph[6] notes the resemblances between the play and *Fidelio*. The common people in the same play receive their full due from B. Scheller.[7] *The Two Noble Kinsmen* is taken to be Shakespeare's final unaided work by P. Leyris.[8]

The most difficult of the poems, *The Phoenix and the Turtle*, is considered by K. T. S Campbell[9] to present the fate of poetry itself which he suggests contains within it its own Nothingness. He sees Shakespeare sublimating the real destruction of the poetic symbol into the concrete image of destruction (i.e. tragedy), with *Lear* being the perfect dramatic reworking of the paradox contained in the poem. *Venus and Adonis* is certainly the poem that has had the sorriest critical handling, and H. Brown[10] makes a valiant attempt to right the balance by denying that the poem is the moral treatise so many critics make it and stressing the dramatic elements in its complex understanding of the conflict of interests felt at a particular moment. In one of the few psychological essays which have any real critical value,

A. Rothenberg[11] examines the imagery in the poem which suggests an overactive, too-loving mother and her resistant, nursing infant.

A new kind of biographical approach to the Sonnets emerges in an article by M. N. Proser,[12] who views the poems as a variety of honest human responses to recognizable experience which leads us to the self of the poet. Among the more detailed work on the individual poems, A. Gurr[13] rather attractively links the crude No. 145 with a 1582 date and the poet's wooing of Anne Hathaway; F. H. Stocking[14] examines the combination of beauty and moral innocence in No. 126 in the light of Renaissance

[1] 'The Grammar of Jealousy: A Note on the Character of Leontes', *Edinburgh Studies in English and Scots*, ed. A. J. Aitken, A. McIntosh, and H. Pálsson (Longman, 1971), pp. 55–65.
[2] 'The Gods of *The Winter's Tale*', *Pacific Coast Philology*, v (1970), 34–8.
[3] 'Shakespeare's Roman Trilogy: The Climax in *Cymbeline*', *Studies in the Literary Imagination*, v (1972), 129–40.
[4] 'Between Fantasy and Imagination: A Psychological Exploration of *Cymbeline*', *Psychoanalysis and Literary Process*, ed. F. C. Crews (Cambridge University Press, 1970), pp. 219–83.
[5] 'Allusion, Theme, and Characterization in *Cymbeline*', *Studies in Philology*, LXIX (1972), 210–16.
[6] '*Cymbeline* und *Fidelio*. Ein Beitrag zur Wechselbeziehung der Künste', *Shakespeare Jahrbuch*, CVIII (1972), 63–80.
[7] 'Die Volksgestalten aus *Cymbeline* im Volkskuntschaffen', *ibid.*, pp. 122–8.
[8] 'Le Chant du Cygne de Shakespeare', *La Nouvelle Revue Francaise*, CCXV (1970), 44–57.
[9] '*The Phoenix and the Turtle* as a Signpost of Shakespeare's Development', *British Journal of Aesthetics*, X (1970), 169–79.
[10] '*Venus and Adonis:* The Action, the Narrator, and the Critics', *Michigan Academician*, II (1969), 73–87.
[11] 'Oral Rape Fantasy and Rejection of Mother', *Psychoanalytic Quarterly*, XL (1971), 447–69.
[12] 'Shakespeare of the Sonnets', *The Critical Survey*, v (1971), 243–54.
[13] 'Shakespeare's First Poem, Sonnet 145', *Essays in Criticism*, XXI (1971), 221–6.
[14] 'Shakespeare's Temperance', *The Hues of English: NCTE 1969 Distinguished Lectures*, pp. 11–32.

ideas of temperateness and permanence; J. R. Russ[1] glosses the 'fickle-glass' of the same sonnet as 'mirror' rather than 'hourglass'; R. Helgerson[2] explicates the opening couplet of No. 128; and D. Stanford[3] notes how an exchange of letters between Samuel Butler and Robert Bridges anticipates some of the attitudes of later critics to the poems.

While it is an accepted truism that much of Shakespeare's poetry is deeply rooted in country life, few scholars have much first-hand knowledge of rural diversions. T. R. Henn[4] is one of the exceptions, and in his new book he everywhere displays a love and longstanding knowledge of country sports as well as an experience of war. After an introductory chapter on the degree of specialization in vocabulary of various field sports, Henn deals with specific areas. There is an exemplary discussion of hawking and the way such knowledge can illuminate various passages in the plays, a rather less rewarding one on the ritual of the hunt, a brilliant demonstration of the ways Shakespeare employed metaphors derived from angling, archery, and horsemanship, and a fascinating description of the organization and methods of the Elizabethan army and the many ungainly weapons it used. A final essay discusses how such imagery becomes a part of the fabric of a single play in *Antony and Cleopatra*. Altogether a book full of insight and esoteric knowledge, and with a nice (new?) piece of biographical evidence implied in Henn's analysis of the equestrian imagery which reflects the knowledge of the groom rather than the expert rider.

The language of the plays receives a good deal of welcome attention. Anne Barton[5] and T. Hawkes[6] both consider Shakespeare's attitude to man's capacity for verbal communication, with Barton ranging widely to display the many functions of language located in characters as different as Richard II and Falstaff, and Hawkes showing the tensions between language

as a social force and as oral dimension. Interestingly, both critics see the tragedies reflecting Shakespeare's unfriendly scrutiny of the word, though one might think the evidence they offer could just as easily indicate merely a deeper exploitation of its powers.

A number of critics have tried to follow Shakespeare's other explorations of his art. J. L. Simmons[7] traces the playwright's search for reality of representation beyond artifice between *Love's Labour's Lost* and *Lear*, while M. M. Mahood[8] claims that the contradictions, repetitions, false starts and ghost characters offer us a glimpse into an adventurous mind feeling its way into dramatic materials during the act of composition. J. Rees[9] also has doubts that Shakespeare worked into each play a carefully articulated intellectual scheme and illustrates how the busy dramatist handled one basic story which has its origin in a crime and pursues the consequences of this act. Other writers stress the limitations imposed by the theater. In a worthwhile essay, I.-S. Ewbank[10] argues that the relationship between what is said and what is seen in the plays is an everchanging one; and on the same subject

[1] 'Time's Attributes in Shakespeare's Sonnet 126', *English Studies*, LII (1971), 318–23.

[2] 'Shakespeare's Sonnet CXXVIII', *Explicator*, XXVIII (1970), 6–48.

[3] 'Robert Bridges and Samuel Butler on Shakespeare's Sonnets: An Exchange of Letters', *Shakespeare Quarterly*, XXII (1970), 329–35.

[4] *The Living Image. Shakespearean Essays* (Methuen, 1972).

[5] 'Shakespeare and the Limits of Language', *Shakespeare Survey 24* (Cambridge University Press, 1971), pp. 19–30.

[6] 'Shakespeare's Talking Animals', *ibid.*, pp. 47–54.

[7] 'Shakespearean Rhetoric and Realism', *Georgia Review*, XXIV (1970), 453–71.

[8] 'Unblotted Lines: Shakespeare at Work', *Proceedings of the British Academy*, LVIII (1972), 1–16.

[9] 'Revenge, Retribution, and Reconciliation', *Shakespeare Survey 24* (Cambridge University Press, 1971), pp. 31–6.

[10] '"More Pregnantly than Words": Some Uses and Limitations of Visual Symbolism', *ibid.*, pp. 13–18.

D. Mehl[1] perceptively examines the various functions visual translation of verbal metaphors can serve. Both K. Muir[2] and T. J. B. Spencer[3] remind us in well-written papers that we can never afford to forget how intrusive is the physical theatre's presence in the plays as they have come down to us. C. Leech[4] uses indications of locality as a starting-point for a far-reaching discussion of how the very idea of place contributes to a play's structure and effect. The problems besetting the translation of the plays into film are considered by J. Fuegi[5] who assesses the claims of various Shakespeare films to be called art.

Aspects of the challenge Shakespeare offers to the classics are taken up in three articles. In a scrupulously-researched piece, J. Freehafer[6] sifts the evidence of Hales of Eton's defence of Shakespeare against neo-classical attack. However, just how differently the plays can be viewed in the light of classical values is illustrated by A. Cairncross,[7] who sees the playwright generally favouring the Stoic, Cynic, and noble man, while being fascinated by the manipulator; and by J. Arthos,[8] who claims that Shakespeare modified the pessimism of the Ancients to produce an attitude to man quite alien to theirs. A far more modern view of man lies behind both A. Kuckhoff's[9] survey of favorable reactions to Shakespeare during the French Revolution, and R. Rohmer's[10] consideration of the relationship between the hero and the common people in the plays and in Goethe's *Egmont*. Also from Germany is an excellent number of the *Deutsche Shakespeare-Gesellschaft West Jahrbuch*. The volume is devoted to reports rising out of the 1970 Frankfurt Convention which clearly attempted to bring stage and study together in lively discussions of Shakespeare's treatment of history,[11] Shakespeare and the plastic arts,[12] and of Shakespeare in the modern theatre.[13] It also contains one of the most thorough examinations of the problems of translating the plays

into German and of some of the solutions tried by such translators as Fried, Eschenburg, Schröder, Dorothea Tieck, and Gundolf.[14] There are two particularly good general contributions by J. Haehlen[15] and H. Heun.[16]

Shakespearian criticism has now become so large in volume that it is almost a separate subject. P. Murray[17] provides the general reader

[1] 'Visual and Rhetorical Imagery in Shakespeare's Plays', *Essays and Studies* (1972), 82–100.

[2] 'Shakespeare the Professional', *Shakespeare Survey 24* (Cambridge University Press, 1971), pp. 37–46.

[3] 'Shakespeare: The Elizabethan Theatre-Poet', *Elizabethan Theatre I*, ed. D. Galloway (Macmillan, 1970), pp. 1–20.

[4] 'The Function of Locality in the Plays of Shakespeare and his Contemporaries', *Elizabethan Theatre I*, pp. 103–16.

[5] 'Explorations in No Man's Land: Shakespeare's Poetry as Theatrical Film', *Shakespeare Quarterly*, XXIII (1972), 37–50.

[6] 'Shakespeare, the Ancients, and Hales of Eton', *ibid.*, pp. 63–8.

[7] 'Shakespeare and the Harp of Man', *Forum*, IX (1971), 70–3.

[8] 'Shakespeare and the Ancient World', *Michigan Quarterly Review*, X (1971), 149–63.

[9] '"Die Revolutionäre hielten es mit Shakespeare." Zur Shakespeare-Rezeption in Frankreich zur Zeit der bürgerlichen Revolution', *Shakespeare Jahrbuch*, CVIII (1972), 81–90.

[10] 'Volk und Held bei Shakespeare und Goethe', *ibid.*, pp. 91–6.

[11] 'Bericht der Arbeitsgruppe zum Thema "Shakespeares Historien und die Gesichte". Leitung H. Viebrock', *Deutsche Shakespeare-Gesellschaft West Jahrbuch* (1971), pp. 10–11.

[12] 'Bericht der Arbeitsgruppe zum Thema "Shakespeare und die bildende Kunst." Leitung H. Oppel', *ibid.*, pp. 7–9.

[13] 'Shakespeare und das moderne Theater – Eine Konfrontation auf der Bühne. Bericht über Aufführung and Diskussion. Von B. Engler', *ibid.*, pp. 18–22.

[14] See the articles by U. Suerbaum, R. Stamm, H. Gidion, B. Engler, G. Hoffmann, H. Schwaz, H. Schelp, *ibid.*, pp. 23–117.

[15] 'Die Übersetzung des dramatischen Inhaltes', *ibid.*, pp. 118–26.

[16] 'Shakespeares Wortspiele in modernen deutschen Übersetzungen. Eine Stilbetrachtung', *ibid.*, pp. 149–68.

[17] *The Shakespearian Scene* (Longman, 1969).

with a good guide to the major landmarks and trends in the criticism over the past forty years or so. He divides his study into character studies of one kind or another, dramatic imagery, religious approaches (with *Lear*, *Hamlet*, and *Measure for Measure* being singled out for special treatment), and the historical approach. Although scholars will find nothing new here, teachers of English and undergraduates at Finals time will find useful this always readable and admirably clear survey. Some of the approaches dealt with by Murray are given two cheers by C. T. Harrison,[1] who notes that only when critical methods are not absorbed in their own motives and are infused with commonsense are they at all enlightening. A. C. Bradley earns the tribute of a book-length study from K. Cooke.[2] After a rather unsatisfactory attempt to evoke the man behind the book, she demonstrates just how far 'Bradley is oversimplified so that he can assume the role of adversary' and proceeds to give the lie to most of the hostile attitudes taken to his work. Bradley's Victorianism, the origins of his critical theories, his lack of theatrical awareness, his moralizing are all carefully scrutinized; there is an excellent survey of the work of both those critics who have used his work as their Aunt Sally and those who have used his essays as a starting-point for their own; and there is a good concluding chapter on the continuing appeal of the style, manner, and approach of *Shakespearean Tragedy*. In fact, although Cooke tends to protest too much, she seems to have fixed Bradley's place in the Shakespearian Pantheon with some accuracy. A living critic who is one of the strongest competitors for the comedy niche in the same edifice is Northrop Frye. However, R. Berry[3] has his doubts about just how accurate are Frye's typical comic structures when tested against all of the comedies. The criticism of two foreign writers is also given some attention: Lessing was clearly influenced by Shakespeare, and

E. M. Batley[4] considers the evidence found in the German dramatist's questioning of Aristotle's principles of tragedy and his defining of an aesthetic concept of Nature in terms of spiritual and psychological values. The first collection in English of Pushkin's critical writings, made by T. Wolff,[5] contains much to interest Shakespearians. The plan of the book is chronological, so that through the editor's interspersed commentary and Pushkin's own letters and articles, one can trace the Russian poet's progressive understanding of the plays (which he read in French translations and preferred to the Bible), and the way their influence made itself felt in works like *Boris Godunov*, *Evgeny Onegin*, and *Angelo*. There are comments on some thirteen of the plays as well as on individual characters, including a fascinating piece on Falstaff in which Pushkin claims to have known just such a man in his youth. Two more recent works of criticism are newly available in paperback: G. Wilson Knight's seminal work, *The Shakespearian Tempest*[6] and P. Edwards' well-received 1968 study of Shakespeare's efforts to turn experience into art.[7]

It is an earlier critic who is the subject of a truly magisterial work of scholarship by D. A. Fineman,[8] who gives us a full-dress edition of all Morgann's writings on Shakespeare. The text of the *Essay on Falstaff* is printed from the

[1] 'Common Sense as Approach', *Sewanee Review*, LXXIX (1971), 1–10.
[2] *A. C. Bradley and his Influence in Twentieth-Century Shakespeare Criticism* (The Clarendon Press, Oxford, 1972).
[3] 'Shakespearean Comedy and Northrop Frye', *Essays in Criticism*, XXII (1972), 33–40.
[4] 'Rational and Irrational Elements in Lessing's Shakespeare Criticism', *Germanic Review*, XLV (1970), 5–25.
[5] *Pushkin on Literature* (Methuen, 1971).
[6] University Paperbacks, Methuen, 1971.
[7] *Shakespeare and the Confines of Art* (University Paperbacks, Methuen, 1971).
[8] *Maurice Morgann. Shakespearian Criticism* (The Clarendon Press, Oxford, 1972).

copy of the 1777 edition that contains Morgann's own interleaved revisions all of which Fineman places after the essay but keyed to the points of their intended insertion in the text. There is in addition a long introduction which discusses Morgann's life, the responses to his work from Mrs Thrale to Alfred Harbage, the conception and revisions of the *Essay*, its bibliographical history, and a superb analysis of the critical ideas and attitudes found in it. Extensive notes detail the connections between almost every point Morgann makes and the arguments of contemporary and later critics. The volume also contains Morgann's commentary on *The Tempest* to which Fineman accords the same meticulous scholarly treatment. Altogether a book that is a major contribution to the history of Shakespearian criticism and a most sumptuous piece of presswork.

2. SHAKESPEARE'S LIFE, TIMES, AND STAGE

reviewed by NIGEL ALEXANDER

In 1968, when Professor G. E. Bentley brought the long labour of *The Jacobean and Caroline Stage*[1] to its successful conclusion, it was evident that it would inevitably become the basis for many fresh studies of English Renaissance drama. It is a pleasure to record that Professor Bentley himself has used his own unique command of the material to give us, in *The Profession of Dramatist in Shakespeare's Time*,[2] a concise and illuminating account of the working conditions enjoyed, or endured, by professional dramatists between 1590 and 1642.

'Professional' is here the key term since this is an aspect of their work that has only recently received scholarly examination. As Professor Bentley writes, 'their professionalism has received comparatively little attention because their productions have commonly been examined as literary phenomena rather than as working scripts for professional actors in a professional theatre'. Some of the material used in the book is, therefore, already available but it has never before been so clearly applied to this particular subject.

It is a fascinating description of a world where dramatists were not considered worthy of mention as literary figures by that 'great frequenter of plays' John Donne and where *The Wise Man of West Chester* and *Bellendon* were of as much concern to Philip Henslowe as *The Jew of Malta* and *Dr Faustus*. From this description there emerges the 'normal' pattern of the work of the men whose scripts Sir Thomas Bodley was anxious to exclude from his library since such 'baggage books' would create a scandal.

It was this normal pattern which dictates the order in which John Webster places his fellow dramatists in the epistle which he wrote for *The White Devil* in 1611. It is not an order of literary merit but a Jacobean hierarchical order and, therefore, Chapman, the translator of Homer, and Jonson, the author of court masques, naturally precede those who were merely regular professional dramatists, Shakespeare, Dekker, and Heywood. Events such as the publication of the Jonson folio in 1616, the founding of Dulwich College, and the publication of the Shakespeare folio in 1623, helped to raise the status of the profession a little but

[1] The Clarendon Press, Oxford, 1941–68.
[2] Princeton University Press, 1971.

it is important to remember that 'the playwright and his professional environment were less esteemed than most readers of Shakespeare, Jonson, Ford, and Webster are likely to assume'.

That few of the dramatists themselves regarded their work as 'literary' may be gathered from their attitude to publication. Nine plays of John Fletcher were published in quarto during his life-time but only one has the full literary apparatus of a signed address to the reader, a dedication, and commendatory verses. Fletcher and his friends published *The Faithful Shepherdess* because it had been a failure on the stage and they felt that it deserved better consideration. Like this play, four of the other published works had been written for the boys' companies. The other four were written for the King's Men but there is no hint that Fletcher had a hand in their publication. What is remarkable is the small number of his plays which did reach print and which reflects some arrangement between the poet and his dramatic company – a practice which seems to have been followed by other regular professionals like Shakespeare, Massinger, and Heywood while dramatists like Marston, writing for the boy companies, or Ford and Jonson, who do not seem to have remained attached for long to any one company, observed no such restraint.

Equally interesting is the normal pattern of revision of plays which had been some time in the repertory. If a play had sufficient theatrical appeal to be kept in the repertory then it was probable that it would be revised for one of its revivals. It is clear that Shakespeare's plays follow this normal pattern and, as Professor Bentley points out, in sixteen of the texts there are clear differences in the text which go beyond printing-house variants and point to revision in the course of production.

This pattern of professional life is shown in an examination of the status of the dramatists, their relationship with the acting companies, the kind of pay they received and the contracts they were obliged to enter into, the nature of the censorship over their activities exercised by the authorities as well as in a consideration of the difficult questions of collaboration, revision, and publication. It is to be hoped that a paperback edition of this instructive and important work will soon be published as it should form part of the basic reading of any student of Renaissance drama.

Another enormous task, of the greatest benefit to scholarship, takes a notable step forward with the publication of Part II of the second volume of *Early English Stages 1300–1660*[1] by Professor Glynne Wickham. It is a volume which complements *The Jacobean and Caroline Stage* since it does not attempt to duplicate the detailed description of all the known facts concerned with all the London theatres from the death of Shakespeare to the closing of the theatres in 1642 which is contained in Volume VI of that work. The work offers 'a study of the events in the year 1597 that led to the virtual abandonment of the Swan, the demolition of the Theatre, the costly adaptations to the Boar's Head Inn and the building of the first Globe and the first Fortune'. Next the volume examines the continuance of the multi-purpose game house, the building of the Hope as such a house, and the various schemes to convert cockpits and equestrian establishments into theatres. Finally it is concerned with the advent of the proscenium-arched stage introduced by Inigo Jones at court in 1604 for the *Masque of Blackness* – some ten years before the building of the second Globe – and with the development of private theatres.

The volume thus naturally begins with a study of the performance by Lord Pembroke's

[1] Routledge and Kegan Paul and Columbia University Press, 1972.

Men of *The Isle of Dogs* by Thomas Nashe and Ben Jonson in 1597 which provoked an Order from the Privy Council condemning both authors and actors to a spell in prison and authorising the City Council to demolish all playhouses in and around London. It is a remarkable state of affairs that, despite this order, the Privy Council were prepared to connive at the resumption of plays at the Curtain, the Rose, and other places, and, only a year later, at the building of the Globe on Bankside. It is this crisis in the theatre, which lasted from 1597 until 1604, which largely contributed to the growing professionalism studied by Bentley. It is, therefore, closely connected with the new Jacobean settlement and, as Professor Wickham argues, 'concern with London's playhouses, public and private, has assumed so great an interest that it has been allowed to eclipse the central realities of the drama of the period. These were, first, that public performances were justified from 1574 onwards as a means of "exercising" or rehearsing in preparation for performances at court where emblematic scenic devices were regularly provided at great cost by the Revels Office; and, secondly, that as an extension of this premise, no actor after 1603 who was not in the service of the royal family had any right to act in London at all'. On this thesis, then, it is the performances at court which provide the historical context of the Elizabethan and Jacobean drama and which determine the artistic principles which govern play construction and stage convention throughout the period.

When Volume 1 of this work was published in 1959 R. A. Foakes, reviewing it in *Shakespeare Survey 13*,[1] described it as 'the most ambitious and important book since Chambers' *Elizabethan Stage*'. Its full significance has now become clear. It is a major work of historical scholarship of the first importance to anyone who desires to approach an understanding of the nature and significance of the Renaissance drama. It is significant that both Bentley and Wickham acknowledge the help and support of the late Professor F. P. Wilson. We must believe that it would have pleased him to see the knowledge which he laboured to accumulate placed so securely in the hands of scholars in works which must rank with any, and surpass many, of the great scholarly achievements of the past.

Neither scholar, however, would claim that the last word had been said upon the subject. It is, therefore, interesting and instructive to turn to C. J. Sisson's study of *The Boar's Head Theatre*[2] which, in smaller compass, disputes many of the conclusions reached by Professor Wickham. The book was substantially completed by Professor Sisson before his death in 1966 and it has subsequently been edited and seen through the press by Stanley Wells. We have reason to be grateful to him for completing this selfless and demanding task because this book gives us, as Sisson's earlier articles did not, a complete range of evidence and reference for his views on the Boar's Head. Professor Wickham, for example, follows Herbert Berry's scholarly article 'The Playhouse in the Boar's Head Inn, Whitechapel' in *Elizabethan Theatre I* edited by David Galloway[3] in believing that theatrical activity did not start in earnest at the Boar's Head until 1598 – which allows him to interpret it as a result of the Privy Council's decree of 1597. Sisson traces its theatrical connections back to 1557 and argues that it must have been operating as a going theatrical concern from 1594. If Herbert Berry and Glynne Wickham appear, at the moment, to offer a clearer and more coherent interpretation of the evidence, it is still extremely valuable to have so uncompromising a statement of the old traditional view of the development of the English theatre through the inn

[1] Cambridge University Press, 1960.
[2] Routledge and Kegan Paul, 1972.
[3] Toronto, 1969.

yard. Full account of Sisson's evidence will have to be taken before that view can be completely superseded.

Victor Bourgy[1] directs our attention to one of the most important roles performed by actors upon early English stages between 1495 and 1594. This is a sober and serious account of the role and nature of the Fool which still does justice to the fact that, above all else, he was a comic figure designed to provoke laughter and encourage attendance at the theatre. Dr Bourgy is thus particularly severe on the heavily-moralized account offered by Bernard Spevack in *Shakespeare and the Allegory of Evil.* Distinguishing the roles of fool, Vice, and clown, the book offers us a combination of theatrical history and psychological interpretation. This is a necessary union with such a subject but inevitably a slightly uneasy one. It is, however, a distinctive contribution to an important and too often neglected subject.

Public office is the concern of Joel Hurstfield in 'The Paradox of Liberty in Shakespeare's England.'[2] He discusses the tensions generated at the time, and recorded in the plays, between the growth of power and the limitations placed upon its exercise. In that conflict, he argues, liberty was at that time preserved. The discussion of legality is pressed even further by G. T. Buckley asking the somewhat strange question 'Was Edmund Guilty of Capital Treason?'[3] – the crime of which Albany accuses him in *King Lear.* This might seem a blatant example of the documentary fallacy but the question is shown to have considerable relevance to the structure of the play. It is unlikely, and it is dramatically and obviously unlikely, that Albany would have difficulty in sustaining this particular charge against Edmund, whatever his other crimes. But it is the grave and capital nature of this charge which forces the guilty Edmund to fight, confess, and die in this doubtful quarrel without availing himself of the many defences and resources which seem open to him. Goneril's cry, 'This is practice, Gloucester' is thus strictly accurate, for Albany has finally over-reached the schemes of Edmund with his own strategic accusation of treason.

A less helpful application of legal terminology is to be found in O. Hood Phillips, *Shakespeare & The Lawyers.*[4] It is claimed on the dust jacket that this book 'gives a comprehensive survey of what Shakespeare wrote about the law and lawyers, and what has been written, particularly by lawyers, about Shakespeare's life and works in relation to the law'. This claim is not, unfortunately, borne out by the text of the book. It is a wide ranging and knowledgeable survey of everything that has been written by commentators who were also lawyers such as Malone, Maitland, Rushton, Clarkson and Warren, and Keeton. Certain select passages are chosen from their arguments for discussion and comment. It is thus a specialized annotated bibliography which has been rather misguidedly offered in book form and since it is neither one thing nor the other it is maddening to use. What is particularly disappointing is the enormous waste of the fine legal and critical talents of the author who is clearly capable of giving us that badly-needed survey of what Shakespeare wrote about the law and lawyers – but the anxious reader or commentator seeking comprehensive coverage will not find it in the present volume.

In an important article on Shakespeare's language, 'ME ou in Shakespeare',[5] Fausto Cercignani offers evidence against the view of Kökeritz that ME ou and ME ǭ had been completely levelled in Shakespeare's speech.

[1] *Le Bouffon sur la scène anglaise au 16ᵉ siècle* (Paris, OCDL, 1969).

[2] *Essays and Studies,* ed. T. S. Dorsch (1972), 56–82.

[3] *Shakespeare Quarterly,* XXIII (1972), 87–94.

[4] Methuen, 1972.

[5] *Studia Neophilologica,* XLIII (1971), 435–45.

Jean Jofen provides further comment on 'Polonius the Fishmonger'[1] by arguing that the phrase had perhaps a religious basis in Elizabethan England – citing a report in which the Company of Fishmongers complained of butchers who sold meat on Fridays. Thomas P. Harrison[2] draws attention to the fact that Shakespeare describes glowworms as having fiery or shining eyes in *A Midsummer Night's Dream*, III, i, 73, and *Venus and Adonis*, line 621. The light provided by the English glowworm is clearly in its tail but it is argued that Shakespeare may have been familiar with travellers' reports of the West Indian glowworm which does have two bright patches on either side which could easily be taken for eyes.

A number of notes and articles establish references, suggest sources and parallels, or offer explanations of difficulties. '*All's Well That Ends Well* and the Galenico-Paracelsian Controversy'[3] by Richard K. Stensgaard draws attention to the fact that the King's fistula (a plague-like symptom) is treated by chemical, and therefore Paracelsian, rather than Galenic, herbal, methods. The course of treatment pursued by Helena is, however, generally irregular and opposed to any of the orthodox schools. It is suggested that this is part of the play's deliberate tone. Keith Rinehart detects a parallel between Cleopatra's eagerness for news of Octavia in III, iii and Elizabeth's questions about Mary Queen of Scots in 'Shakespeare's Cleopatra and England's Elizabeth'.[4] Falstaff's description of Prince John in 2 *Henry IV*, IV, iii, 96–101 is studied by Jurgen Schafer in 'When They Marry They Get Wenches',[5] who concludes that a distinction is made between Prince John, whose 'thin drink' has made his complexion turn cold, and Prince Hal who has not neglected his diet and thus turned his naturally cold complexion into an energetic one.

E. B. Lyle finds 'Two Parallels in *Macbeth* to Seneca's *Hercules Oetaeus*'[6] arguing that

Macbeth's challenge to Banquo's ghost at III, iv, 99–105 is reminiscent of Hercules' description of the pain he endures through the poison (lines 1,377–95) and that Deianira's speech at lines 1,260–1 is glanced at in 'For Banquo's issue have I filed my mind' (III, i, 63–7). The Duke's treatment of Lucio is considered by J. W. Scott in '*Measure for Measure* and Castiglione'[7] and judged not to be so harsh as at first appears since it possibly is a reference to the Spanish custom, mentioned in Book II of *The Courtier*, of freeing a man led to execution if a common prostitute begged him for a husband.

'Yet Another Source for Othello's "Base Indian"'[8] is traced by Katherine Duncan-Jones to Gasgoigne's *The Steele Glas* while T. Sipahigil offers 'Lewkenor and Othello: An Addendum'.[9] The addendum is to Malone and Kenneth Muir's observation that Shakespeare might have made use of Sir Lewis Lewkenor's translation from Cardinal Gaspar Contarini's *The Commonwealth and Governement of Venice* (1599), pointing out that Lewkenor's book suggests a background of the urgency of war which is present in the play but conspicuously absent from Matteo Bandello's novella.

Philip C. Kolin detects 'A Shakespearian Echo in Dekker's *Old Fortunatus*',[10] arguing that I, i, 118–19 are a recollection of 'He jests at scars that never felt a wound' (*Romeo and Juliet*, II, ii, 1). A more convincing echo-sounding technique is employed by MacD. P. Jackson in 'Shakespeare's *Sonnets*, *Parthenophil and Parthenope*, and *A Lover's Complaint*.'[11]

---

[1] *Notes and Queries*, XIX (1972), 126–7.
[2] 'Shakespeare's Glowworms', *Shakespeare Quarterly*, XXII (1971), 395–6.
[3] *Renaissance Quarterly*, XXV (1972), 173–88.
[4] *Shakespeare Quarterly*, XXIII (1972), 79–86.
[5] Ibid., XXII (1971), 201–11.
[6] *English Studies*, LIII (1972), 109–12.
[7] *Notes and Queries*, XIX (1972), 128.
[8] Ibid., 128–9.   [9] Ibid., 127.
[10] Ibid., 125.   [11] Ibid., 125–6.

He comments on Claes Schaar's[1] detection of a relationship between Shakespeare's Sonnet 119 and Number 49 in Barnes's *Parthenophil and Parthenope*. Jackson now argues for the precedence of the sonnet by Barnes and points out that lines 316–17 of *A Lover's Complaint* are also an echo of the same sonnet by Barnes. 'A Biblical Allusion in Sonnet 154'[2] by Ronald W. Jaeger draws attention to the Geneva Version of *The Song of Solomon* 8: 7 'Muche water can not quench love, nether can the floods drowne it.' Ian Donaldson[3] argues that the language of *Venus and Adonis* makes it probable that Shakespeare had access to John Astley's *The Art of Riding* (1584).

David Greer suggests a new setting for Silence's song at 2 *Henry IV*, v, iii, 77, in 'Music for Shakespeare's *Samingo*: Lasso versus Anon'.[4] Dr Sternfeld[5] some time ago gave a bibliographical history of a chanson of Orlando di Lasso which seemed related to Silence's song. There is, however, a parody of the song in a seventeenth-century manuscript with an anonymous setting and it is now suggested that the parody has retained the original setting. In 'Shakespeare's Cornetts'[6] John W. Sider draws attention to the fact that the wooden or ivory cornett of the sixteenth century had finger-holes instead of valves and was therefore used for very different musical effects than anything suggested by its modern counterpart.

'*The New Inn* and the Profilation of Good Bad Drama'[7] by Richard Levin offers some interesting developments in a current important controversy. This paper attacks the view that, in English drama, 'all errors must be the result of conscious artistry' since if every obviously bad play that we know turns out on inspection to contain bad writing for ironic or parodic effect where are all the bad plays that were being thus pilloried? A later number of *Essays in Criticism* carries a reply by R. A. Foakes, 'Mr Levin and Good Bad Drama',[8] which establishes beyond reasonable doubt that Marston's *Antonio and Mellida* uses deliberate parody of its own plot in order to establish its tone. Mr Levin's question, however, is a pertinent one and the onus of proof must lie with those who claim to perceive ironic effects. Both articles are contributions to a debate about the nature and role of the children's companies which is clearly of the greatest importance to our understanding of drama after 1600.

In this context Chapman's *Bussy* plays have always remained a difficult problem. In an important article, 'The Revised *Bussy D'Ambois* and *The Revenge of Bussy D'Ambois*',[9] Albert G. Tricomi argues – as against the views of Parrott – that *Bussy* was revised at the same time as the *Revenge* was written. This revision was necessary to create an effective double play since '*The Revenge of Bussy D'Ambois* realizes most completely its dramatic potential and its ethical impact only when the revised version of *Bussy D'Ambois* has been played before it.' This is the most persuasive account of a difficult relationship that has yet been offered.

English Studies contains a review article by Keith Brown on 'Number Symbolism and Structural Patterning'[10] which must itself be counted a useful contribution to a continuing debate and again focuses attention upon the numerical pattern in the Sonnets traced by Alastair Fowler in his book *Triumphal Forms*.[11]

---

[1] *Elizabethan Sonnet Themes and the Dating of Shakespeare's Sonnets* (Lund Studies in English, XXXII, 1962).

[2] *Notes and Queries*, XIX (1972), 125.

[3] 'Adonis and his Horse', *Notes and Queries*, XIX (1972), 123–5.

[4] *Shakespeare Quarterly*, XXIII (1972), 113–16.

[5] *Ibid.*, IX (1958), 105–16.

[6] *Ibid.*, XXII (1971), 401–4.

[7] *Essays in Criticism*, XXII (1972), 41–7.

[8] *Ibid.*, XXII (1972), 327–9.

[9] *English Language Notes*, IX (1972), 253–62.

[10] *English Studies*, LIII (1972), 40–7.

[11] *Triumphal Forms: Structural Patterns in Elizabethan Poetry* (Cambridge University Press, 1970).

This has hardly yet received the attention it deserves since, if correct, it offers a mathematical basis for believing that the printed order of the Sonnets is correct and that vain attempts to discover another order which will unlock the riddle could usefully be abandoned. Brown naturally draws attention to a number of objections which can be urged against the method employed but it is one which may be expected to yield more dramatic results.

English Literary Renaissance is now clearly established as a major journal and its editors are to be congratulated on the care and thought which have distinguished their selection of articles and topics. Sidney has seldom received as much attention as other Renaissance artists and it is pleasant, therefore, to have a complete number devoted to his achievement. In studying that artistry the distinguished contributors provide an important survey of many topics of interest to scholars. My own personal predilections happened to be best served by the articles by A. C. Hamilton and O. B. Hardison Jr, but it seems certain that scholars are soon likely to be familiar with all the references in this important number.[1]

Webster has been more readily recognised than Sidney as a man whose works repay study but the effect of Ralph Berry's *The Art of John Webster*[2] is to take a massy sheet of lead and wrap it round the reader's heart. Mr Berry disclaims any intention of writing a major study of Webster since that would involve a study of Webster as collaborator and other as yet unresolved topics. Instead this is a study of the three plays which are usually, without serious question, ascribed solely to the dramatist. He then proceeds upon the assumption that 'Webster's dramatis personae seem to draw on a communal hoard of concepts and images, which represent the intellectual substance of his plays'. This 'substance' can then 'properly be analysed in certain broad groups. Webster's plays are intellectually assembled

structures that can be intellectually dismantled.' Unfortunately this is exactly what has been achieved. The book seems filled with pieces of an intellectual structure that has been dismantled according to the best precepts of imagistic criticism but which has never been assembled into anything like a working intellectual argument or a piece of dramatic writing for the stage. This is important since it is exactly in this area that Webster's achievement seems most vulnerable to criticism.

It is, therefore, a book from which many incidentally valuable things may be learnt but it leaves one without any real grounds for increasing one's respect for Webster as either intellectual assembler or dramatist. For example Mr Berry gives us this as his 'final statement' of the themes of *The Duchess of Malfi*:

The play depicts man as prone to evil and error, but the state of evil is apprehended imaginatively not theologically. Man's errors are embodied in a series of *peripeteias* which attain a philosophical status, the concept of an 'absurd' universe. Irony is elevated to a philosophy.

[1] *English Literary Renaissance*, II (1972), containing:

F. J. Levy, 'Philip Sidney Reconsidered', 5–18.
Charles S. Levy, 'The Sidney-Hanau Correspondence', 19–28.
John Buxton, 'A New Letter from Sir Philip Sidney', 28.
A. C. Hamilton, 'Sidney's *Arcadia* as Prose Fiction in Relation to its Sources', 29–60.
Robert W. Parker, 'Terentian Structure and Sidney's Original *Arcadia*', 61–78.
John Buxton, 'Sidney and Theophrastus', 79–82.
O. B. Hardison Jr, 'The Two Voices of Sidney's *Apology for Poetry*', 83–99.
Richard A. Lanham, '*Astrophil and Stella*: Pure and Impure Persuasion', 100–15.
Myron Turner, 'The Disfigured Face of Nature: Image and Metaphor in the Revised *Arcadia*', 116–35.
Nancy R. Lindheim, 'Vision, Revision and the 1593 Text of the *Arcadia*', 136–47.
William L. Godshalk, 'Recent Studies in Sidney', 148–64.

[2] The Clarendon Press, Oxford, 1972.

It reads as if it had been devised by Tom Stoppard for his recent polemic 'Playwrights and Professors'[1] and it tells us little or nothing about the art of John Webster.

'Shakespeare, the Ancients and Hales of Eton'[2] by John Freehafer examines the implications of Dryden's 1666 report of Hales's defence of Shakespeare against other poets and the ancients. Arthur Murphy's Shakespearian criticism is examined by Roy E. Aycock in 'Shakespearian Criticism in the Gray's Inn Journal'.[3]

Among studies of productions Kathleen M. D. Barker's 'Macready's Early Productions of *King Richard II*'[4] is of interest while, in 'William Poel',[5] Edward N. Moore gives an unusual and fascinating account of this pioneer of modern stage production. It is a little disconcerting to find that in 1914 Poel was attempting to relate *Hamlet* to the case of Essex and therefore produced the play with Gertrude dressed as Elizabeth and such minor details as the Ghost, Hamlet's 'to be, or not to be' soliloquy, and the Gravediggers cut in case they should interfere with the general design. It is fortunate that, in general, Poel was a man who respected Shakespeare's design.

A Bridges-Adams Letter Book edited by Robert Speaight[6] studies the work of an important twentieth-century director and provides a great deal of useful information about some interesting productions as well as the texts of some broadcast talks not readily available elsewhere.

Peter Brook's 1950 production of *Measure for Measure* with the Royal Shakespeare Company is studied by Herbert Weil Jr in his extremely important paper 'The Options of the Audience: Theory and Practice in Peter Brook's *Measure for Measure*'.[7] Weil points out that Brook cut his text in a fashion that inevitably favours the Duke as an all-controlling figure who can do no wrong – and suggests that no-one can watch the complete exchange

between Lucio and Vincentio without feeling that authority to some extent called in question. This paper, delivered in rather different form at the 1971 Vancouver Conference, is part of a projected book on Shakespeare's comedies. Readers of this article are likely to await its publication with impatience.

It is slightly disturbing to find that the hermaphrodite form of the taped interview has penetrated the pages of *Shakespeare Survey*. Even if what John Barton and Gareth Lloyd Evans had to say to each other was of the greatest possible relevance such comments as 'I understand what you are saying and, indeed, I agree with it' hardly enhance our understanding of the problems of 'Directing the Problem Plays'.[8] Question and answer seem here to proceed on strictly parallel lines and the reader is left to pursue an irregular course in an endeavour to extract the gist of what he thinks must have been actually said on tape if what he has in front of him is to make sense. Barton is a director whose views on Shakespearian production are of the greatest possible interest and they deserve nothing less than the selfless devotion with which Truffaut taped Hitchcock.

As a matter of stage economy Anthony J. Lewis argues in '"Who's There?": Shakespeare's Most Economical Description of Time'[9] that the phrase 'Who's there?' is Shakespeare's most economical description of time since it both establishes the time as night or darkness and creates a tone of uneasiness which approaches a sense of evil. 'Enter Macduffe with Macbeth's Head'[10] by William

[1] *Times Literary Supplement*, 13 October 1972, 1,219.
[2] *Shakespeare Quarterly*, XXIII (1972), 63–8.
[3] *Year Book of English Studies*, II (1972), 68–72.
[4] *Shakespeare Quarterly*, XXIII (1972), 95–100.
[5] *Ibid.*, 21–36.
[6] The Society for Theatre Research, n.d.
[7] *Shakespeare Survey 25* (Cambridge University Press, 1972), 27–35.   [8] *Ibid.*, 63–71.
[9] *Notes and Queries*, XIX (1972), 122–3.
[10] *Theatre Notebook*, XXVI (1972), 75–7.

Ingram establishes an extremely important effect in the staging of *Macbeth*. The apparitions which Macbeth sees in the Cauldron scene are a bloody child, a child crowned with a tree in his hand, and an armed head. This prefigures Macbeth's destruction at the hands of the bloody child, Macduff, after the child crowned, Malcolm, has brought the forest to Dunsinane. The moment when Macbeth prepares to take the field against Malcolm is, arguably, the first time that we see him with a helmet on his head in the play. The resemblance to the armed head and to the head later displayed upon a pole ought to be clearly evident. This is exactly the kind of visual symbol which is Dieter Mehl's concern in 'Visual and Rhetorical Imagery in Shakespeare's Plays'.[1] This is a suggestive survey which resembles earlier articles of Mehl's on emblems in Renaissance drama and it seems time for a more substantial demonstration.

In 'Originality in Shakespearian Production'[2] J. R. Brown argues that it is time now to trust the actor rather than the director, advice which is rather drearily confirmed by the accounts of Shakespeare productions and festivals for 1971 in *Shakespeare Quarterly*[3] or Richard David's[4] review of the Stratford season. The short account and impressive list of productions in Germany recorded by Karl Brinkmann[5] makes one wonder if the theatres of Europe are perhaps performing better Shakespearian service than their Anglo-Saxon counterparts.

John Fuegi undertakes an extremely important task in his survey of Shakespearian films 'Explorations in No Man's Land: Shakespeare's Poetry as Theatrical Film'[6] and his interesting defence of the aesthetic soundness of Olivier's balance of real and unreal in his version of *Hamlet*.

The work of modern adaptors is recorded in 'Charles Marowitz directs an *Othello*'[7] which,

together with the rock version *Catch My Soul*, might be cited as evidence that *Othello* was now the play that affected the modern consciousness even more powerfully than *King Lear* – despite Edward Bond's own interesting and powerful *Lear* described in a number of important articles in *Theatre Quarterly*.[8]

As a corrective to these more extravagant and erring spirits the reader may be finally directed to a simple and unpretentious work edited by Ina Schabert whose *Shakespeare-Handbuch* is comprehensive, clear and, in general, accurate.[9]

[1] *Essays and Studies*, ed. T. S. Dorsch (1972), 83–100.

[2] *Theatre Notebook*, XXVI (1972), 107–15.

[3] *Shakespeare Quarterly*, XXII (1971), containing:
Robert Speaight, 'Shakespeare in Britain', 359–64.
B. W. Jackson, 'Shakespeare at Stratford, Ontario, 1971', 365–70.
E. G. Hill, 'The 1971 Season at Stratford, Connecticut', 371–5.
Robin Carey, 'Oregon Shakespeare Festival, 1971', 377–80.
J. H. Crouch, 'The Colorado Shakespeare Festival, 1971', 381–4.
Lynn K. Horobtez, 'Shakespeare at the Old Globe, 1971', 385–7.
H. R. Courson Jr, 'Shakespeare in Maine: Summer, 1971', 388–92.
W. C. Haponski, 'The 1971 Champlain Shakespeare Festival', 393–4.

[4] 'Of an Age and for All Time: Shakespeare at Stratford', *Shakespeare Survey 25* (Cambridge University Press, 1972), 161–70.

[5] *Deutsche Shakespeare-Gesellschaft West Jahrbuch* (1971), 191–205.

[6] *Shakespeare Quarterly*, XXIII (1972), 37–49.

[7] *Theatre Quarterly*, II (1972), 68–81.

[8] *Theatre Quarterly*, II (1972), containing:
Edward Bond, 'Drama and the Dialectics of Violence', 4–14.
Arthur Arnold, 'Lines of Development in Bond's Early Plays', 15–19.
Gregory Dark, 'Edward Bond's *Lear* at the Royal Court', 20–31.

[9] Kroner, Stuttgart, 1972.

© NIGEL ALEXANDER 1973

3. TEXTUAL STUDIES

reviewed by RICHARD PROUDFOOT

Charlton Hinman follows his facsimile of the First Folio with the 1600 Quarto of *Much Ado About Nothing*, published as No. 15 of the Clarendon Press Shakespeare Quarto Facsimiles.[1] The copy reproduced is the fine one in the Capell collection at Trinity College, Cambridge, which contains all recorded variant formes in their corrected state, with the trivial exception of a single turned letter in outer D. This is the first volume in the series to be numbered with the Through Line Numbering of the Hinman Folio facsimile, adapted to cover the few places where the quarto text includes lines omitted from the folio. The introduction explains the conventions used in this adaptation and also presents evidence for the setting of the text from Shakespeare's foul papers by Valentine Simmes's Compositor A, 'a compositor who, though reasonably competent, is likely to have been responsible for a considerable number of minor departures from his copy'. Twelve perfect copies of the quarto were collated in the preparation of the facsimile, a thirteenth, in the Bodmer Library, having been, at the time, unavailable (a problem unlikely to face future scholars since the establishment in 1971 of the Bodmer Foundation, in accordance with the wishes of the late Dr Martin Bodmer).

Three new volumes in the New Penguin Shakespeare span the entire range of Shakespeare's work.[2] J. W. Lever has edited *The Rape of Lucrece*, presenting a text which seldom departs from the Quarto of 1594 and a stimulating introduction which should do much to help new readers of the poem to bring it into meaningful relation to Shakespeare's mature tragic writing. He proposes a new punctuation for line 135, to read 'That what they have, not that which they possess', for the quarto's

'...have not, that...', which makes sense if *possess* is understood as 'take' or 'acquire', in opposition to *have*. There seems to be less to recommend the hyphenation of 'Tarquin stained' at line 1743, where the sense is adequate without it.

Henry VIII is the latest of the histories to be edited by A. R. Humphreys. Much of his introduction is given over to a judicious account of the play as the collaborative work of Shakespeare and Fletcher, an emphasis which, as so often, goes hand in hand with a qualified approval of the play's achievement. It is healthy to be reminded, with reference to some of the more ambitious critical attempts to discern unifying themes in the play, that these 'controlling ideas' may sometimes be 'likelier to reflect the critic's anxiety to perceive unity and meaning than to show the forms of genuine structure'. As if to compensate for the qualifications of the introduction, the edition also contains a full and admirably annotated list of 'Further Reading'. The text calls for little comment: in common with other volumes in the series (but not *Lucrece*) its modernisations include that of *moe* to *more*.

King Lear, a key volume in any Shakespeare, has been edited with great verve and vigour by G. K. Hunter, who helped to launch the New Penguin Shakespeare with his *Macbeth*. His *Lear* accepts the folio as its basic text, but readily incorporates quarto readings where good reason can be found to prefer them to those of the folio, on the assumption that, for all its obvious deficiencies, the quarto text is 'in the main...quite closely derived from an

[1] Oxford, 1971.
[2] *The Rape of Lucrece: Henry VIII* (Harmondsworth, 1971): *King Lear* (1972).

authoritative original'. Equally optimistic is the view that the press corrections found in the twelve extant copies of the First Quarto constitute a complete picture of the process of stop-press correction. Nevertheless, as a final list of familiar readings rejected from this edition reveals, Hunter accepts fewer quarto readings than most modern editors of *Lear*. For instance, the assumed general superiority of the folio leads to the adoption of such readings as the following: 'for *qualities* are so weighed', Q *'equalities'*, I, i, 5; *'Being* oil to fire', Q *'Bring'*, II, ii, 75; 'I would have made *him* skip', Q *'them'*, v, iii, 275; or the assignment to Edmund of what in the quarto is the final line of Goneril's part (v, iii, 158). Usually a reason is given in the notes for preferring a Q reading to a feasible reading from F, but there are exceptions, such as *possesses*, F *professes*, I, i, 74, or 'KENT Why Fool?' for F '*Lear*. Why my Boy', I, iv, 98. At v, iii, 291, Q's *sees* is accepted as providing the better sense but no mention is made of the possibility that it is no more than a variant spelling of F's *saies*. Reassignment of lines in IV, vii produces a sensible division between Q's Doctor and the Gentleman to whom his lines are assigned in F, but the transformation of F's Gentleman in I, v into a Knight seems slightly fussy. Several corrected Q readings are accepted in IV, i and ii, two of the scenes in which F is thought to have been set from a copy of Q which had the inner forme of sheet H in its uncorrected state. This procedure is certainly right in IV, ii (set from Q H3v, 4), but in IV, i and in III, vii (set from Hlv, 2) it is more problematic. The latter two Q pages contain seven variants: F prints the corrected readings of two, *annoynted* and *stelled*, III, vii, 57, 60; it further corrects one corrected reading, *buoy'd*, line 59 (Q corr. *bod*); it alters two of the readings entirely, *as his bare*, line 58 (Q corr. *on his lowd*); and it prints one reading in its uncorrected form, *poorely led*, IV, i, 10. The remaining Q variant on H2, *rogish*

madnes¦ (uncorr.), *madnes* (corr.), III, vii, 103, is in a passage omitted from F. In the passage contained in these two Q pages Hunter, though using the argument that F was set from the uncorrected state of Q to defend his adoption of the corrected Q reading at IV, i, 10, *parti-eyed* (Q corr. *parti, eyd*), prefers F to corrected Q elsewhere in these pages. This procedure is not only slightly inconsistent, but is perhaps open to question in the case of *bare*, III, vii, 58, which has all the appearance of a folio sophistication and where the uncorrected reading of Q, *lou'd*, suggests the possibility that the true reading was *lone* and that even the quarto correction was mistaken guesswork. Altogether, the assumption that uncorrected Q copy of these pages underlies the F text seems assailable, or at least hardly sufficient to support *parti-eyed* in the face of F's retention of the uncorrected Q reading.

Hunter's introduction and commentary will lead readers of the play straight into a lively understanding of it as an enactment of experience and endurance in which 'we cannot separate the plot from the poetic pattern'. A constant alertness to stage requirements and opportunities gives the notes great life and freshness, if it occasionally leads to over-ingenuity, as when Kent's lines 'If Fortune brag of two she loved and hated / One of them we behold' are taken to refer not to one man but to two, Lear and Kent himself: 'Each beholds *One* – they are looking at one another.' Again, Edgar's 'The safer sense will ne'er accommodate his master thus' *may* not bear the meaning usually assigned to it, 'Nobody sane would go around like that', but it seems rash to reject this interpretation without even a reference to the possible echo of 'unaccommodated man', which might strengthen the association of *accommodate* with clothing. In the same scene, IV, vi, the phrase 'whose face between her forks presages snow' is oddly misread: 'the *face between her forks* is her private parts'. The true sense is surely rather that indicated by the transposition 'whose face presages snow between her forks'. These are, however, minor criticisms of an edition in which the editor makes the fruits of his learning extremely palatable to a wide range of readers and never stands between them and the play.

The indefatigable T. H. Howard-Hill draws near to the end of his labour of concording the plays of Shakespeare from the texts of the good quartos and the First Folio. With *Hamlet* still to come, presumably from the Second Quarto, the Oxford Shakespeare Concordances are nearly complete and it is possible to summarise what has been done and to see more clearly than before what is still to do. The concordances cover the folio texts of twenty-five plays and the quarto texts of eleven more. The additions this year are F *Coriolanus, Antony and Cleopatra,* and *Cymbeline* and Q *Titus Andronicus, Romeo and Juliet* (1599), *Troilus and Cressida* and *Pericles.*[1] Earlier quarto plays are *Love's Labour's Lost, A Midsummer Night's Dream, The Merchant of Venice* and *Much Ado About Nothing* among the Comedies and *Richard II* and the two parts of *Henry IV* among the Histories. In addition to the concordance each volume has brief prefatory notes, including a compositor analysis (where one is available) and a list of such misprints as have been corrected before concording (and these are very few).

In spite of criticisms which can be made of several details of layout, for instance, the separation of different spellings of the same word in the alphabetical sequence of entries, and one or two questionable editorial decisions, especially the ambiguous form of the entries *w* and *y* for the superscript abbreviations of *with, which, you, ye* and *that,* the fact remains that we now have a set of concordances to the only texts of Shakespeare which will not change, rather than to an edited text. At this stage it becomes necessary, however, to point out the limitations inherent in the plan of the Oxford series. The most serious of these is the incompleteness of the textual record which inevitably follows from the choice of one only of the texts of, say, *Richard III,* and *Lear* (F) or *Troilus and Cressida* (Q), as the basis for the concordance. As they stand, these volumes omit substantial portions of the plays in question, *Richard III,* IV, ii, 96–113, the whole of *Lear,* IV, iii, and the Prologue to *Troilus.* Other large casualties include *Richard II,* IV, i, 162–320, a passage omitted from the First Quarto presumably on political grounds, and *Titus Andronicus,* III, ii, a scene first printed in the folio. Apart from such large gaps, the choice of one text only has excluded all the variants between quartos and folio which have so great a significance for editors of such plays as *Othello, Lear* or *Hamlet,* where the possibility exists of two independent authoritative texts. It is equally desirable that the poems and sonnets should be added and perhaps also the 'hard core' of the dramatic apocrypha, at least the *More* fragment, *Edward III* and *The Two Noble Kinsmen.*

The first and last of these categories of omissions can be easily supplied; the second is more difficult, as there are good grounds for excluding some of the many variants where little doubt exists that one reading is erroneous (though equally good arguments could have been found for admitting more editorial correction into the texts already concorded). The place for these omitted readings would seem to be not in further separate and expensive volumes but in a consolidated concordance in which the material already published should also be rearranged with rather more thought for the convenience of the user. Such a consolidated concordance was envisaged at the outset: it is to be hoped that the project will be completed by its publication.

Several recent publications concern them-

[1] Oxford, 1972.

selves broadly with the problems of editing or with topics concerning the publication and editing of Shakespeare. P. H. Davison[1] contemplates the possibility that editors are in need of a new paradigm of textual criticism: this need he deduces from the various discontentments with the present state of textual scholarship expressed, for example, by James Thorpe and D. F. McKenzie. His plea for a closer relation between editorial principles and the broader currents of thought which characterise our time is liberating, if it pushes its scientific analogies rather hard, and his emphasis on the limits of textual bibliography will come as a relief to some editors. Although it is strictly true to state that 'it is simply not possible to wait until one has all the information before one comes to a conclusion in bibliography or editing', there is room for a distinction between impatience and the decision to draw realistic limits. A further distinction which is never made is that between different types of edition aimed at different readerships. The restiveness in the face of the domination of bibliography in textual studies which informs Davison's essay is expressed at greater length by James Thorpe in his *Principles of Textual Criticism*.[2] Neither writer is addressing himself to editors of Shakespeare in the first instance, but both provide healthy reminders that, in Davison's words, all editors face 'problems that are humanistic, not scientific or enumerative'. G. Thomas Tanselle[3] explores 'the way in which a critical *edition* is, in itself and of necessity, also a critical *study*' and illustrates the infrequency with which bibliographical analysis can provide editors with more than 'valuable assistance, taken in conjunction with literary evidence, for reaching a final decision'. Perhaps his most striking statement of the new humility in textual studies is that 'an edition may conceivably be "definitive" in terms of its scholarly method and of the material assembled in it; but – except perhaps in the most simple

cases – "definitive" is not an adjective which can meaningfully be applied to the actual text of an edition, since decisions about an author's final intention are more often matters of judgement than matters of fact'.

In another paper,[4] Tanselle appears in his more familiar role as the upholder of bibliographical orthodoxy. His systematic and comprehensive paper on editorial apparatus is an act of homage to Fredson Bowers, but makes its own valid contributions to the subject, of which the most appealing is the suggestion that a separate list should draw attention to the new readings in any edited text, especially where these involve rejection of copy-text readings. If Tanselle's descriptive approach prompts the thought that any layout of apparatus can be made to sound useful or not by a careful choice of emphasis, he nevertheless raises questions which every editor, for whatever audience, has to face and provides a fair array of the available answers. Two statements at the beginning of the essay, however, do seem to confuse issues: these are references to 'a variorum edition' as one which 'must *by definition* include apparatus which records variant readings' and to 'Greg's *rationale for choosing* a copy-text'. 'By definition' a variorum edition is *editio cum notis variorum*, that is, with the notes of various scholars, whatever the term may have come to mean in current usage; Greg's rationale, likewise, was more of the uses to which a copy-text, as he defined it, should be put than of the methods of selecting it.

A. S. Cairncross[5] returns to the vexed

[1] 'Science, Method, and Textual Criticism', *Studies in Bibliography*, XXV (1972), 1–28.
[2] San Marino, 1972.
[3] 'Textual Study and Literary Judgement', *Papers of the Bibliographical Society of America*, 65 (1971), 109–22.
[4] 'Some Principles for Editorial Apparatus', *Studies in Bibliography*, XXV (1972), 41–88.
[5] 'Shakespeare and the "Staying Entries"', *Shakespeare in the Southwest: Some New Directions*, ed. T. J. Stafford (El Paso, 1969), 80–93.

question of the 'staying' entries of certain plays of Shakespeare on the Stationers' Register. His main thesis, which differs essentially from that first propounded by A. W. Pollard in *Shakespeare's Fight with the Pirates*, is that James Roberts, so far from being the ally of Shakespeare and his company in attempting to restrain unauthorised publication of their plays, should rather be cast in the role of 'the pirate king', the most dangerous to them of a group of stationers which also included Edward Blount, William Jaggard and Thomas Walkley. 'Staying' of copies is shown to have been a method employed by the Stationers' Company to restrict the piratical practices of their own unruly members: the backing of the Lord Chamberlain for the players gave them adequate incentive to use it in defence of plays. Conjecture is pushed dangerously far when Cairncross alleges beyond the possibility of demonstration that 'Roberts's privilege to print the players' bills gave him the chance of picking up manuscripts, but made it wise for him to conceal such activities'. As a whole, though, the picture that he paints is convincing as an account of conflicting business interests and of the area in which players and printers who opposed each others' interests had most need to reach mutually profitable compromise and most opportunity to bring pressure on each other to achieve it, the printers by publishing 'bad' texts, the players by withholding the 'true and perfect coppie'. At least this hypothesis gives a plausible account of Roberts's position in the case of *Hamlet*, when, according to Cairncross, he 'entered a bad text in 1602, transferred it (though not through the Register) to Nicholas Ling to publish, had the printing meantime done by Simmes, but reserved for himself any later, and safer, printing such as that of Q2'.

The statistical approach to Shakespeare is applied to new ends by Christopher Spencer,[1] who has used a computer to analyse and classify 457 major and 2,126 minor variants in sixty-three editions of *The Merchant of Venice* in order to establish 'the dependence of each edition upon its predecessors' and 'the contribution of each edition to the developing and to *the modern text* of the play' (my italics: this notional text is represented by the editions of Peter Alexander and of G. Blakemore Evans, which is as yet unpublished). The general conclusions are as might have been expected: the 'modern text' is heavily dependent on editions before 1800; the early drift away from reliance on the quartos was reversed by Capell; textual theory had little impact on editorial practice until the twentieth century. More interesting is the demonstration, in relation to this last conclusion, that even editors such as those of the Old Cambridge Shakespeare who wrongly supposed that Heyes's Quarto of 1600 was derived from the Jaggard-Pavier reprint of 1619, produced texts which adopted more readings from it than from what we now know to be Q2. A final note does belated justice to the press reader who corrected proof of Q3, 1637. Two corrected readings introduced by him anticipate the conjectures of later editors: at IV, i, 281, 'I wou'd lose all, I, sacrifize them all', he added the comma after the second *I*, implying the sense 'Ay', which is generally thought to have been first suggested by Pope; at III, ii, 113, 'In measure *reine* thy joy' (uncorr. *raine*) anticipates Johnson's conjecture, *rein*.

Christopher Spencer and John W. Velz[2] draw attention to copies of Theobald's first edition of Shakespeare (1733) and Warburton's edition (1747) in the Folger Shakespeare Library (apart from Volume 6 of Warburton, lost when on loan to Dr Johnson and now in the library of the University College of Wales,

[1] 'Shakespeare's *Merchant of Venice* in Sixty-Three Editions', *Studies in Bibliography*, XXV (1972), 89–106.
[2] 'Styan Thirlby: A Forgotten "Editor" of Shakespeare', *Shakespeare Studies*, VI (1970), 327–33.

Aberystwyth) which contain annotations by the eighteenth-century scholar Styan Thirlby, Fellow of Jesus College, Cambridge, who contributed to Theobald's edition and annotated three separate editions of Shakespeare with a view to producing his own edition. The first of these, Pope's first edition (1723–5), is no longer extant. Examination of his copious notes on *The Merchant of Venice* (mostly in Theobald) and *Julius Caesar* (most in Warburton) reveals that 'Thirlby is informative on the meaning of Elizabethan locutions, calls attention to possible ambiguities...and untangles the grammar of difficult passages'. In his use of 'analogies in phrasing or contexts' he anticipated an important technique of later eighteenth-century editors. He should be credited with at least two brilliant emendations in *The Merchant*, *page* for *rage*, II, i, 35, which he supplied to Theobald, and the addition of a comma after *was* in the stage direction which opens II, v, '*Enter the Jew and his man that was the Clown*', which J. Dover Wilson rediscovered in 1926. The authors conclude, 'if his edition had been published, the notes would have rivalled Johnson's in their solidity and common sense, the text might have rivalled Capell's in its excellence, and – for some plays – the annotation would probably have been fuller than that in any edition before Reed's Variorum of 1803'. As it was not, the neglect which has attended the memory of Thirlby is perhaps excusable.

It is hard to see why anyone thought it worth-while to publish W. S. Kable's monograph on *The Pavier Quartos and the First Folio* in the form in which it appears as the second of the *Shakespeare Studies Monographs*.[1] The argument has been published as a double article in *Studies in Bibliography* and the tables of spellings which make up more than half of the book are set out without references to the play in which they occur, let alone to the precise line, so that there is no way of knowing either whether the record is complete and accurate or whether given forms occur in patterns indicative of possible interpretations other than Kable's own. The validity of his argument that the habits of Jaggard's Compositor B can be accurately described on the basis of the 1619 Quartos depends, in any case, upon the inadequately tested hypothesis that B was the sole setter of these plays and the extension of the argument to the First Folio similarly depends upon undue reliance on Hinman's compositor analysis for that book. Should any substantial revision of the compositorial pattern in either be urged, the basis of this study would be shaken.

A much more rigorous method is adopted by Warren B. Austin in a monograph only obliquely related to Shakespeare studies[2] in which he sets out to prove, on the evidence of a computer analysis of carefully-selected linguistic and stylistic details and patterns, that the true author of *Greene's Groatsworth of Wit* (1592), and therefore of our first vivid glimpse of William Shakespeare, player and poet, was not Robert Greene but Henry Chettle. The trouble with this theory is that Chettle is known to have prepared this posthumous work of Greene for the press and that we have no way of knowing how much, or what kind of, editorial revsion he was called upon to perform. The linguistic facts revealed by Austin's study are open to more than one construction: Chettle's revision may virtually have constituted authorship (or at least co-authorship) without carrying the implication of fraud or imposture alleged by Austin. Nor is it easy to see how the possibility that Chettle may have written the 'Shake-scene' passage could open the way to fundamental reappraisal of that

[1] Shakespeare Studies Monograph Series, ed. J. Leeds Barroll, II (Dubuque, Iowa, 1970).

[2] *A Computer-Aided Technique for Stylistic Discrimination: The Authorship of 'Greene's Groatsworth of Wit'*. US Department of Health, Education, and Welfare: Office of Education, Bureau of Research. Final Report: Project No. 7–G–036 (1969).

passage: its obscurities are verbal and do not depend for their elucidation on the incontrovertible identification of the author.

Peter M. W. Blayney[1] takes a fresh and challenging look at *The Book of Sir Thomas More* and produces a new account of the possible chronology of revisions undergone by that long-suffering document. He points out a few details which escaped even the keen eye of Greg. The verso of folio 9 (the second 'Shakespeare' leaf), though previously described as blank, in fact bears the speech prefix *all* written twice. A worm-hole in the misplaced additional leaf numbered folio 6 corresponds to holes in folios 18 and 19 and indicates that folio 6 was once loosely placed between them, where the additional lines written on it belong. His interesting suggestions include a reduction in the share of the authorship generally assigned to Antony Munday and a tentative identification of Henry Chettle as a left-hander. He argues for revision in two stages as the hypothesis that makes best sense of the complicated textual facts. Hand D's contribution belongs to the first revision and once consisted of three leaves, of which only the second and third survive as folios 8 and 9. Blayney is least convincing on the subject of the likely chronology of the revisions, where he attaches undue weight to the existence of certain verbal similarities between various parts of the play, including Hand D's addition, and Chettle's *Kind Heart's Dream*, which was entered on the Stationers' Register on 8 December 1592. He makes no allusion to stylistic arguments for a very much later dating of the other shorter Shakespearian addition on folio 11*.

Andrew S. Cairncross[2] attempts 'to carry the identification process a little farther' for Hinman's 'F compositors C and D'. He suggests that C is distinguished from D by his preference for *wee'll* over *weele* (etc.) and by his practice of running-on stage directions that extend to more than one line where D usually centres the final line if it is short. These, along with a few more spellings, are used to outline a far-reaching revision of Hinman's conclusions: 'C is there at the beginning of the Folio, and disappears after *King John*. D comes in with quire F, works exclusively from a new case (z) in quire H, and from quire K to quire Q; and ends with quire V. Compositor A's share in the Comedies is much less than supposed, C's much greater'. Sceptics may feel like replying 'It may be so, but if he says it is so he is, in telling true, but so.' Within the space of a short article, Cairncross can do no more than invite a reappraisal of the evidence. His own presentation of it lacks the precision and especially the extended comparison between compositorial patterns without which his conclusions can be accepted as no more than intriguing possibilities, to be verified or modified by further investigation. Alan E. Craven[3] detects the work of three compositors in the three Shakespeare quartos printed by Peter Short and characterises their habits under the names of A, B and C. A set some of sheets H to M in the First Quarto of *Richard III* (1597); B set the eight pages which are the sole survivors of Q0 of 1 *Henry IV* (1598); while the whole of Q1 of that play (1598) was set by C. To carry full conviction, his identifications would need to be verified by reference to a larger body of the output of Short's shop in 1597–8.

Silvano Gerevini[4] reviews the controversy about the printer's copy for folio *Richard III* as it has developed since his own earlier contribution to it in 1957 in *Il testo del Riccardo III di*

[1] '*The Booke of Sir Thomas Moore* Re-Examined', *Studies in Philology*, LXIX (1972), 167–91.

[2] 'Compositors C and D of the Shakespeare First Folio', *Papers of the Bibliographical Society of America* 65 (1971), 41–52.

[3] 'The Compositors of the Shakespeare Quartos Printed by Peter Short', *Papers of the Bibliographical Society of America*, 65 (1971), 393–7.

[4] 'Ancora sul Testo del "Riccardo III"', *English Miscellany*, 21 (Rome, 1970), 11–33.

Shakespeare.[1] He expresses his scepticism of the hypothesis of J. K. Walton that F was set throughout from corrected Q3 and maintains that a new and full collation of the first six quartos and the folio would provide evidence for mixed copy made up of Q3 and Q6. Neil Taylor[2] corrects and extends the record of variants in the double setting of sheet E in *2 Henry IV*, 1600, as it is given in M. A. Shaaber's New Variorum edition, but confuses the nature of the resetting by speaking of 'the two issues of 1600'. R. Levin[3] supports Q1 at *Romeo and Juliet*, II, iv, 145–6, where the Nurse's 'If hee stand to anie thing against mee, Ile take him downe if he were lustier than he is' seems to him (as it has to many editors, G. I. Duthie among them) to lose its bawdy point in the Q2 version 'And a speake any thing against me, Ile take him downe'. In the same play, III, iii, 51, J. C. Maxwell[4] proposes 'determine me' as a likely emendation of Q2's 'Briefe, sounds, *determine* my weale and wo', and as an alternative to Q5/F 'determine of' which is 'stylistically unobjectionable'. D. A. Carroll[5] interprets the honeysuckle in Nicholas Ling's device on the title-page of the first two quartos of *Hamlet* as an anagram of *Nicholas-Honisocal*, claiming that 'Whatever the spelling, the pun was clearly intended'. Using the evidence of an ornamental head-piece, J. A. Lavin[6] identifies the printer of *Hamlet*, Q3 as George Eld, not, as Greg suggested, Valentine Simmes, who parted with the ornament in question in 1607 to Henry Ballard from whose shop it passed to Eld in 1609. Kenneth Muir[7] points out the frequency of internal rhymes in *Cymbeline* and suggests that such rhyming is a possible further differentiating feature between the portions of *Henry VIII* and *The Two Noble Kinsmen* assigned respectively to Shakespeare and Fletcher. Its presence in Theobald's *Double Falsehood* could argue in favour of the ultimate derivation of that heavily-adapted play from the lost *Cardenio*, itself, perhaps, a Shakespeare–Fletcher collaboration. Warren B. Austin[8] considers the sonnet by 'Phaeton *to his friend* Florio' printed in Florio's *Second Fruits*, 1591, rejecting the suggestion of Shakespeare's authorship first made by William Minto in 1885 and proposing Thomas Nashe as a better candidate on slight but plausible internal and external grounds.

[1] Pavia, 1957.

[2] 'Variants in the Quarto of *2 Henry IV*', *Library*, 5th series, XXV (1970), 249–50.

[3] 'A good Reading from the Bad Quarto of *Romeo and Juliet*', *Review of English Studies*, XXIII (1972), 56–8.

[4] '*Romeo and Juliet*, III.ii.51', *Notes and Queries*, n.s. XIX (1972), 125.

[5] 'The Publisher's Device on the Early *Hamlet* Quartos', *Papers of the Bibliographical Society of America*, 64 (1970), 449.

[6] 'The Printer of *Hamlet*, Q3', *Studies in Bibliography*, XXV (1972), 173–6.

[7] 'A Trick of Style and Some Implications', *Shakespeare Studies*, VI (1970), 305–10.

[8] 'Thomas Nashe's Authorship of a Sonnet Attributed to Shakespeare', *Shakespeare in the Southwest: Some New Directions*, ed. T. J. Stafford (El Paso, 1969), 94–105.

© RICHARD PROUDFOOT 1973

INDEX

INDEX

INDEX

Joyce, James, 92
Judges, A. V., 71n.

Kable, W. S., 182
Kaufmann, R. J., 158
Kay, C. M., 157
Ker, W. P., 76n.
Knight, G. Wilson, 89, 127n., 151, 162, 167
Knights, L. C., 76
Knowles, Richard, 112n., 114n., 115n.
Kodama, J. H., 153
Kökeritz, H., 171
Kolin, Philip C., 172
Koppenfels, W. von., 154
Kuckhoff, A., 166
Kyd, Thomas, 1, 41,

La Bruyère, 89
Lanham, Richard A., 174n.
Lascelles, Mary, 69–79, 120
Lasso, Orlando di, 173
Lavin, J. A., 184
Lawes, William, 33
Lawrence, D. H., 8
Lawrence, W. W., 119
Leavis, F. R., 123n.
Lee, Sir Sidney, 107
Leech, Clifford, 1–9, 166
Leggatt, A., 155
Leimberg, I., 163
Lengler, R., 161
Lessing, G. E., 167
Lever, J. W., 9, 122, 126, 127n., 177
Levin, Harry, 89–94
Levin, Richard, 4, 173, 184
Levy, F. J., 174n.
Lewis, Anthony J., 175
Lewkenor, Sir Lewis, 172
Leyris, P., 164
Liddell, Mark Harvey, 82n., 85
Lindeheim, Nancy R., 174
Ling, Nicholas, 184
Lloyd Evans, Gareth, 175
Lockhart, Calvin, 148–9
Lodge, Thomas, 113, 115
Long, E. T., 74n.
Lowes, John L., 99n.
Lucas, F. L., 4
Luce, Morton, 72n.
Luther, Martin, 49
Lyle, E. B., 172
Lyly, John, 153
Lynche, Richard, 112n.

McAlindon, T., 155
Machiavelli, Niccolo, 49
McIntosh, A., 164n.
Mack, Maynard, 9, 96
McKellen, Ian, 140
McKenzie, D. F., 180

McKerrow, R. B., 45n.
McLuskie, K., 163
McNeir, W. F., 158, 163
McPeek, J. A. S., 154
Magarshack, David, 22n.
Magee, W. H., 155
Mahood, M. M., 165
Malone, Edmond, 71, 91, 172
Manley, F., 157
Mann, Thomas, 163
Margaret, Queen of Scotland, 44
Marlowe, Christopher, 3, 6, 8, 9, 54, 103, 108
Marston, John, 9, 55, 57, 99, 153, 169, 173
Mary, Princess, 44n.
Mary, Queen of Scots, 36n., 41, 46, 48
Marx, Karl, 92
Masefield, John, 103
Massinger, Philip, 5, 9, 169
Matthews, Brander, 119
Maxwell, Baldwin, 9
Maxwell, J. C., 105, 184
Mehl, D., 155, 161, 166, 176
Meiss, Millard, 115n.
Melville, Herman, 89, 91, 94
Meres, Francis, 108
Michelangelo, 60, 116
Middleton, Thomas, 4, 5, 7, 8, 9, 39, 54, 56, 57, 66
Milton, John, 114
Milward, P., 162
Mincoff, Marco, 13–14, 113n., 117n.
Minto, William, 184
Miyauchi, B., 159
Molière, J.-B., 90, 94
Monmouth, Geoffrey of, 35, 36n., 41, 42, 43
Montaigne, M. de, 49
Moore, Edward N., 175
Morgan, W. W., 154
Morgann, Maurice, 167–8
Morley, Christopher, 140, 142
Morris, Ivor, 23, 24
Muir, Edwin, 76
Muir, Kenneth, 5, 71, 72, 82, 166, 172
Mulcaster, Richard, 38n., 45n.
Mulryne, J. R., 9
Munday, Anthony, 35, 39, 43, 45, 47, 103, 183
Munro, John, 44n.
Murdock, D., 161
Murphy, Arthur, 175
Murray, P., 166–7
Murry, J. Middleton, 103
Musset, Alfred de, 9

Nabokov, Vladimir, 89
Nashe, Thomas, 170, 184
Nichols, John Gough, 39n., 74
Nicoll, Allardyce, 3, 4, 9

Nosworthy, J. M., 20n., 81, 82–4, 85n.
Nunn, Trevor, 139, 140, 141, 148

Olivier, Lord, 150, 176
Oppel, H., 163
Ornstein, Robert, 4, 6, 8
Ortego, P. D., 158
Overmyer, J., 162
Ovid, 104, 107, 108
Owst, G. R., 76 n.

Palmer, D. J., 154
Palsson, H., 164n.
Panofsky, Erwin, 57
Parker, Robert W., 174n.
Parmigianino, 50, 54
Parrott, T. M., 4, 173
Paul, Henry N., 85n.
Peacham, Henry, 98
Pearce, F. M., 154
Percy, Thomas, 40
Perrett, Wilfred, 36n., 41n.
Perugino, 54
Pettet, E. C., 98
Phillips, O. Hood, 171
Pierce, R. B., 156
Poel, William, 147, 175
Pollard, A. W., 181
Pontormo, 50, 51, 54, 55
Pope, Alexander, 181, 182
Pope-Hennessy, John, 112n, 116n.
Proser, M. N., 164
Prosser, Elinor, 23, 25n., 161
Proudfoot, Richard, 177–84
Püschel, U., 162
Pushkin, 167
Pyle, F., 161

Quiller-Couch, Sir Arthur, 119

Rabkin, N., 163
Rackin, P., 159
Raleigh, Sir Walter, 103, 114n., (ob. 1610)
Raleigh, Sir Walter (ob. 1922), 73
Raphael, 54, 65
Reaske, C. R., 153
Redgrave, Corin, 147
Redgrave, Sir Michael, 147
Rees, Joan, 34, 36, 165
Reid, S., 155
Ribner, Irving, 7
Rice, John, 45
Richards, I. A., 9
Richmond, H. M., 152, 164
Ridler, Anne, 119n.
Riehle, W., 158
Riggs, David, 157
Righter, Anne, 16
Rinehart, Keith, 172
Roberts, James, 181

187